SINGLE MOTHERS
AND THEIR
CHILDREN

To our children: Sara, Jay, Lisa, Anna, and Lynn.

SINGLE MOTHERS AND THEIR CHILDREN

A New American Dilemma

Irwin Garfinkel
Sara S. McLanahan

The Changing Domestic Priorities Series
John L. Palmer and Isabel V. Sawhill, Editors

THE URBAN INSTITUTE PRESS · WASHINGTON, D.C.

Copyright © 1986
THE URBAN INSTITUTE
2100 M Street, N.W.
Washington, D.C. 20037

Library of Congress Cataloging in Publication Data

Garfinkel, Irwin.
  Single mothers and their children.

  (Changing domestic priorities series)
  Bibliography: p.
  1. Single parents—Government policy—United
States.   2. Working mothers—Government policy—
United States.   3. Family policy—United
States.   I. McLanahan, Sara.
II. Title.   III. Series.
HQ759.915.G37   1986   362.8′2   86-23413
ISBN 0-87766-405-6
ISBN 0-87766-404-8 (pbk.)

Printed in the United States of America
9 8 7 6 5 4 3 2 1

THE URBAN INSTITUTE is a nonprofit policy research and educational organization established in Washington, D.C., in 1968. Its staff investigates the social and economic problems confronting the nation and government policies and programs designed to alleviate such problems. The Institute disseminates significant findings of its research through the publications program of its Press. The Institute has two goals for work in each of its research areas: to help shape thinking about societal problems and efforts to solve them, and to improve government decisions and performance by providing better information and analytic tools.

Through work that ranges from broad conceptual studies to administrative and technical assistance, Institute researchers contribute to the stock of knowledge available to public officials and to private individuals and groups concerned with formulating and implementing more efficient and effective government policy.

Conclusions or opinions expressed in Institute publications are those of the authors and do not necessarily reflect the views of other staff members, officers or trustees of the Institute, advisory groups, or any organizations that provide financial support to the Institute.

THE CHANGING DOMESTIC PRIORITIES SERIES

Listed below are the titles available in the Changing Domestic Priorities Series

Advisory Board of the
Changing Domestic Priorities Project

CONTENTS

TABLES

FIGURES

FOREWORD

This book is part of The Urban Institute's Changing Domestic Priorities Series, a collection of volumes that assess the impact and significance of the changes in domestic policy that have occurred under the Reagan administration and analyze the critical economic and social issues facing the nation during the 1980s and beyond.

One of these issues is the rapid increase of families headed by women. During the last past twenty-five years the proportion of children living in such families has more than doubled from one in ten to more than one in five. Concern about this trend stems from the fact that these families are much more likely to be poor or to experience sharp drops in income than other families and from a belief (and some evidence) that the children of single parents are less likely to be successful as adults than those who grow up in two-parent homes.

The trends discussed in this book have altered the public debate about poverty and the welfare system. In particular, the tradition of providing public assistance to women with children is now being called into question. Although such assistance improves their economic position and enables them to stay home with their children, it also fosters long-term welfare dependence and may encourage or facilitate marital instability or out-of-wedlock births. Thus, in the process of providing greater economic security to families headed by women, the nation may have unwittingly increased the dependence of these families on government and contributed to the very growth that now seems so problematical. Irwin Garfinkel and Sara McLanahan call this tension between the desire to provide economic security to such families and the need to stem their growth and dependence on government "the new American dilemma."

The authors point out that the resolution of this dilemma requires answers to some difficult questions. Has welfare, in fact, caused an increase in the number of single-mother families? Has welfare dependence grown to the point that it is morally corrosive to the recipients and fiscally unacceptable to the public? Do other solutions, such as encouraging mothers to work, make sense in light of what is known about the effects on their children?

After reviewing the social science literature on these and related questions, the authors conclude that the welfare system has been a minor cause of the growing number of single-mother families, that the majority of mothers on welfare remain dependent on government assistance for a long time, and that this dependence could have harmful effects and is, in any case, increasingly unacceptable in a society in which most mothers work and self-reliance is highly valued. They also conclude that a mother's employment is unlikely to have adverse effects on her children and could actually be beneficial. In sum, although they reject the idea that the welfare system has been a major reason for the rising number of mothers who head families, they nevertheless prefer work over welfare as the best solution to the "new American dilemma." They go on to note that most women on welfare cannot command high enough wages to lift their families out of poverty even when they work full-time. Thus they believe it will be necessary to supplement the earnings of these women with both increased child support payments from fathers and some form of government assistance.

Garfinkel and McLanahan also examine the effects of a number of recent policy changes on these single mothers with children. They document how the inflation of the 1970s and the budget cuts of the early 1980s have resulted in substantial reductions in public benefits available to these families and discuss the current administration's preferred strategy—requiring welfare mothers to work if they have no preschool-age children. Based on recent experiences with voluntary as well as mandatory work programs, the authors are cautiously optimistic about the potential of employment and training initiatives to increase the earned income of mothers now on welfare. An even more significant recent development, in their view, is the increased emphasis being placed on the enforcement of the child support obligations of absent parents. They estimate that more adequate child support awards and tougher enforcement of these awards could greatly reduce poverty and welfare dependence.

The authors end the book with a discussion of their own policy recommendations. These include the adoption of a new child support system, a conversion of the personal exemptions in the tax system to child-and-adult allowances, and a substitution of work for welfare as the primary source of income for women heading families. These recommendations are both innovative and likely to be controversial.

With concerns about poverty and welfare reform once more on the national agenda, this book makes an especially timely contribution. While not everyone will agree with its specific conclusions, readers will benefit from its thoughtful presentation of the issues and careful weighing of the available evidence.

John L. Palmer
Isabel V. Sawhill
Editors
Changing Domestic Priorities Series

ACKNOWLEDGMENTS

This book would not have been possible without help from many people. The authors are grateful to Andrew Cherlin, David Ellwood, Robert Lampman, and Isabel Sawhill for their detailed reviews of the original manuscript and their many thoughtful suggestions. Larry Bumpass and James Sweet made available their files from the Public Use Samples of the U.S. Census, 1940 through 1980, and helped locate and interpret information on numerous demographic events. Other colleagues who provided comments on specific chapters are Mary Jo Bane, Brett Brown, Glen Cain, Sheldon Danziger, Peter Gottchalk, Robert Haveman, Ann Orloff, and Michael Wiseman. Don Oellerich and Quintin Sullivan provided valuable research assistance. Karen Wirt and Priscilla Taylor edited various drafts of the manuscript, and Felicity Skidmore improved the readability of the final version with unusual speed and skill.

The support of the Carnegie Corporation of New York, the Ford Foundation, and the John D. and Catherine T. MacArthur Foundation is gratefully acknowledged.

ABOUT THE AUTHORS

Irwin Garfinkel is a professor in the School of Social Work and the Institute for Research on Poverty, University of Wisconsin-Madison. From 1975 through 1980 he was the director of the Institute for Research on Poverty and from 1982 through 1985, he was director of the School of Social Work. He has done research on the causes of and remedies for poverty. In particular, he has studied the benefits and costs of alternative kinds of government transfers. His most recent work focuses on child support. In conjunction with officials at the Wisconsin Department of Health and Social Services, he developed a proposal for a new child support assurance system that is being tried on a demonstration basis in the state. Garfinkel is currently evaluating the outcomes of the demonstration.

Sara S. McLanahan is a professor in the Department of Sociology and the Institute for Research on Poverty at the University of Wisconsin-Madison. She teaches sociology of the family, medical sociology, and sociology of the life course and has published numerous articles on the feminization of poverty, the intergenerational consequences of family disruption, and the effects of parenthood on psychological well-being. She was also a single mother for ten years.

CHAPTER 1

THE NEW AMERICAN DILEMMA

This book is about families headed by single women with children and the public policies that affect their lives. Few topics could be of greater importance to the nation's future. Half of all American children born today will spend part of their childhood in a family headed by a mother who is divorced, separated, unwed, or widowed.[1]

Not surprisingly, national concern about these families has grown in proportion to the increase in their prevalence. In 1960 only one of every twelve children lived in a family headed by a woman. By 1983 more than one of every five children lived in such a family.[2] Rapid change per se is somewhat frightening, especially when the cause and the extent of the change are not clear. Furthermore, prudence directs a nation to examine closely the causes and consequences of rapid change in the living arrangements of its children.

Concern also stems from the serious economic and social problems of these families. About half of them are poor and dependent on welfare. The mothers and children in such families also have poorer than average mental health and use a disproportionate share of community mental health services. Most important, perhaps, compared with children who grow up in two-parent (husband-wife) families, the children from mother-only families are less successful on average when they become adults. They are more likely to drop

1. L. Bumpass, "Children and Marital Disruption: A Replication and Update," *Demography*, vol. 21 (February 1984), pp. 71-82.

2. U.S. Bureau of the Census, "Household and Family Characteristics, March 1983," *Current Population Reports*, series P-20, no. 388 (Washington, D.C.: U.S. Government Printing Office, 1984).

out of school, to give birth out of wedlock, to divorce or separate, and to become dependent on welfare.

In view of the seriousness of the problems associated with this type of family and the recent explosion in its prevalence, it is not surprising that the government's policy toward mother-only families has recently been scrutinized and debated by policymakers as well as by the general public. Although most observers agree that something must be done, there is no general agreement about what direction policy should take or how the various reform strategies should be implemented.

Some argue that government is not doing enough. These critics point to the recent "feminization" of poverty as evidence of government neglect; they argue that most, if not all, of the problems cited earlier could be alleviated if the economic insecurity of mother-only families were reduced. Strategies for improving their standard of living range from increasing welfare benefits to establishing more universal programs of family and child support.[3] Others believe that government has already done too much. They argue that recent increases in the prevalence and welfare dependence of mother-only families are a direct result of the expansion of social programs during the 1960s, and that the best way to alleviate the problem is to prevent formation of such families by reducing benefits or eliminating programs.[4]

Both sides have a point. Some, perhaps most, of the problems of families headed by single women with children stem from their very low incomes. Through government policy it is possible to raise the incomes of these families and thereby reduce the adverse effects of poverty on the mothers and children. But increasing their incomes will make such families more dependent on the government and, by making the status of single parenthood more attractive, will increase their number. This is the policy dilemma: should government policy give priority to reducing the economic insecurity of mother-only families or to reducing their prevalence and dependence?

Both options entail costs to society. Increasing the incomes of such families would certainly reduce short-term suffering but might create suffering for more people in the long run. Reducing incomes might reduce prevalence

---

3. For the most thorough analysis of the income-testing issue, see Irwin Garfinkel, ed., *Income-Tested Transfer Programs: The Case For and Against* (New York: Academic Press, 1982); Irwin Garfinkel and Liz Uhr, "A New Approach to Child Support," *The Public Interest* no. 75 (Spring 1984), pp. 111-22, detail a proposal for a new child support assurance system. For proposals to expand welfare, see Sar A. Levitan, Martin Rein, and David Marwick, *Work and Welfare Go Together* (Baltimore, Maryland: Johns Hopkins University Press, 1972); and Henry Aaron, *On Social Welfare* (Cambridge, Massachusetts: Abt Books, 1980).

4. George Gilder, *Wealth and Poverty* (New York: Basic Books, 1981) and Charles Murray, *Losing Ground: American Social Policy, 1950-1980* (New York: Basic Books, 1984).

and dependence, but at the expense of the people who currently live in those families. Resolving the dilemma involves making hard choices on the basis of incomplete knowledge. The choices also are inherently difficult because they involve conflicts among values that are fundamental to American culture—compassion, self-reliance, and self-interest. The dilemma exists not just because of competition among groups with conflicting values but because of conflicts within individuals over which value to maximize.

Ultimately the choices among government priorities are political decisions; however, social scientists can have an important role in shaping and informing the political debate. Social scientists can identify the important questions and provide information on the direction and size of the consequences associated with particular strategies, and thus help policymakers arrive at a more enlightened resolution to the dilemma.

In the following section we outline the questions that we believe must be answered in order to resolve the dilemma. We also identify the points at which the values of self-reliance, compassion, and self-interest conflict and the points at which they converge.

Empirical Questions Relevant to the Dilemma

The dilemma about whether to give priority to increasing economic well-being or to reducing prevalence and dependence consists of two parts: (1) the relation between economic well-being and prevalence and (2) the relation between economic well-being and dependence.

Well-being and Prevalence

It is clear that increasing the incomes of families headed by single women will reduce some if not all of their present problems; it might also reduce the negative consequences associated with growing up in such a family. Economic theory, however, tells us that increasing their incomes will also enlarge the proportion of women and children who live in such families. Which strategy is best—increase economic well-being and encourage prevalence or reduce well-being and discourage prevalence?

Some people have argued that low income is the only problem confronting families headed by single women. They claim that this type of family is a viable alternative to the nuclear family form, and that if incomes were the same, the life opportunities of children from one- and two-parent families would also be the same. If this is true, the only argument against raising incomes is that the economic costs to the rest of society are too great. The decision is a question of values. Compassion for such women and their children argues for increasing their incomes; taxpayer self-interest argues for limiting public aid.

But what if income does not account for much of the disadvantage associated with living in a mother-only family, and if increasing income has a large effect on prevalence? Then the long-term costs for future generations outweigh the short-term benefits accruing to those who currently live in such families. In this case, compassion and taxpayer self-interest both point in the direction of reducing prevalence by limiting aid.

An enlightened resolution to this part of the dilemma requires answers to a host of empirical questions: how much does prevalence increase with increased benefits or decrease with decreased assistance? How much would increased benefits reduce the handicaps of children in such families? For each particular kind and amount of benefit increase, one must know how great is the improvement in the well-being of the children and the mother compared with the increase in prevalence. The slogan "Relieving It Breeds It" is not sufficient to make the case against improving the conditions of such families. Some methods of improving conditions might lead to very large improvements in the future well-being of children and to trivial increases or even decreases in the number of children affected. Presumably these methods would be preferred to others that have small effects on increasing future well-being but large effects on reducing prevalence.

One must also consider the fact that transfer programs are not the only, or even the major, source of raising incomes among single women with children. Quite apart from transfer policy, increases in the participation of women in the labor force during the past century have contributed both to the growing economic independence of women and to the increasing prevalence of mother-only families. At least some of the change in labor supply is due to expanded demand for female labor, which is independent of the change in family structure.[5] In addition, some people argue that the growth of black families headed by single women with children is more a reflection of declining opportunity for men than of rising opportunity for women.[6] Thus, another question must be addressed: how large is the effect of changes in income transfer policy as compared with broader changes in the social structure?

---

5. Valerie Kincade Oppenheimer, *The Female Labor Force in the United States: Demographic and Economic Factors Governing Its Growth and Changing Composition*, Population Monograph Series 5 (Berkeley, California: University of California, Institute of International Studies, 1970).

6. W. J. Wilson and K. M. Neckerman, "Poverty and Family Structure: The Widening Gap between Evidence and Public Policy Issues," paper prepared for the conference entitled Poverty and Policy: Retrospect and Prospects, Williamsburg, Virginia, December 6-9, 1984.

One last point: it is not always clear that the costs of an increase in prevalence exceed the benefits. As a general matter, we believe that two parents can do a better job of raising children than one parent. It does not follow, however, that two parents are always preferable to one. To take an extreme example, in cases in which the child or mother is being physically or sexually abused by the father, that child or mother would almost certainly be better off living apart from the abusive parent. Improving the economic status of families headed by single women may increase prevalence by encouraging the breakup of abusive relationships, but who would say that the children in such families were worse off?

Well-being and Dependence

The second part of the dilemma facing policymakers arises from the conflict between increasing economic well-being and reducing dependence. Economic theory maintains that if government assumes more responsibility for the economic well-being of the children in families headed by women, parents will assume less responsibility. More specifically, increasing incomes through government benefits will reduce the incentive of the mothers to work and will increase their reliance on public welfare. It may also reduce the support provided by the noncustodial fathers.

Some people argue that dependence on welfare is not harmful in and of itself. All human beings are dependent to a greater or lesser extent on other people or institutions. Children are dependent on their parents. Many people over age sixty-five are dependent on Social Security. Many wives are dependent on their husbands, and even breadwinners are dependent on their jobs for their livelihood. Dependence in this sense has given rise to the description of people with inherited wealth as having "independent means." Such an argument treats all forms of dependence as the same and as basically benign. The dilemma over whether to increase economic well-being or reduce dependence is viewed as a dispute over how much society is willing to spend.

Others disagree, noting that the consequences of dependence vary with its degree of "legitimacy." If a particular group—such as children or disabled people—is not expected to be self-supporting or if a particular person's loss of independence is viewed as involuntary or of short duration, society views the dependence as legitimate. But if dependence occurs among people who are expected to be independent, society takes a dim view.[7]

---

7. Lee Rainwater, "Stigma in Income-Tested Programs," in Garfinkel, *Income Tested Transfer Programs*; Gilder, *Wealth and Poverty*; and Murray, *Losing Ground*.

At the heart of the dilemma is the question of whether single women with children should work to support themselves. Clearly, the more that mothers work to support themselves, the less help the rest of us have to provide. Furthermore, in this case, self-interest is reinforced by the value of self-reliance. When our current federal system of aiding single women with children was begun as part of the New Deal legislation, the prevailing wisdom was that mothers should stay at home and take care of their children. Most of them did. Since then, expectations and mores about mothers' working have changed. Today more than half of married mothers work outside the home at least part of the day. Given the change in norms, it is not surprising that welfare recipients are often viewed as lazy and undeserving. And yet welfare programs discourage single women with children from working.

To determine whether welfare is the best way to reduce the economic insecurity and poverty of these families, one needs to answer several questions. What are the effects of welfare programs on the economic and psychological well-being of beneficiaries and their children? Do the extra income and the model of independence provided by the working mother make up for the reduced time spent with the child, or are children better off when mothers stay at home? What are the effects of welfare and mothers' working on intergenerational dependence? What other ways does society have to increase the economic well-being of these families and how do their psychological and economic consequences vary? These are types of questions we address in this book.

Why the Need for a New Book

This book is similar in many ways to a book published by The Urban Institute a decade ago. *Time of Transition: The Growth of Families Headed by Women*, by Heather Ross and Isabel Sawhill, addressed many of the same questions and dilemmas raised in this book and reached many of the same conclusions. Why do we need a new book on the same subject?

One justification is that scientific knowledge has increased greatly in the interim. We now know much more about the growth and dynamics of poverty, headship by single women, and welfare dependence than we did a decade ago. It is worth asking whether the major conclusions of *Time of Transition* are still valid in light of the new evidence. Even if the conclusions were identical, our study would serve the function of confirming the findings of a major book.

But empirical confirmation is not the only justification. Some of the conclusions are different ten years later. First, Ross and Sawhill stressed that, from the women's point of view, female headship was a time of transition between two different, but nevertheless traditional, types of two-parent families. They found that the average experience lasted from three to five years and most often ended in remarriage. Our estimates, in contrast, indicate that the length of time has become considerably longer, averaging about five years for white families and seven years for blacks in 1984. From the children's point of view, these represent long periods of time. Furthermore, a large and growing minority of black children are born to never-married women and can expect to spend their entire childhood in a mother-only family.

Second, although we agree with Ross and Sawhill that the major problems of female-headed families are poverty and economic insecurity, we differ somewhat on the question of whether poverty is a time of transition. When Ross and Sawhill wrote their book over ten years ago, the general wisdom was that poverty and welfare dependence were relatively common experiences—affecting about 25 percent of American families—and lasted only a short time. This description is still true for most families who experience poverty; but we now know that a substantial minority are poor and dependent for long periods of time.

We differ also in our interpretation of integenerational consequences. Ross and Sawhill reported rather small effects on the socioeconomic achievement and future marital stability of offspring from mother-only families. Recent research suggests that the effects may be much greater. This new evidence on the long-term economic dependence of single mothers and the long-term effects on children is part of what makes the central dilemma of our book both new and disturbing.

With these exceptions, our findings reinforce those of Ross and Sawhill. Both books conclude that increases in welfare benefits contributed to, but were not the major cause of, the growth of mother-only families. For middle-income groups, and therefore for most white families, the increase in women's employment opportunities and concomitant economic independence appear to have been the most important cause. For low-income groups, and therefore most black families, poverty and a decline in employment opportunities for unskilled black men appear to be the principal factors.

Ross and Sawhill do not analyze the history of public aid to mother-only families, so we are unable to compare conclusions in this area. With respect to current public policy recommendations, however, three of four major conclusions are similar. Both books conclude that the public enforcement of private child support obligations should be a high government priority. *Time of Transition* was one of the first major analyses to stress the importance of child support; and in subsequent work Sawhill developed the first estimates of the economic effects of alternative guidelines for establishing child support obligations. Both books also stress the importance of increasing employment opportunities for poor men and poor women as a means of improving the economic status of mother-only families while simultaneously minimizing the increase in the number of such families.

Finally, both books stress the importance of subsidizing the earnings of poor families headed by both men and women as a means of reducing poverty without encouraging family dissolution. The recommended means for achieving this end are different in one critical respect. Ross and Sawhill suggested that the Aid to Families with Dependent Children (AFDC) program might be expanded to provide cash benefits to poor two-parent as well as one-parent families and to those who were working as well as those who were not. We recommend that the earnings of poor families be subsidized through separate nonwelfare programs such as a universal child support assurance program and a universal child-and-adult allowance program. Furthermore, we recommend the use of work relief rather than cash relief as the principal method of aiding those who are able to work but are unable to find employment.

A Guide to the Book

This book is subtitled "A New American Dilemma," but the dilemma we focus on is timeless and universal. So why do we characterize it as new and American? One reason is that both the prevalence of mother-only families in the United States and the amount of aid provided to them have risen remarkably in the past twenty years. The second reason is to point out our debt to Gunnar Myrdal, whose *American Dilemma* is the classic scientific work on the problem of race relations in America.[8] As Myrdal predicted, American race relations have undergone a revolution to bring practice more in conformance with the American creed, and a sizable middle class has developed within the black population. At the same time, the unprecedentedly high rates of single-mother headship among black families poses a new race relations dilemma. Whereas nearly 45 percent of white children will spend part of their youth in a family headed by a woman, the figure for black children is an astounding 86 percent.[9] Clearly, blacks have a greater-than-average stake in how the dilemma over these families is resolved; yet, because whites are an overwhelming majority in the population, whites will have the stronger influence. Finding a sensible and fair solution to this new American dilemma will require all the wisdom the nation can muster.

In this book, as discussed at the outset, we focus on three characteristics of families headed by single women with children: their economic well-being,

---

8. Gunnar Myrdal, *An American Dilemma* (New York: Random House, 1942).
9. Bumpass, "Children and Marital Disruption."

their prevalence, and their welfare dependence. These three characteristics correspond to the three elements of the major policy dilemma and they serve as an organizing framework for the book.

In chapter 2 we provide empirical evidence to document our claim that the problems of mother-only families warrant immediate national attention. Most of the discussion is devoted to problems of poverty and welfare dependence. What proportion of single mothers who head families are poor and for how long? What are the sources of income for such families and why are they so poor? What are the long-term consequences for children of growing up in such a family, and what proportion of these consequences is due to poverty and economic instability?

Chapter 3 documents the trends in prevalence and analyzes the demographic components of the growth of mother-only families. What proportion of our nation's women and children are affected and for how long? What caused the recent explosion in mother-only families? How much of the growth is due to broad changes in social structure, such as increases in women's labor force participation, and how much is due to changes in public policy, such as increases in public assistance?

Chapters 4 and 5 focus on both previous and current public policies toward mother-only families. By tracing the history of policies from the colonial days through 1980, chapter 4 seeks to understand how the dilemma of whether to give priority to increasing the economic well-being or to reducing the dependence and prevalence of single women with children has been resolved in the past. Chapter 5 examines the policies of the Reagan administration and the Congress and estimates their effects on the economic well-being, welfare dependence, and prevalence of mother-only families.

Chapter 6, the last chapter, begins with a summary of our findings. It concludes with an argument that enlightened self-interest, compassion, and self-reliance would all be best served by shifting away from such heavy reliance on income-conditioned cash welfare toward a greater reliance on universal benefits to supplement the earnings of single mothers. The universal benefits include child support assurance, child allowances, and adult allowances. Such benefits need not entail any additional costs to the taxpayers if they were designed as a substitute rather than as a supplement for the current tax-transfer system. We argue that cash relief should be reserved for persons who are permanently unable to work or who are temporarily without a job. Such a strategy would simultaneously increase economic well-being and reduce welfare dependence and prevalence.

CHAPTER 2

PROBLEMS OF MOTHER-ONLY FAMILIES

Families headed by single women with children are the poorest of all major demographic groups regardless of how poverty is measured. Their economic position relative to that of other groups, such as the aged and disabled, has actually declined during the past two decades. Mother-only families are also subject to numerous other forms of economic and social instability, such as income loss, residential moves, and changes in employment and household composition. These disruptions—many of which are related to marital breakup—are a source of continual psychological stress and may lead to clinical depression in children as well as mothers.

Why are mother-only families so poor, and why is their socioeconomic situation so unstable? The data on income show that the economic status of these families varies somewhat according to whether the women are widowed, divorced, separated, or never married, but is systematically much lower than that of two-parent families. We conclude that poverty and economic insecurity are a consequence of three factors: (1) the low earnings capacity of single mothers, (2) the lack of child support from noncustodial fathers, and (3) the meager benefits provided by public assistance programs.

Poverty and economic insecurity are serious problems in their own right. Some analysts, however, go even further to argue that the families headed by single women are creating an "underclass" in American society. According to this view, offspring from such families are more likely to drop out of school, be unemployed, and themselves form mother-only families than are children who grow up with two parents. Evidence on intergenerational poverty indicates that, indeed, offspring from such families are far more likely to be poor and to form mother-only families than are offspring who live with two parents most of their preadult life. Evidence also indicates that income accounts for a substantial part—but not all—of the intergenerational trans-

11

mission of poverty. Not surprisingly, the greatest effect of income is on educational attainment and occupational status. Even after income is taken into account, however, children who grow up in mother-only families are still far more likely to become single parents themselves than are offspring who grow up in two-parent households. Why? Is it lack of supervision, the absence of a male role model, or something about the type of people who form such families that makes the difference? Most important, what can policymakers do to minimize the disadvantages for children who grow up in such families? To answer the policy question, it is necessary to learn whether the children do better, other things equal, if their mothers work or if they stay home and take care of their children full time.

Maternal employment appears to have no negative consequences for preschool-age children. Working for pay clearly has a positive effect on economic well-being. There is also some evidence of a positive role-modeling effect of employment outside the home. However, single mothers who have jobs are different from those who do not in other important ways, which may also influence the development of their children. One must be cautious in generalizing about the effects of employment on families headed by single women without further evidence.

In the last section of the chapter we examine the question of whether welfare programs designed to aid mother-only families are actually contributing to long-term poverty and dependence by encouraging the development of attitudes and values that retard economic mobility. The evidence is mixed. Some researchers say that being on welfare lowers recipients' self-esteem and feeling of control over one's environment—efficacy—which, in turn, reduces the future earnings and economic achievement of offspring. Others find no evidence of stigma and no evidence of change in the attitudes of the families after they go on welfare. On balance, we would be surprised if welfare were proved to have done more harm than good because, without welfare, families headed by women would have been much poorer and their incomes even less stable.

Poverty

Approximately one out of every two mother-only families is poor, according to the official government definition of poverty. Trends in the prevalence of poverty among mother-only families, two-parent families, the aged, and the disabled are reported in figure 1 for the years 1967 through 1982. These data are based on the official definition of poverty and include income from cash-transfer programs such as Aid to Families with Dependent Children (AFDC), Social Security, and disability insurance.[1]

Mother-only families have had substantially higher poverty rates than other groups for the past fifteen years, and the gap between them and the next poorest groups (the disabled and the aged) has increased because the poverty rates of the disabled and the aged have declined over the period. The contrast depicted in figure 1 is exacerbated by the fact that the number of mother-only families grew dramatically during the 1970s (see chapter 3), which caused the size of this subgroup to increase relative to the size of other poor households or families.[2] In 1967, 21.4 percent of the nonaged poor were living in mother-only families as compared with 41.4 percent in two-parent families. By 1978, the proportions were reversed: more than 35 percent of the poor were living in mother-only families, compared with 29.8 percent in two-parent families. In that year Pearce introduced the concept of the "feminization of poverty" to capture this phenomenon.[3] About half of the feminization of poverty between 1967 and 1978 was due to increases in the number of mother-only families and half to improvement in the living standards of other groups.[4]

Figure 1 also indicates that a large number of two-parent families have been cast back into poverty, presumably as a result of the recent recession. If normal economic growth resumes, the situation of two-parent families should improve markedly, whereas economic growth by itself is unlikely to be of much help to mother-only families, given their greater dependence on nonmarket sources of income.

The numbers reported in figure 1 are based on the official definition of poverty, which counts only the cash incomes of families. If the value of in-kind benefits is counted along with cash transfers, the overall decline in

1. Christine Ross, "Trends in Poverty, 1965-1983," paper prepared for the conference entitled Poverty and Policy: Retrospect and Prospects, sponsored by the Institute for Research on Poverty, held at Williamsburg, Virginia, December 6-8, 1984. Data for 1984 poverty rates come from U.S. Bureau of the Census, "Money Income and Poverty Status of Families and Persons in the United States: 1984," *Current Population Reports*, series P-60, no. 149 (Washington, D.C.: U.S. Government Printing Office, 1985), tables 15 and 18, pp. 21 and 28. Unless otherwise stated, what we refer to as mother-only families are what the Census counts as independent households headed by single women (unwed, separated, divorced, or widowed) with children under age eighteen.

2. Irwin Garfinkel and Sara McLanahan, "The Feminization of Poverty: Nature, Causes and a Partial Cure," Institute for Research on Poverty paper 776 (Madison, Wisconsin: University of Wisconsin, 1985).

3. Diana Pearce, "The Feminization of Poverty: Women, Work and Welfare," *Urban and Social Change Review* (February 1978), pp. 28-36.

4. Garfinkel and McLanahan, "The Feminization of Poverty."

FIGURE 1

POVERTY RATES FOR MOTHER-ONLY FAMILIES, THE AGED, THE DISABLED, AND
TWO-PARENT FAMILIES, 1967–82

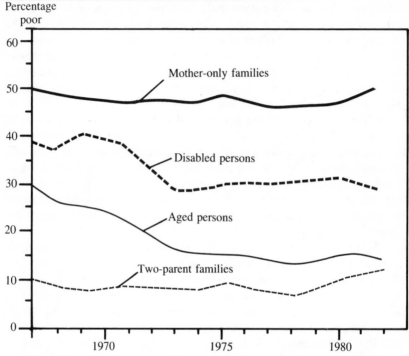

SOURCE: U.S. Bureau of the Census, *Current Population Survey* for the years shown.

poverty between 1967 and 1979 is greater than figure 1 suggests, and the proportion of mother-only families who were poor in 1982 is lower. This is because a large proportion of mother-only families receive noncash benefits in the form of food stamps, medical assistance, and housing subsidies. The Bureau of the Census estimates that, depending on how in-kind benefits are valued, the proportion of mother-only families classified as poor in 1983 ranged from 29 percent to 41 percent. Nevertheless, they remain much poorer than the aged, the disabled, and two-parent families. Even the lower estimate (29 percent) far exceeds the comparable poverty rates for aged (2.5 percent to 11.0 percent including in-kind transfers) or for two-parent families (9.1 percent to 10.9 percent including in-kind transfers).[5]

---

5. U.S. Bureau of Census, "Estimates of Poverty including the Value of Noncash Benefits: 1984," technical paper 55 (Washington, D.C.: U.S. Government Printing Office, August 1985), table 2.

Not only are mother-only families more likely to be poor than other groups, but also the dynamics of their poverty experience are different. Duncan and his colleagues found that nearly a quarter of the population was poor for at least one year during the decade from 1967 to 1978. They also found considerable turnover in the poverty population, with most of the people who became poor remaining poor for less than two years.[6] Among mother-only families, however, poverty lasts much longer and is more severe. Bane and Ellwood found that during the late 1970s the average length of time in poverty for children in families headed by single women was 7.0 years. This compares with 4.6 years for children in two-parent families. For black children the difference was even greater: 12 years for those in families headed by single women, compared with 6 years for those in two-parent families.[7]

These differences are in good part because the factors associated with becoming poor and getting out of poverty are different for the two family types. For example, a change in the earnings of the father is the primary cause of poverty in two-parent families (accounting for more than 40 percent of two-parent families who enter poverty). In contrast, changes in family structure—marital disruption and out-of-wedlock births—are the major factor for mother-only families. Bane and Ellwood have shown that only 13 percent of all new spells of poverty in mother-only families began with a decline in the women's earnings, whereas more than 50 percent began with a change in family structure. Changes in family structure are somewhat less important for ending poverty in such families than for beginning it. Similarly, changes in the mother's earnings are more important for ending poverty in such families than for beginning it.

Economic and Social Instability Following a Divorce

Poverty is not the only source of stress for mother-only families. Even those who do not fall below the poverty line experience substantial economic instability and loss of income as a result of divorce. Duncan and Hoffman report that the income of these women and children one year after a divorce is only 67 percent of their predivorce income.[8] Because two separate house-

---

6. G. Duncan, R. Coe, and M. Hill, "The Dynamics of Poverty," in G. Duncan, ed., *Years of Poverty, Years of Plenty* (Ann Arbor, Michigan: University of Michigan, Survey Research Center, 1984), pp. 33–70.

7. Mary Jo Bane and David Ellwood, "Slipping Into and Out of Poverty: The Dynamics of Spells," unpublished paper (Cambridge, Massachusetts: Harvard University, August 1982).

8. Greg J. Duncan and Saul D. Hoffman, "A Reconsideration of the Economic Consequences of Marital Dissolution," *Demography*, vol. 22 (November 1985), pp. 485-98. In another study of the economic consequences of divorce based on California court records, Lenore Weitz-

holds are more expensive to maintain than one, we would expect both parties to experience a drop in living standards after a divorce, but the drop for divorced mothers is much greater than the drop for divorced fathers. The implications of these findings for child support policy are discussed in the section that follows.

In addition, following a divorce, women and children undergo numerous other changes in roles and social position, which involve loss of social status as well as loss of family and friends. Changes in residence are perhaps the most common form of social instability in newly formed mother-only families. One study shows that about 38 percent of divorced mothers and their children experience a residential move during the first year after a divorce.[9] Subsequently household moves drop off rapidly to about 20 percent a year on average—still about one-third higher than the rate for moves in two-parent families. Changes in residence not only require adjustment to new neighborhoods and living conditions; they may also mean the loss of important social networks and support.

Changes in employment are also common. In an effort to recoup some of their income loss, many divorced and separated mothers enter the labor force for the first time or increase their working hours. Duncan and Hoffman found that the proportion of mothers who worked 1,000 or more hours per year increased from 51 percent before divorce to 73 percent after divorce. The average divorced mother earned $8,937 in 1981 dollars the year after divorce, compared with $5,829 the year before divorce.[10] When a mother makes a substantial change in her working hours, this change in itself is stressful for her as well as her children. If her children are young, child care arrangements must be made, and both mother and child are likely to experience anxiety about the new situation.

In addition to experiencing changes in residence and working hours, divorced and separated mothers are more likely to experience job changes, changes in their household composition, and unemployment than are the fathers in two-parent families. Data from the Michigan Panel Study of Income Dynamics (PSID) found that unemployment was three times more common among single mothers during the first three years after a divorce or separation

---

man reports that divorced women and their children experience a 73 percent decline in income compared to a 42 percent increase among divorced fathers. See Lenore J. Weitzman, *The Divorce Revolution* (New York: The Free Press, 1985).

9. Sara McLanahan, "Family Structure and Stress: A Longitudinal Comparison of Two-Parent and Female-Headed Families," *Journal of Marriage and the Family* (May 1983), pp. 347-57.

10. Duncan and Hoffman, "A Reconsideration of the Economic Consequences of Marital Dissolution."

than among fathers in two-parent households, and job changes were about one-and-a-half times more common. Family composition changes, such as another adult or child moving in or out, also were about one-and-a-half times more common among mother-only families, even five years after marital disruption.[11]

Social and economic instability have direct implications for the mental health of these families. Research on stressful life events indicates that changes in social roles or status may lead to increases in psychological distress and anxiety.[12] Undesirable and involuntary changes are thought to be the most stressful, particularly when they involve the disruption of social networks and support systems. Not surprisingly, epidemiological surveys show that single mothers report substantially higher rates of anxiety and depression than do married women and men; and facility utilization statistics show that mother-only families with children consume a disproportionate share of community mental health services.[13] According to Guttentag and her colleagues, the mental health service utilization rates of preschool-age children in mother-only families are four times as great as those of children in two-parent families; for children between the ages of seven and eighteen, the rates are twice as high. Much of the variation in psychological distress appears to be caused by differences in income and economic instability. The Michigan PSID data also indicate that single mothers are much more likely to experience declines in psychological well-being than are married men with children and that most of the relative decline could be explained by differences in income.[14]

Causes of Poverty and Economic Instability

Families headed by single mothers are poor for three reasons: because the earning power of the primary breadwinner (the mother) is relatively low; because the contribution of other family members—the noncustodial father in particular—is low; and because public transfers to women who head such families, with the exception of those to widows, are quite meager.

The sources of income for two-parent and mother-only families are reported in table 1 for whites and table 2 for blacks. As these tables show, the

11. McLanahan, "Family Structure and Stress."

12. B. Dohrenwend and B. Dohrenwend, eds., *Stressful Life Events: Their Nature and Effects* (New York: Wiley, 1974).

13. Marcia Guttentag, Susan Salassin, and Deborah Belle, *The Mental Health of Women* (New York: Academic Press, 1980).

14. Sara McLanahan, "Single Mothers and Psychological Distress: A Test of the Stress and Vulnerability Hypotheses," in J. Greenley, ed., *Research in Community and Mental Health*, vol. 5 (Greenwich, Connecticut: J.A.I. Press, 1985).

TABLE 1

AVERAGE INCOME OF WHITE FAMILIES IN 1982, BY TYPE OF FAMILY

(Percentage Reporting Income in Parentheses)

Income	All Two-Parent Families	All Mother-Only Families	Mother-Only Families			
			Widowed	Divorced	Separated	Never Married
Earned income of household head	21,932	7,666	5,098	9,556	6,070	4,568
	(94)	(70)	(54)	(81)	(64)	(52)
Mean for those reporting	23,230	10,866	9,359	11,833	9,475	8,709
Pensions	273	119	851	37	30	31
	(4)	(2)	(15)	(1)	(0)	(2)
Mean for those reporting	7,187	5,059	5,613	4,472	5,571	2,885
Other unearned income	1,609	702	2,878	524	385	258
	(77)	(47)	(61)	(52)	(40)	(26)
Mean for those reporting	2,049	1,493	4,687	1,004	961	978
Earnings by other family members	6,377	928	2,132	874	755	511
	(70)	(22)	(41)	(23)	(19)	(8)
Mean for those reporting	9,159	4,283	5,239	3,850	4,072	6,044

Alimony and child support	227	1,246	174	1,797	1,022	238
	(13)	(40)	(9)	(55)	(33)	(13)
Mean for those reporting	1,814	3,129	1,968	3,260	3,099	1,763
Social Security	289	961	6,493	273	414	369
	(5)	(15)	(86)	(6)	(7)	(7)
Mean for those reporting	5,843	6,471	7,574	4,306	5,890	5,075
Public assistance	107	1,007	173	784	1,445	1,837
	(3)	(29)	(9)	(23)	(40)	(53)
Mean for those reporting	3,076	3,430	1,878	3,392	3,608	3,496
Food stamps	67	392	176	299	575	642
	(7)	(32)	(17)	(26)	(44)	(52)
Mean for those reporting	1,022	1,205	1,056	1,158	1,293	1,205
Total cash income[a]	30,814	12,628	17,799	13,845	10,122	7,812
	(100)	(100)	(100)	(100)	(100)	(100)

SOURCE: U.S. Bureau of the Census, *1983 Current Population Survey* (Washington, D.C.: U.S. Government Printing Office, 1983). As noted, our definition of family is the Census definition of households with children.

a. Total cash income is the sum of all categories shown except food stamps. For some reason, this sum differs from the original total variable in the *Current Population Survey* data tape for some groups. The largest difference is found among the white two-parent households, where the figure we obtained is $220 higher. For black two-parent households the difference is $50. For households headed by women the differences are either zero or within the margin of rounding error.

TABLE 2

AVERAGE INCOME OF BLACK FAMILIES IN 1982, BY TYPE OF FAMILY
(Percentage Reporting Income in Parentheses)

Income	All Two-Parent Families	All Mother-Only Families	Mother-Only Families			
			Widowed	Divorced	Separated	Never Married
Earned income of household head	13,508 (86)	5,363 (58)	2,454 (34)	7,660 (71)	4,967 (56)	4,939 (56)
Mean for those reporting	15,710	9,276	7,207	10,736	8,825	8,821
Pensions	232 (4)	93 (2)	568 (9)	61 (1)	79 (1)	36 (1)
Mean for those reporting	5,670	4,946	6,510	4,745	5,571	2,885
Other unearned income	849 (54)	251 (25)	367 (20)	389 (38)	184 (23)	196 (21)
Mean for those reporting	1,559	1,000	1,808	1,027	792	954
Earnings by other family members	8,096 (75)	827 (17)	1,818 (34)	888 (19)	511 (15)	783 (13)
Mean for those reporting	10,732	5,002	5,409	4,693	3,328	5,958

Alimony and child support	253	322	123	613	284	236
	(13)	(19)	(11)	(28)	(18)	(16)
Mean for those reporting	1,940	1,698	1,145	2,150	1,610	1,431
Social Security	639	563	3,207	315	384	328
	(11)	(15)	(69)	(8)	(12)	(10)
Mean for those reporting	5,743	3,873	4,679	3,734	3,142	3,420
Public assistance	336	1,710	952	1,264	1,813	1,999
	(12)	(50)	(36)	(34)	(53)	(59)
Mean for those reporting	1,940	1,698	1,145	2,150	1,610	1,431
Food stamps	1,502	863	581	613	1,001	963
	(15)	(57)	(47)	(43)	(61)	(63)
Mean for those reporting	1,502	1,514	1,241	1,425	1,636	1,514
Total cash income[a]	23,913	9,128	9,489	11,187	8,221	8,517
	(100)	(100)	(100)	(100)	(100)	(100)

Source: Same as table 1.

a. Same as table 1.

average income of two-parent families in 1982 was about two-and-one-half times as large as the average for mother-only families. Total income was $30,814 for white two-parent families, compared with $12,628 for white families headed by single mothers. For blacks the pattern was much the same, although income levels were lower in both types of families. The average income for black two-parent families was $23,913, compared with $9,128 for black mother-only families.

Low Earnings Capacity

The major source of income both for two-parent families and for mother-only families, except those headed by widows, is the earnings of the primary breadwinner. Since approximately 60 to 70 percent of total income comes from this source, the ability of single women with children to earn income is a critical determinant of their economic status. Because of differences in labor force participation and wages, female breadwinners earn only 35 percent as much as fathers in two-parent families.

The tables also show that single mothers participate in the labor force substantially less than married fathers. Participation in the labor force ranges from 34 percent of widows who are black to 81 percent of divorced mothers who are white. The significance of not working is profound. Ellwood has shown that only about 6 percent of single mothers who worked full time year-round during the previous decade were poor in any given year, as compared with more than 70 percent of nonworking women.[15] These findings should not be interpreted to mean, however, that if all single mothers worked full time, only 6 percent of them would be poor. To some extent, the apparent advantage of working mothers reflects the selection process that channels women with higher earnings capacity into the labor force and women with lower capacity into homemaker status. On this point, Sawhill has found that women on welfare in the early 1970s had very low earnings capacity and that even if they worked full time, more than half would still earn less than their welfare grants. Another quarter would earn up to $1,000 more than their grants, and one-quarter would earn $1,000 or more than their grants.[16] Although the Sawhill study has not been replicated with more recent data, there is good reason to believe that even if women on welfare worked full time

15. David Ellwood, "Working Off Welfare: Prospects and Policies for Self-Sufficiency of Female Family Heads," unpublished manuscript (Cambridge, Massachusetts: Harvard University, 1985).

16. Isabel Sawhill, "Discrimination and Poverty among Women Who Head Families," *Signs*, vol. 2 (Spring 1976), pp. 201-11.

year-round, most still would be either unable to earn their way out of poverty or able to do just marginally better. For example, a woman working 2,000 hours a year at the minimum wage of $3.35 an hour would earn only $6,700 a year, which is less than the 1985 poverty level for a family of two ($7,050). To earn more than the poverty level for a family of three ($8,850), a woman working 2,000 hours a year would have to earn more than $4.40 an hour.

Why are the wages of single mothers so low? In part it is because they are mothers and as such have invested a substantial amount of their time and energy in child care. Compared with fathers, mothers are less likely to have worked continuously since leaving school and are less likely to have received on-the-job training, both of which have a strong positive effect on wage rates. More important perhaps, a large proportion of poor, single mothers bore their first child as teenagers. Moore and Burt have estimated that nearly 60 percent of all women on welfare in 1975 had been teenage mothers. Early childbirth is associated with lower education and higher fertility, both of which limit the development of skills and relevant experience and reduce earnings capacity.[17]

Differences in education and work experience, however, cannot account for all the difference in the wages of fathers and mothers; thus some of the lower earnings of nonmarried mothers must be due to other factors. It is well known that among full-time year-round workers, women earn about 60 percent as much as men and this ratio has remained relatively constant for the past thirty years. Estimates of the proportion of the wage gap due to differences in human capital (education, work experience, and work commitment) generally range from 10 to 44 percent, which suggests that over half of the gender wage gap is due to something other than differences in productivity, presumably discrimination.[18]

---

17. Kristin A. Moore and Martha R. Burt, *Private Crisis, Public Cost: Policy Perspectives on Teenage Childbearing* (Washington, D.C.: Urban Institute, 1982). See also Richard Wertheimer and Kristin A. Moore, "Teenage Childbearing: Public Sector Costs," final report to the National Institute for Child and Human Development (Washington, D.C.: Urban Institute, 1982). Also see Sandra L. Hofferth, "Long-Term Economic Consequences of Early Childbearing," in Hofferth and Hayes, eds., *Teenage Pregnancy and Childbearing: A Review of Research* (Washington, D.C.: National Academy of Science Press, forthcoming 1987).

18. A. S. Blinder, "Wage Discrimination: Reduced Form and Structural Estimates," *Journal of Human Resources*, vol. 8, no. 4 (Fall 1973), pp. 436-55; Jacob Mincer and Solomon Polachek, "Family Investments in Human Capital: Earnings of Women," *Journal of Political Economy*, vol. 82, (March-April 1974), pp. 76-108; Mary Corcoran and Greg Duncan, "Work History, Labor Force Attachment, and Earnings Differences between the Races and Sexes," *Journal of Human Resources*, vol. 14 (Winter 1979), pp. 3-20. For more complete reviews of this literature see Francine D. Blau, "Occupational Segregation and Labor Market Discrimination," in B. F.

Inadequate Child Support

Low income among families headed by single women also is due to the fact that in most cases only one parent contributes to the family income. Not only does the major breadwinner in such families have a lower earnings capacity than the major breadwinner in two-parent families, but also the ratio of dependents to earners is higher. Tables 1 and 2 showed that a substantial portion of income in two-parent families is attributable to "earnings by other family members," primarily the earnings of the mother. Earnings of other family members account for about 21 percent of the total family income in white two-parent families and for about 34 percent of the income in black two-parent families.

In families headed by single mothers, the contribution from the father appears under the category of "alimony and child support." According to our estimates, only about 40 percent of absent white fathers and 19 percent of absent black fathers pay child support. Of those who pay, the average amount received annually is $3,129 for white mothers and $1,698 for black mothers. Support payments from the absent father account for about 10 percent of the income of single white mothers and for about 3.5 percent of the income of single black mothers. These numbers are much smaller than the contributions of fathers in two-parent families and also much smaller than the contributions from the secondary earner in two-parent families.

Why is child support such a small share of single mothers' income, and how much more should absent fathers contribute? Parents are obligated by law to support their children. When a parent lives with a child, this obligation is normally met through the course of everyday sharing. When a parent does not live with the child, the obligation is supposed to be discharged through child support—a transfer of income from the noncustodial to the custodial parent.

When a family separates, it loses the economies of scale that result from living together in one household. Two homes must be bought or rented, furnished, heated, and maintained, rather than one. Therefore even if all noncustodial fathers paid a reasonable amount of child support, such payments would not fully compensate for the economic contribution of a father in the house. Nevertheless, most noncustodial fathers do not pay even a reasonable amount of child support. National data on child support awards indicate that only about 60 percent of the children who live with their mothers and are

Reskin, ed., *Sex Segregation in the Workplace: Trends, Explanations, Remedies*, (Washington, D.C.: National Academy Press, 1984); and Donald J. Treiman and Heidi I. Hartmann, eds., *Women, Work and Wages: Equal Pay for Jobs of Equal Value* (Washington, D.C.: National Academy Press, 1981).

potentially eligible for child support receive an award at all. (There are no comparable data on the child support obligations and payments of noncustodial mothers.) Of those with an award, only half receive the full amount due. Nearly 30 percent receive nothing. Furthermore, even among parents with the same financial ability to pay child support, awards vary dramatically. At one extreme, children are well provided for; at the other extreme, children receive nothing.

Exactly what share of the cost of raising a child should be borne by the absent parent depends, of course, on value judgments. To obtain an idea of the effect of child support on the poverty status of families headed by single mothers (excluding widows), Garfinkel and Ollerich simulated the effect of collecting child support equal to 17 percent of the noncustodial parent's gross income for one child, 25 percent of income for two children, 29 percent for three children, 31 percent for four children, and 33 percent for five or more children. Those estimates indicated that the poverty gap—the difference between the incomes of poor families headed by single mothers and the amount of money they would need to move above the poverty level—would be reduced by 27 percent.[19] Additional payments might also result in behavioral changes that further reduce the poverty gap. For example, by providing a stable source of income that is not means-tested, child support might help a welfare mother to obtain a job and work her way out of poverty.

Meager Public Transfers

A final cause of poverty in mother-only families is the relatively meager transfer benefits provided by the government to such families. When the benefits available to widows are compared with those available to other single women who head families with children, the inadequacy of the latter becomes obvious. Whereas 51 percent of all families headed by single mothers are poor, only 34 percent of families headed by widows are poor. A large part of the difference is directly traceable to the differences between Survivors' Insurance—the program that aids widows—and Aid to Females with Dependent Children (AFDC)—the program that aids other mother-only families. Tables 1 and 2 showed that white widows are far better off than any other group of single mothers, not because they earn more, but because they receive a much larger proportion of their income through public benefits.

19. The Garfinkel and Ollerich estimates assume that all eligible custodial parents have an award and that awards are paid in full. See Donald Ollerich and Irvin Garfinkel, "Distributional Impact of Alternative Child Support Systems," *Policy Studies Journal*, vol. 12, no. 1 (September 1983), pp. 119-29.

There are two major reasons. First, the proportion of all widows who receive Survivors' Insurance is much larger than the proportion of other female heads of families who receive welfare. As table 1 and 2 indicated, nearly 90 percent of all widows who are white and 70 percent of those who are black receive Survivors' Insurance. Only 23 percent of white and 34 percent of black divorced women receive welfare, and the proportion for separated and never-married white and black women who receive welfare ranges from 40 to 59 percent. Second, the average Survivors' Insurance benefit is much higher than the average welfare benefit—nearly double for whites, more than double for blacks.

Benefits for divorced, separated, and never-married mothers and their children could be made more similar to benefits to widows either by increasing benefit levels or by making benefits available to single mothers regardless of income. Increasing the benefits would be consistent with a policy decision to enable poor mothers to stay home and rear their children. Extending benefits without income limits to all single mothers would be consistent with a policy decision to supplement the earnings of single mothers because they were expected to work.

By drastically reducing benefits as earnings increase, welfare programs replace rather than supplement earnings. Even when the AFDC program contained better work incentive provisions than is now the case, the gains from working were slight. After deductions for work-related expenses, families receiving AFDC benefits lost two-thirds of each dollar earned. They lost about another quarter of each dollar earned in food stamp benefits. If they lived in public housing, their rents increased. And if they earned enough to leave welfare, they faced the prospect of losing a valuable health insurance policy in the form of Medicaid.

In short, what the government gives in welfare benefits with one hand, it takes away with the other. As a consequence, single mothers who have low earnings are faced with an all-or-nothing situation: become dependent on welfare or work full time and achieve a marginally better economic position—assuming that a full-time job and suitable child care can be found.

Intergenerational Consequences of Mother-Only Family Structure

Much of the present concern in our society about the increase in the number of families headed by women arises from two beliefs: that family experiences have important implications for the well-being of children, and that large-scale changes in family structure will have a negative influence on the character and behavior of future generations of Americans. Some people focus on the considerable economic hardship and emotional stress of families headed by single mothers and want the government to play a major role in at least mitigating their problems. Others blame mother-only families for what they perceive to be a deterioration of American values and a threat to the nuclear family itself. The latter view, which was the subject of considerable controversy in the mid-1960s, has been revived in the 1980s both by Auletta and by Gilder in their discussions of the growth of an underclass in America.[20]

What happens to children who live in such a family? Do they perform less well in school or exhibit more symptoms of psychological distress? More important, what happens to those children when they become adults? Are they more likely to be poor? Are they more likely to contribute to families headed by women themselves and thereby perpetuate the cycle of dependence?

The literature on the consequences of family structure for children is large, and we do not attempt to cover all of it in this chapter. Rather, we limit our focus to outcomes that are directly related to long-term socioeconomic well-being, including educational attainment, economic attainment (occupational status and earnings), and family formation behavior.[21] It should be made clear at the outset that much of the literature on family structure and attainment does not distinguish between mother-only and father-only families, but only between one-parent and two-parent families. Because the majority of one-parent families are mother-only families, the one-parent versus two-parent comparisons primarily reflect differences between mother-only and two-parent families. When we quote results that do address one or the other form of single parenthood, we make that explicit.

Effects on Socioeconomic Attainment

Studies of family structure and its consequences on educational achievement greatly outnumber studies of other outcomes. Such an emphasis appears

---

20. Ken Auletta, *The Underclass* (New York: Random House, 1982); and George Gilder, *Wealth and Poverty* (New York: Basic Books, 1981).

21. For major reviews of the literature, see Heather L. Ross and Isabel Sawhill, *Time of Transition: The Growth of Families Headed by Women* (Washington, D.C.: Urban Institute, 1975); Marybeth Shinn, "Father Absence and Children's Cognitive Development," *Psychological Bulletin*, vol. 85 (1978), pp. 295-324; Elizabeth Herzog and Cecilia Sudia, "Children in Fatherless Families," in B. Caldwell and H. Ricciuti, eds., *Review of Child Development Research*, vol. 3 (Chicago: University of Chicago Press, 1973); E. Mavis Hetherington, "Children and Divorce," in R. Henderson, ed., *Parent-Child Interaction: Theory, Research and Prospect* (New York: Academic Press, 1981); and E. Mavis Hetherington, Kathleen A. Camara, and David L. Featherman, "Achievement and Intellectual Functioning of Children in One-Parent Households," in J. Spence, ed., *Achievement and Achievement Motives* (San Francisco, California: W. H. Freeman, 1983).

reasonable because educational success is a strong predictor of a range of adult outcomes, including occupational status, earnings, and marital stability.

Cognitive Ability and Educational Achievement. Research on cognitive ability indicates that membership in a one-parent family has a negative, but relatively weak, effect on IQ scores. After examining thirty studies of IQ differences, Hetherington, Camara, and Featherman noted that the scores of children in single-parent families ranged from one to seven points lower than those of children in two-parent households.[22] Given that the standard deviation on IQ test scores is fifteen points, they concluded that this difference is quite small. Their results with respect to cognitive achievement tests were similar. Children in one-parent families scored lower than children in two-parent families on quantitative as well as verbal tests, but the differences were less than one school year. Unlike the evidence from IQ and achievement tests, their results with respect to aptitude tests were mixed. Boys from families headed by single parents scored lower than average on quantitative tests; whereas girls from such families scored higher than average on verbal tests.

The biggest differences in the performance of schoolchildren appear in teacher evaluations—such as grade point averages and behavioral assessments—both of which show substantially lower scores for children from one-parent families. The disparity between the subjective indicators and standardized test scores can be interpreted in two ways: either children from such families are more likely to underachieve or they are less successful in adapting to teacher expectations. Morrison has noted that teacher ratings are often based on perceptions of whether a student is obedient and conforming to the norm rather than on academic mastery.[23] Because children of divorcing parents may act out their anger and disappointment for some time after the separation, they are also more likely to be perceived as uncooperative by teachers.

In addition to conducting research on the relation between family structure and intellectual capacity and achievement, researchers have also investigated the relation among family structure, the likelihood that children will drop out of high school, and, more generally, the children's educational attainment. In a recent study based on the Michigan PSID, McLanahan found that living in a mother-only family decreased the likelihood of completing high school by about 5 percentage points for white children and 13 percentage points for blacks.[24] These differences represent substantial proportional de-

---

22. Hetherington, Camara, and Featherman, "Achievement and Intellectual Functioning."

23. E. Morrison, "Under-Achievement among Adolescent Boys Considered in Relation to Passive Aggression," *Journal of Educational Psychology*, vol. 60 (1969), pp. 168-73.

24. Sara McLanahan, "Family Structure and the Reproduction of Poverty," *American Journal of Sociology*, vol. 90 (January 1985), pp. 873-901.

creases in the likelihood of graduation: about 42 percent for whites and 70 percent for blacks. Shaw and also Krein and Beller have reported similar results, using data on mothers and daughters from the National Longitudinal Survey (NLS).[25] Krein and Beller found that living in a single-parent family decreases the educational attainment of sons by about 0.5 of a school year and attainment of daughters by about 0.2 of a year. Their estimates were based on the children's spending an average of 6.7 years in a single-parent family. For offspring who spend their entire childhood in such a family, the estimated effects would be greater: 1.8 years for boys and 0.6 year for girls.

Studies of educational attainment based on cross-sectional surveys have consistently found that offspring from single-parent families are disadvantaged with respect to years of schooling completed. Duncan, Featherman, and Duncan, in their analysis of the Occupational Changes in a Generation (OCG) 1962 data, reported that growing up in a two-parent family added between 0.6 and 1.2 years of school to the educational attainment of white males and about 0.4 to 0.8 year to that of blacks.[26] Featherman and Hauser, using 1972 OCG data, found somewhat smaller differences: males from single-parent families obtained about 0.6 to 1.0 year less education than males from two-parent families.[27] Similar results were reported for a sample of Canadian males and females born during the same period.[28]

Occupational and Economic Attainment. Children from single-parent families are also disadvantaged with respect to occupational status and other indicators of economic well-being. In their analysis of the 1962 OCG data, Duncan and his colleagues found that the occupational status scores of offspring from such families were lower than those of offspring from two-parent families. Among whites, the average score for males from two-parent families was 45.12, compared with 40.28 for males from single-parent families. Among blacks, the scores were 21.80 and 17.93, respectively.[29] Featherman and Hauser have reported similar differences using 1972 OCG data. They point

25. Lois Shaw, "Does Living in a Single-Parent Family Affect High School Completion for Young Women?" (Columbus, Ohio: Ohio State University, Center for Human Research, 1979); and Sheila F. Krein and Andrea Beller, "Family Structure and Educational Attainment of Children: Differences by Duration, Age, and Gender," paper presented at the annual meeting of the Population Association of America, San Francisco, California, April 3-5, 1986.

26. Otis Dudley Duncan, David Featherman, and Beverly Duncan, *Socioeconomic Background and Achievement* (New York: Seminar Press, 1972). The data came from the social supplement to the March 1962 *Current Population Survey*.

27. David Featherman and Robert M. Hauser, *Opportunity and Change* (New York: Academic Press, 1978).

28. Hetherington, Camara, and Featherman, "Achievement and Intellectual Functioning."

29. Duncan, Featherman, and Duncan, *Socioeconomic Background and Achievement*.

out that differences in status are due both to differences in educational attainment and to differences in the returns to education.[30]

Children from single-parent families also have lower earnings in young adulthood and are more likely to be poor. Hill, Augustiniak, and Ponza have shown that living with a divorced or separated mother for two years or more (1) reduces wages for white and black men, (2) reduces economic well-being for white men and women and black men, and (3) increases welfare dependence for white men and women.[31] The results for welfare dependence are supported by McLanahan, who found that having lived in a mother-only family approximately triples the probability of becoming a welfare recipient, for whites as well as blacks:[32] for whites from 0.01 to 0.03, and for blacks from 0.05 to 0.14.

Family Formation Behavior. Perhaps the strongest evidence for intergenerational effects comes from research on family formation behavior. Numerous studies have shown that daughters who grow up in single-parent families are more likely to marry early and have children early, including both marital and out-of-wedlock births. They are also more likely to divorce than are daughters from two-parent families. In early research based on data from the 1970 National Fertility Study, Bumpass and Sweet found that parents' marital disruption increased the likelihood of daughters' marital disruption by about 60 percent. Whereas the disruption rate averaged 0.15 for the population at large, for daughters of single parents it was 0.24.[33] Heiss reported similar results for blacks but concluded that overall the effect of parents' marital disruption was small, especially among lower-income families.[34]

More recently, McLanahan and Bumpass have presented even stronger evidence that daughters from one-parent families are more likely to become single heads of similar families themselves. Using data from the 1982 National Survey of Family Growth, they concluded that family structure has a strong and consistent effect across a wide range of indicators. Among whites, daughters of single parents are 53 percent more likely to marry as teenagers, 111 percent more likely to have children as teenagers, 164 percent more likely to

30. Featherman and Hauser, *Opportunity and Change*.

31. Martha Hill, Sue Augustiniak, and Michael Ponza, "The Impact of Parental Marital Disruption on the Socioeconomic Attainments of Children as Adults," unpublished paper (Ann Arbor, Michigan: University of Michigan, Institute for Social Research, 1985).

32. Sara McLanahan, "Family Structure and Dependency: Early Transitions to Female Household Headships," Institute for Research on Poverty paper 807-86 (Madison, Wisconsin: University of Wisconsin, 1986).

33. Larry L. Bumpass and James A. Sweet, "Differentials in Marital Instability: 1970," *American Sociological Review*, vol. 37 (December 1972), pp. 754-66.

34. Jerald Heiss, "On the Transmission of Marital Instability in Black Families," *American Sociological Review*, vol. 87 (February 1972), pp. 82-92.

have a premarital birth, and 92 percent more likely to dissolve their own marriages. The pattern is similar for blacks (although the effects are about half as strong) with one exception: family structure is not related to early marriage.[35] Similar results were found by Hogan and Kitagawa in a study of black adolescent girls in the Chicago area. These researchers found that young black women from mother-only families were about 50 percent more likely to become pregnant than were young women from two-parent families.[36]

Reasons for the Intergenerational Consequences of Family Structure

As noted, the appropriate policy prescription to alleviate these negative effects depends on the relative importance of the economic deprivation itself, outside employment of the mother and absence of the father as explanatory factors.

Economic Deprivation. Given that mother-only families are concentrated at the lower end of the income distribution, and that children from poor families are more likely to be poor when they grow up, it would be surprising if the offspring of female-headed families were *not* worse off in adulthood than were offspring from two-parent families. This reasoning, combined with the fact that much of the early research on intergenerational consequences did not control for income while looking for other explanations, has led some people to conclude that low income can account for *all* of the relative disadvantages of children from such families.

Several explanations can be offered for why economic deprivation might lead to lower achievement among offspring. First, poor families have less money to invest in children's educational activities. Family income has a powerful influence on children's participation in extracurricular activities, length of and distance traveled on vacations, and attendance at summer camps,

---

35. Sara S. McLanahan and Larry Bumpas, "Intergenerational Consequences of Family Disruption," paper presented at the annual meeting of the Population Association of America, San Francisco, California, April 3-5, 1986. The Family Growth Survey data do not provide information on family income and therefore differences in income between one- and two-parent families are not controlled. In a separate study based on the PSID data, however, McLanahan found that income differences did not explain variations in family formation behavior. See also McLanahan, "Family Structure and Dependency: Early Transitions to Female Household Headship."

36. Dennis P. Hogan and Evelyn M. Kitagawa, "The Impact of Social Status, Family Structure, and Neighborhood on the Fertility of Black Adolescents," *American Journal of Sociology*, vol. 90 (January 1985), pp. 825-56. The Hogan and Kitagawa study controls for differences in family income. Also see Dennis P. Hogan, "Structural and Normative Factors in Single Parenthood among Black Adolescents," unpublished paper (Chicago, Illinois: University of Chicago, Department of Sociology, 1985).

all of which are positively related to school achievement.[37] Economic necessity may also promote the premature assumption of adult responsibilities.[38] Specifically, offspring from low-income families are more likely to leave school early to earn money for their families and to care for younger siblings than are offspring in middle-income families. This hypothesis does not assume that early departure from school is due to poor performance or negative behavior in general. On the contrary, children who leave school prematurely to fulfill adult roles may be highly responsible. Their responsibilities, however, are directed toward family survival rather than individual achievement.

Finally, as already documented, low income is associated with numerous forms of instability and chronic stress that might be expected to undermine the achievement of children. Poor single mothers who head families experience frequent unemployment and are more likely to live in unsafe neighborhoods, where delinquency rates are high and the quality of schools is low.[39]

But what evidence is there to demonstrate that income per se can account for the negative association between family structure and attainment? It is unfortunate that much of the research on mother-only families does not adequately control for income, making it impossible to identify the separate influences of income and family structure. Even the research on adult attainment, which is based on relatively sophisticated models, is limited because of a lack of information on family income in childhood or adolescence. Although the attainment studies typically control for the education and occupational status of the mother and father, or family head, these controls are not adequate when comparing one- and two-parent families. Because one-parent households are generally headed by women and because women earn considerably less than men of similar occupational and educational status, controlling for the latter variables is not enough to control for differences in family income.

Nevertheless, some studies do have good income information, and these provide support for the economic deprivation hypothesis. In particular, income appears to be important in explaining differences in school performance and

37. Barbara Heyns, "The Influence of Parental Work on Children's School Achievement," in S. B. Kamerman and C. D. Hayes, eds., *Families That Work: Children in a Changing World* (Washington, D.C.: National Academy Press, 1985), pp. 229-67.

38. Robert Weiss, "Growing Up a Little Faster: The Experience of Growing Up in a Single-Parent Household," *Journal of Social Issues*, vol. 35 (1979), pp. 97-111; and Glen H. Elder, Jr., *Children of the Great Depression* (Chicago: University Press, 1974).

39. Ruth Brandwein, Carol Brown, and Elizabeth Fox, "Women and Children Last: The Social Situation of Divorced Mothers and Their Families," *Journal of Marriage and the Family* (August 1974), pp. 498-514.

high school dropout rates. In their summary of the research on intellectual achievement, Hetherington and her colleagues have concluded that when socioeconomic status was taken into account, previous differences in one- and two-parent households tended to disappear. With respect to high school graduation, McLanahan has reported that differences in income explain about half of the association between family structure and matriculation among whites (though not among blacks); Shaw has found similar results using the National Longitudinal Survey data, although in a more recent analysis, Krein and Beller did not.[40]

Income appears to be much less important in accounting for differences in family formation behavior. McLanahan found that family income during adolescence explained very little about the tendency of daughters of single mothers in the Michigan PSID data to become heads of such families themselves.[41] Similarly, Hogan and Kitagawa have reported that social class did not account for fertility differences among black female teenagers in Chicago.[42] Given these findings, it seems reasonable to assume that increasing the incomes of single mothers would alleviate at least some of the educational disadvantages now associated with being a member of a female-headed family, but would not have much of an effect on out-of-wedlock births or on the perpetuation of mother-only families.

The Absence of a Parent. Aside from economic deprivation, the most commonly stated explanation is that negative outcomes are due to the consequences of parental absence for the socialization and supervision of children. The traditional version of this argument stresses the absence of the father or the loss of the male role model and its consequences for psychosexual development. For sons, the absence of the father is thought to undermine sex-role identity, and for both sons and daughters, it is thought to interfere with cross-sex relationships. For both sexes it is thought to reduce analytical thinking as reflected in mathematical aptitude scores.[43]

Although traditional theory has generally stressed the absence of the father, it can be argued that the role model presented by a single mother heading the family is the critical link in intergenerational instability. Stated another way, marital dissolution or single parenthood may have more legitimacy among offspring reared by single women than among other groups. In

40. McLanahan, "Family Structure and the Reproduction of Poverty"; Shaw, "Does Living in a Single-Parent Family Affect High School Completion for Young Women?"; and Krein and Beller, "Family Structure and Educational Attainment of Children."
41. McLanahan, "Family Structure and Dependency."
42. Hogan and Kitagawa, "The Impact of Social Status."
43. Hetherington, Camara, and Featherman, "Achievement and Intellectual Functioning."

both cases, theory suggests that the effects will be stronger the longer the father is absent, and strongest when the father has never been present at all.

Other researchers emphasize the importance of parental supervision in determining the behavior and achievement of children. Here the critical factor is the absence of a parent in general rather than the absence of the father, because the one remaining parent has less time and presumably less energy for monitoring and supervising than two parents have. People who support this position also argue that disruption of the parent's marriage or single parenthood may be most harmful to offspring when they are in adolescence, because this is the period when they are becoming sexually active and are making important decisions about stopping or continuing school. In their study of young black women in Chicago, for example, Hogan and Kitagawa found that adolescent girls in mother-only families were more likely to become pregnant than girls in two-parent families, both because they became sexually active at an earlier age and because their parents exercised less supervision over their dating.[44]

The evidence in support of the parental absence hypotheses suggests that growing up without a mother is just as bad as growing up without a father. Although the number of single-parent families headed by a man is quite small, some studies have looked specifically at this subgroup. Featherman and Hauser, for example, found that male offspring from families headed by a single man complete between 0.85 and 1.5 fewer years of school than offspring from two-parent families, compared with 0.75 fewer for those in families headed by a single woman.[45] Using 1980 census data, Bumpass has also found that offspring in one-parent families are less likely to be in school at age seventeen than are those in two-parent families, regardless of the sex of the single parent.[46] Finally, McLanahan and Bumpass report no difference in the negative outcomes between one-parent families headed by a man and those headed by a woman for a variety of indicators, including early marriage, early birth, out-of-wedlock birth, and divorce.[47]

Maternal Employment. In the past some analysts have argued that the negative consequences associated with living in a mother-only family were due as much to the mother's working as to the father's absence. Maternal employment has been viewed negatively because it reduces the mother's participation in the child's educational activities as well as her monitoring and supervising of extracurricular activities. According to this argument,

44. Hogan and Kitagawa, "The Impact of Social Status."
45. Featherman and Hauser, *Opportunity and Change*.
46. Larry Bumpass, personal communication to authors, November 15, 1985.
47. McLanahan and Bumpass, "Intergenerational Consequences of Family Disruption."

single mothers are more likely to work than married mothers, rendering their offspring doubly disadvantaged: they spend less time with their fathers because they live in a different place, and less time with their mothers because the mothers work.

The question of whether a mother's employment is bad for children and whether employment can account for the problems of offspring in mother-only families is of critical importance to policymakers. Much of our present welfare system is based on the idea that mothers should be encouraged to stay home and take care of their children, at least until the children are in school. This was the prevailing ideal in the 1930s when the Social Security and AFDC programs were initiated, and it has continued to receive support from numerous policymakers and administrators.

But things have changed since the 1930s, as noted in chapter 1, and many of these changes have called into question the assumption that single women with children should not work. First, married mothers with children, including those with preschool-age children, have entered the labor force in large numbers, especially since 1960. Working at least part-time is now the norm rather than the exception. Should single women with children be treated differently? Second, a large proportion of single women with children are already employed, and those who work are better off in terms of income than those who do not. Although selectivity is clearly a part of the difference here, and although employment would not lift all mother-only families out of poverty, it is not clear that our current welfare system, which has a high tax on work, is the best way to supplement their incomes.

To make an enlightened policy choice, we must know how much good or how much harm is associated with maternal employment. If working has no negative consequences for children, few people would argue that single mothers should stay home and limit their activities to household work. But if employment of these mothers *is* bad for their children, and if it increases the likelihood that their daughters will become heads of such families in the future, many people would argue for continuing to discourage work.

The research on employment of mothers has been summarized recently in two excellent reviews. Hoffman has concluded that there is no evidence that maternal employment has harmful effects on the children and some evidence that the effects are positive, especially for daughters.[48] Heyns has reached similar conclusions.[49] Focusing specifically on studies of minority and low-income families, Heyns has noted that most of the research shows

---

48. Lois Hoffman, "Maternal Employment: 1979," *American Psychologist*, vol. 34 (October 1979), pp. 859-65.
49. Heyns, "The Influence of Parental Work."

that the economic benefits of the mother's employment outweigh the costs. In her own work on fifth- and sixth-grade black children in Atlanta, Heyns found that the mother's employment was positively related to increases in the children's achievement test scores during the summer.[50] Similar results have been reported by Woods, who studied fifth graders in a North Philadelphia ghetto school; by Reiber and Womach, who studied children in Head Start programs in Houston, Texas; and by Kriesberg, who looked at families in poverty in New York State.[51]

Studies of adolescents or high school students are less positive with respect to the effect of work. Using data from the High School and Beyond Study, which sampled sophomores and seniors in 1981, Milne and her colleagues reported that the mother's working has negative effects on reading and mathematics scores; Krein and Beller, using the NLS youth sample, report that the mother's working has negative consequences for the educational attainment of sons.[52]

The literature on the mother's working must be interpreted with caution. In particular, one should be cautious about positive findings. First, since working is highly correlated with earnings capacity, any positive effect may be due simply to selection into the labor force. This would be especially true of mothers of young children where selection would be the strongest (due to the high costs of child care) and where observed effects are most positive. Second, positive effects may simply be due to higher income since mother-only families in which the mother works are clearly better off than those in which she stays home. Heyns notes that most of the difference between children of working and nonworking mothers disappears once income is taken into account.[53] This does not mean that the positive benefits of earned income are unimportant but simply that the mother's working itself may not have any particular benefits beyond those of income. Finally, it is possible that positive effects may come about through a "modeling effect," rather than through

---

50. Barbara Heyns, *Summer Learning and the Effects of Schooling* (New York: Academic Press, 1978); for a conflicting view, see F. F. Chevy and E. L. Eaton, "Physical and Cognitive Development in Children of Low-Income Mothers Working in the Child's Early Years," *Child Development*, vol. 48 (1977), pp. 158-66.

51. M. B. Woods, "The Unsupervised Child of the Working Mother," *Development Psychology*, vol. 6 (1972), pp. 14-25; M. Rieber and M. Womach, "The Intelligence of Preschool Children as Related to Ethnic and Demographic Variables," *Exceptional Children*, vol. 34 (1967), pp. 609-14; and Lawrence Kriesberg, "Rearing Children for Educational Achievement in Fatherless Families," *Journal of Marriage and the Family*, vol. 2 (1967), pp. 288-301.

52. Ann Milne et al., "Single Parents, Working Mothers, and the Educational Achievement of School Children," *Sociology of Education* (July 1986); and Krein and Beller, "Family Structure and Educational Attainment of Children."

53. Heyns, *Summer Learning and the Effects of Schooling*.

the effect of outside work itself. Some studies have found that the mother's employment and occupational status have positive effects on the career expectations and aspirations of high school girls. One study points out that maternal employment may vary across different ethnic groups, depending on whether it is consistent with cultural norms.[54]

At present we cannot say with certainty that the mother's working has no negative consequences for children. However, there is good reason to believe that the effects on children of preschool and elementary school age are neutral to positive. The fact that Milne and her colleagues find negative effects for high school sophomores and seniors, however, makes this less certain for adolescents.

There is a certain irony in the observation that adolescents may be the children who are more negatively affected by mother's absence, since the concern has clearly been for young children. This suggests that perhaps we may be focusing on the wrong factor when we talk about employment effects. In most cases theory has stressed the importance of the mother's attention for the psychological (cognitive and emotional) development of the child. It is possible, however, that the key factor behind negative outcomes may be supervision rather than interpersonal relationships. Recall that Hogan and Kitagawa have found that supervision of early dating patterns, which is less common in mother-only families, is an important determinant of early pregnancy.

Welfare Dependence and Mother-Only Families

Before concluding this discussion of the problems of mother-only families, we must address the question of whether the current system of aiding single mothers—through AFDC—is creating additional problems for these families at the same time that it is reducing their poverty and economic insecurity. The question of dependence arises because of the high proportion of such families receiving welfare each year and because of the number of years that some of these families are on welfare.

According to the Current Population Survey (CPS), which is conducted annually by the U.S. Bureau of the Census, about one of every three mother-only families received AFDC benefits in 1983. This figure underestimates the prevalence of welfare dependence for at least two reasons. First, we know that the amount of benefits reported by AFDC recipients is about 25 percent

---

54. Anne Macke and William Morgan, "Maternal Employment, Race and Work Orientation of High School Girls," *Social Forces*, vol. 57 (1978), pp. 187-204; see also Heyns, *Summer Learning and the Effects of Schooling*.

less than the government spends on AFDC. Second, the procedure used by the CPS—which is to ascertain family composition as of the date of interview and welfare income as of the previous year—leads to an underestimate of the proportion of female heads of household who received welfare during the past year. If the average annual AFDC caseload of mother-only families for 1983 is compared with the CPS estimate of the number of such families in the same year, the results indicate that about 47 percent, or nearly half, of all female-headed families received some welfare during the year.[55]

Recent studies of the duration of welfare dependence present two seemingly contradictory pictures. One set of studies emphasizes the short-term nature of dependence. Coe, for example, has found that only 6.5 percent of the U.S. population during 1969-78 received welfare for six or more years.[56] Other researchers have found that between 48 percent and 69 percent of all new welfare recipients leave welfare within two years.[57] In contrast, Ellwood has found that 65 percent of recipients of AFDC at any time are in the midst of a welfare spell of eight or more years.[58] He also notes that about 70 percent of families who leave welfare within two years will become dependent again. Which of these two pictures is accurate? The answer is both. A majority of those who go on welfare will be off in less than two years, but a substantial minority—and this minority accounts for a majority of the caseload at any point in time—will be dependent for a long time.

When they are on welfare, the degree of dependence of recipient families is quite high. During the months they receive AFDC benefits, the overwhelming majority of women who had families with children (85 percent) do not work. Most have no other sources of income and are totally dependent on AFDC, food stamps, Medicaid and, less frequently, public housing assistance.

---

55. U.S. Bureau of the Census, "Estimates of Poverty including the Value of Noncash Benefits: 1984," technical paper 55 (Washington, D.C.: U.S. Government Printing Office, 1985).

56. Richard D. Coe, "A Preliminary Empirical Examination of the Dynamics of Welfare Use," in Greg J. Duncan and James N. Morgan, eds., *Five Thousand American Families: Patterns of Economic Progress*, vol. 8 (Ann Arbor, Michigan: University of Michigan, Institute for Social Research, 1981). Coe includes families other than those headed by women and other forms of welfare besides AFDC and food stamps.

57. For a review of the literature see Greg J. Duncan and Saul Hoffman, "Welfare Dynamics and Welfare Policy: Past Evidence and Future Research Directions," paper presented at the Association for Public Policy Analysis and Management meetings, Washington, D.C., October 1985.

58. David Ellwood, "Targeting the Would-Be Long-Term Recipient of AFDC: Who Should Be Served?" unpublished preliminary report (Cambridge, Massachusetts, Harvard University, 1985).

Whether the dependence of these women lasts too long or is too great is largely determined by how society feels about work. If, on the one hand, women who head families with children are expected to work and to be economically independent, even two years may seem a long time. If, on the other hand, they are not expected to work, then duration and degree of economic dependence may not seem like serious problems.

Much of the current concern about welfare dependence arises from the belief that welfare undermines both values of independence and motivation toward economic mobility. This belief is not limited to conservatives or to the current debate. Franklin D. Roosevelt, in his message to Congress in January of 1935, declared, "Continued dependency upon relief induces a spiritual and moral disintegration fundamentally destructive to the national fiber. To dole out relief in this way is to administer a narcotic, a subtle disintegrator of the human spirit. . . . It is in violation of the traditions of America."[59]

In the current debate, welfare is viewed as harmful for two reasons. First, welfare recipients are believed to be stigmatized, and stigma may lead to a loss of self-esteem and poor mental health. Second, welfare is believed to create feelings of helplessness and loss of control over one's life, which may lead to long-term dependence by recipients as well as their offspring. Both arguments suggest that welfare produces a particular set of attitudes or a view of the world that undermines the motivation to achieve and ultimately reduces economic mobility.

Welfare Stigma

When we say that welfare mothers are stigmatized, we mean that society holds negative views about recipients of welfare, and that the welfare mothers come to accept these views about themselves. Theoretical arguments for stigma are based on the high value that society places on independence. As a consequence, people who are dependent are devalued in society's view. Even though we as a society are still somewhat ambivalent about whether mothers should work, nearly everyone agrees that heads of households should support their families. When a woman assumes this role, she implicitly assumes the same obligations.

Ethnographic studies report mixed results on the question of whether welfare mothers feel stigmatized. Some researchers report that welfare mothers are aware of and feel depressed about the negative views people hold

---

59. President Franklin D. Roosevelt, quoted in Josephine Brown, *Public Relief 1929-1939* (New York: Henry Holt and Co., 1935), p. 165.

about them. One former welfare mother, for example, described her experience: "Being on welfare hurt me because I felt as if I were irresponsible. If I were working and bringing home $60 a week, I would know it was my money, and I would feel better about myself. On welfare I began feeling as if I was asking them to give me something I didn't deserve."[60] In another well-publicized study of a long-term black welfare mother, however, Sheehan reported that the woman was not even aware of, let alone affected by, society's negative attitudes.[61]

Good quantitative evidence on the prevalence and severity of stigma is hard to come by. One study, conducted by Handler and Hollingsworth in the late 1960s, found that about half of AFDC mothers reported that they never felt embarrassed or uncomfortable when they were with others who were not on welfare, about 35 percent said they sometimes felt uncomfortable, and about 15 percent said they always felt uncomfortable. Responses were closely correlated with mothers' characterization of community attitudes toward AFDC recipients but not in the expected direction. Those who saw community attitudes as negative or indifferent reported the least embarrassment about their situation.[62]

Rainwater has suggested that stigma is pervasive and that it affects recipients in a variety of ways, only some of which would result in observable effects. According to Rainwater, depression or lower self-esteem is one response to feeling stigmatized; denial is another; and labeling oneself as sick or disabled is a third. Recipients who deny their situation or who assume the sick role would not necessarily report that they felt stigmatized, which may explain the mixed findings in the empirical studies.[63] Rainwater's observations are consistent with epidemiological research showing that welfare recipients report more symptoms of psychophysiological distress (for example, nervous stomach, tension, and high blood pressure) than nonrecipients.[64]

---

60. A. S. Coles, "The Inner Relationships among Work, Welfare and Higher Education: An Exploratory Case Study," unpublished paper (Cambridge, Massachusetts: Harvard University, n.d.).

61. Susan Sheehan, *Welfare Mother* (New York: New American Library, 1977).

62. Joel F. Handler and Ellen J. Hollingsworth, "How Obnoxious Is the Obnoxious Means Test? The Views of AFDC Recipients," Institute for Research on Poverty paper 31 (Madison, Wisconsin: University of Wisconsin, 1967). Because this study was conducted in 1967 and was based on a sample of Wisconsin AFDC recipients that included only one black ghetto, Milwaukee, the results cannot be considered conclusive evidence against the existence of a welfare subculture.

63. Rainwater, "Stigma in Income-Tested Programs."

64. Sharon Berlin and Linda Jones, "Life after Welfare: AFDC Termination among Long-Term Recipients," *Social Service Review* (September 1983), pp. 378-90.

Welfare Dependence

Some people argue that being on welfare leads to a change in attitudes and values (such as loss of motivation to achieve and loss of a sense of control over one's life), which feeds back into a cycle of dependence. Others argue that such attitudes are passed on from one generation to the next, which leads to dependence among the offspring of welfare recipients.

The latter argument is quite similar to the culture-of-poverty thesis outlined by Lewis in his classic case study of poor Puerto Rican families living in the slums. Lewis noted: "Once it [the culture of poverty] comes into existence, it tends to perpetuate itself from generation to generation because of its effects on children. By the time slum children are age six or seven, they have usually absorbed the basic values and attitudes of their subculture and are not psychologically geared to take full advantage of changing conditions or increased opportunities which may occur in their lifetime."[65]

What was originally offered as an explanation for the persistence of poverty is now given as an explanation for the persistence of dependence. In a recent study of participants in a Supported Work program, Auletta described what he calls the "behavioral deficiencies" of the underclass in America. According to Auletta, the underclass—which is made up of street criminals, hustlers, welfare-dependent mothers, and the chronically ill—"operates outside the mainstream of commonly accepted values" and is "responsible for a disproportionate amount of the crime, the welfare costs, the unemployment and the hostility that beset many American communities."[66]

To support the culture-of-dependence argument, at least two sets of relations must be demonstrated. First, it must be shown that a particular set of attitudes reduces economic mobility in adults (or offspring), and second, it must be shown that being on welfare produces such attitudes. With regard to the former, several researchers have demonstrated that future mobility is related to feelings of efficacy, that is, a sense of control over one's life. Andrisani, for example, reports that higher efficacy led to economic progress in both young and middle-aged adults in the NLS survey.[67] Similarly, Hill and her colleagues have shown that both efficacy and motivation to achieve

65. Oscar Lewis, *LaVida, A Puerto Rican Family in the Culture of Poverty: San Juan and New York* (London: Panther Books, 1968), p. 50.

66. Auletta, *The Underclass*, p. 92. See also Ken Auletta, "The Underclass: Part III," *The New Yorker* (November 30, 1981), p. 105.

67. Paul Andrisani, *Work Attitudes and Labor Market Experience* (New York: Praeger Press, 1979). See also Paul Andrisani, "Internal-External Attitudes, Personal Initiative and the Labor Market Experience of Black and White Men," *Journal of Human Resources*, vol. 12 (Summer 1977), pp. 308-28.

are related to certain kinds of mobility.[68] Although Hill and colleagues conclude that overall attitudes have only a small effect on future achievement—
compared with the effect of achievement on attitudes—their results indicate
that efficacy in particular is related to a number of critical outcomes. For
example, they show that black women with high efficacy are about 20 percent
more likely to work their way out of welfare than those with low efficacy,
and that white and black daughters of parents with high efficacy are about
50 percent less likely to go on welfare than daughters of parents with low
efficacy.

Evidence for the belief that being on welfare leads to declines in efficacy
is much weaker. Although numerous studies have shown that welfare recipients have lower self-esteem and lower efficacy than nonrecipients, the studies
have not proved that welfare *caused* such attitudes. People who go on welfare
could have been worse off to begin with. Researchers need to examine changes
in self-esteem and efficacy subsequent to a person's going on welfare. Until
recently, very little has been done in this area; moreover, the studies that
have been done report conflicting results. According to O'Neill and her colleagues at The Urban Institute, there is "nothing to indicate that experience
with AFDC causes significant changes in personal efficacy."[69] In contrast,
Nichols-Casebolt found that going on welfare was associated with declines
in efficacy among black women but not among whites.[70] Somewhat surprisingly, she also found that going on welfare increased self-esteem, which is
counter to what theories of stigma would have predicted.

Our review of the evidence on welfare stigma and dependence suggests
that although welfare recipients have lower self-esteem and lower efficacy,
there is no strong reason to believe that welfare is the cause rather than the

---

68. Martha S. Hill et al., "First Report of the Project: Motivation and Economic Mobility
of the Poor," (Ann Arbor, Michigan: University of Michigan, Institute for Social Research,
1983), tables F. 4 and O.18.

69. June O'Neill et al., "An Analysis of Time on Welfare," report prepared for Assistant
Secretary for Planning and Evaluation, Office of Income Security Policy, U.S. Department of
Health and Human Services, (Washington, D.C.: Urban Institute, June 1984).

70. Anne Nichols-Casebolt, "The Psychological Effects of Income-Testing Income Support
Benefits," unpublished paper (Madison, Wisconsin: University of Wisconsin, Institute for Research on Poverty, 1985). We should note that efficacy and self-esteem may not be the best
measures of dependence. They are, however, the only indicators available in the PSID and the
NLS—the longitudinal surveys used to examine welfare dynamics. For more general discussions
of dependence and the underclass, see William Julius Wilson, "The Urban Underclass in Advanced Industrial Society," in Paul Peterson, ed., *The New Urban Reality* (Washington, D.C.:
Brookings Institution, 1985), pp. 129–60; Nicolas Lemann, "The Origins of the Underclass,"
Atlantic Monthly (June–July 1986), pp. 31–55 (June), 54–68 (July); and Lawrence M. Mead,
Beyond Entitlement: The Social Obligations of Citizenship (New York: Free Press/Macmillan,
1986).

consequence of negative self attitudes. Thus, although the value of self-reliance urges us to seek alternative methods of aiding mother-only families—methods that promote and model independence—little justification exists for imposing alternatives that reduce economic well-being and leave these families worse off.

CHAPTER 3

THE INCREASE IN THE NUMBER OF MOTHER-ONLY FAMILIES, 1940–83

This chapter examines the nature and causes of the dramatic changes in American family structure during the past few decades. The first section describes the prevalence and dynamics of mother-only families in 1983. The more women and children affected and the longer the period of dependence, the more serious are the consequences for children and the long-term implications for family structure.

The second section looks at trends in the growth of mother-only families between 1940 and 1980 and at the major demographic components of this growth. We find that, for whites, the major source of growth in such families has been the increase in the proportion of formerly married mothers—as a result of higher rates of divorce and, more recently, lower rates of remarriage. For blacks the picture is somewhat different. Whereas much of the early growth in such families stemmed from increases in marital disruption, recent growth has come primarily from increases in out-of-wedlock births.

The chapter ends with an evaluation of several explanations for the increasing number of mother-only families, including increases in women's economic independence, decreases in men's employment opportunities, and changes in social norms and attitudes about divorce and single parenthood. Of principal interest to policymakers is the question of whether increases in government benefits during the 1960s and 1970s to mother-only families altered the costs and benefits of marriage enough to account for a large portion of the growth in such families during this period.

We conclude that the increase in welfare benefits can account for some of the growth but that, relative to other factors, its effect is small. For whites the major factor has been the increase in women's labor force participation (and the economic independence that accompanied it); for blacks the major factor has been the decline in employment opportunities among males. We

45

also conclude that social norms and attitudes about single parenthood tend to follow rather than to lead changes in family behavior. Once a trend is established, however, attitudes play an important feedback function in sustaining and augmenting earlier growth.

The Prevalence and Dynamics of Mother-Only Families

In 1983 there were more than 7.2 million families headed by single women with children in the United States. If we ask what proportion of all children were living with a single mother in 1983, the answer is 20.5 percent— 15.0 percent of whites and 51.0 percent of blacks.[1] These numbers are based on cross-sectional data and therefore present only a snapshot of the proportion of children in mother-only families at a given time. The snapshot is the net result of two processes: the rate at which such families are created (the "inflows") and the rate at which such families are dissolved (the "outflows"). Thus the numbers count only families who had entered and *not* left mother-only status as of 1983.

This measure of prevalance is to be sharply distinguished from lifetime prevalence—the proportions of women and children who ever occupy the status. The distinction is important for several reasons. First, because many formerly married mothers remarry and because all mothers change status as their children grow up and leave home, the prevalence figures grossly underestimate the actual number of children who have spent or will spend some portion of their lives in a family headed by a single woman. Recent estimates indicate that about 42 percent of all white children and about 86 percent of all black offspring born in the late 1970s will live in such a family before they reach age eighteen.[2] These staggering numbers highlight the fact that the mother-only family is and will continue to be a common experience in the lives of American women and children.

Second, in addition to underestimating the number of children affected by single parenthood, the snapshot prevalence figures exaggerate racial differences in the likelihood of participation in this type of family. Because blacks become mothers at a younger age and because they are less likely to marry or remarry than whites, the snapshot figures for blacks are closer to lifetime prevalence estimates than they are for whites. Thus, although mother-

1. U.S. Bureau of the Census, "Household and Family Characteristics: March 1983," *Current Population Reports*, series P-20, no. 388 (Washington, D.C.: U.S. Government Printing Office, 1984).

2. Larry Bumpass, "Children and Marital Disruption: A Replication and Update," *Demography*, vol. 21 (February 1984), pp. 71-82. See also Sandra Hofferth, "Updating Children's Life Course," *Journal of Marriage and Family*, vol. 47 (1985), pp. 93-116.

only families as a proportion of all families are nearly four times more common among blacks than whites in the snapshot (55.8 percent versus 17.0 percent), the lifetime prevalence rate is only twice as high for blacks as for whites (86 percent versus 42 percent).

Third, the snapshot reveals little about how long children spend in mother-only families. If the heads of such families marry or remarry quickly, their situation can be viewed as less serious than if they remain single for long periods of time. Moreover, policymakers might be less concerned with the long-term effects on children if they knew that single parenthood was a short-term experience.[3]

Recent estimates indicate that the median length of time spent in a mother-only family is about six years. For black children the duration is much longer. Only 33 percent of black mothers had remarried by ten years after separation.[4] Although these numbers represent a relatively short period in the lives of adult women, the implications for children are clearly much more serious. Six years is a third of the time that most children spend in the parental household.

The estimates just cited are based on data for continuous spells of single parenthood; that is, the length of time between the beginning of single parenthood and marriage or remarriage. For families that experience more than one disruption, the total time spent in a mother-only family may be considerably longer for both mothers and children. Bumpass estimates that approximately one-half of remarriages will end in divorce before the child has reached age eighteen, in which case the children in these families will be exposed to multiple disruptions and longer periods in a mother-only family.[5]

The final limitation of the snapshot approach is that it can lead to misconceptions about the underlying causes of change over time. Because cross-sectional prevalence figures reflect the net effect of entrances into and exits from single parenthood, overall growth can be attributed erroneously to one factor when in fact it is being produced by another, or by a combination of the two. Some commentators, for example, have interpreted the recent growth in the proportion of black children born out of wedlock as an indicator of increases in illegitimacy rates among blacks. This is incorrect; the growth is actually due to declining fertility rates among married black women and to declining marriage rates for young black women. The distinction between the

---

3. This assumes, of course, that the effects of single parenthood are related to duration: the longer the exposure, the worse the effect. If negative consequences are due only to the event of marital disruption itself, differences in duration would be of less concern.

4. Bumpass, "Children and Marital Disruption."

5. Ibid.

static and dynamic pictures of families headed by single women should be kept in mind as we explore the nature and causes of the increase in the number of such families in the next two sections.

Trends in the Increasing Number of Mother-Only Families

Having looked at the prevalence and dynamics of families headed by single women in 1983, we now consider how much growth has occurred during the past forty years and the major causes of that growth. Trends by race are depicted in figure 2 for 1940 to 1984. Since 1975 the data are reported annually.

FIGURE 2

THE PROPORTION OF MOTHER-ONLY FAMILIES IN THE UNITED STATES, 1940–84

Percentage

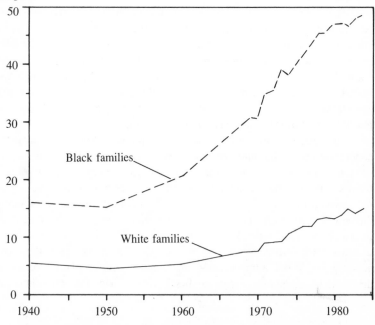

SOURCES: Data for 1940, 1950, and 1960 are taken from the Public Use Sample of the U.S. Bureau of the Census. Data for 1968–84 are from "Household and Family Characteristics," *Current Population Reports*, series P-20, table 1 for each respective year. Rates are computed by dividing the number of families with a female head of household and children under age eighteen by the total number of families with children under age eighteen.

The prevalance for whites is lower than that for blacks throughout the period. However, the trends are similar because the largest increases for both races occurred in the 1960s and 1970s, and the rates of growth were alike. For whites the number of mother-only families grew 37 percent between 1960 and 1970 and 40 percent between 1970 and 1980. For blacks the proportions were 37 percent and 35 percent, respectively. These similarities may seem surprising because many researchers and policymakers have depicted mother-only families as a problem of the black community that has only recently affected whites.

Of particular interest in the figure is the leveling off for both races during the past few years. After increasing rapidly for most of the 1970s, the growth in the number of mother-only families among whites paused during the late 1970s, picked up again in 1981 and 1982, dropped in 1983, and increased slightly in 1984. Among blacks there was no growth between 1980 and 1982, followed by increases in 1983 and 1984.

Whether the more recent numbers indicate a permanent leveling off is not clear. Researchers such as Bane and Ellwood have suggested that the trends in the early 1980s may reflect changes in the living arrangements of the mothers and children rather than declines in single parenthood per se.[6] If, for example, single women with children decided to move in with their parents or other relatives during hard economic times, the number of single mothers heading their own families would decline even though the number of single women with children remained constant. If this was the case, we would expect to find a renewed increase in the number of families headed by single women once economic opportunities improved. In the following section we examine the demographic patterns that underlie the trend in mother-only families from 1940 to 1980. In so doing we focus on the decisions about

---

6. Mary Jo Bane and David Ellwood, "Single Mothers and Their Living Arrangements," unpublished paper (Cambridge, Massachusetts: Harvard University, 1984). The CPS data support the Bane and Ellwood argument for declines in families with children headed by women among blacks. If we include subfamilies as well as primary families, the trend for 1980 to 1983 for blacks is 48.5 percent, 48.9 percent, 52.3 percent, and 55.8 percent, respectively. These numbers show that the 1982 decline in female-headed families was due to a shift in living arrangements. For whites the trend in subfamilies and primary families for the same 1980-83 period is 15.1 percent, 15.8 percent, 17.4 percent and 16.9 percent, respectively, which is similar to the pattern reported in figure 2. The CPS figures however, may underreport subfamilies before 1983, and therefore it is difficult to evaluate the true effect of the shift in living arrangements. Bane and Ellwood estimate that approximately 50 percent of all subfamilies were miscoded in the CPS reports before 1983.

marriage, fertility, and living arrangements that determine whether a woman will be the sole head of her own family.[7]

Women's Paths to Mother-Only Family Headship

The two paths of women to single parenthood and mother-only family headship are shown in figure 3.

The first decision facing a woman is whether to marry. If she remains single, she risks becoming a never-married mother, depending on two ad-

FIGURE 3

PATHS TO SINGLE FEMALE HEADSHIP OF A FAMILY

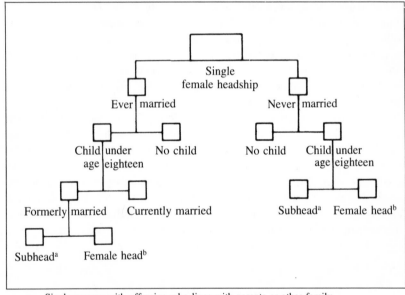

a. Single woman with offspring who lives with parents or other family.
b. Lives independently as family headed by a single woman.

---

7. The trends in female headship as a proportion of all women are somewhat different from the trends described in figure 2. If we focus on the former, the growth rates are, respectively, 0.94, 1.24, 1.27, and 1.25 for whites in each of the last four decades and 1.06, 1.48, 1.50, and 1.29 for blacks. These trends suggest that if we consider the experience of women rather than of children, we find that the growth among whites began in the 1950s and has been quite stable for the past three decades. We also find that growth rates were substantially higher among blacks in the 1950s and 1960s than they were in the 1970s (see tables 3 and 4).

ditional decisions: whether to have a child (or if pregnant whether to have and keep the child) and whether to live independently. For women who marry, the path to heading mother-only families depends on three additional decisions: whether to have a child, whether to end the marriage, and whether to establish an independent household. Because a woman does not always control the decision to end her marriage (in cases of widowhood or desertion, for example), her choices may be limited to whether she becomes a parent and whether she lives independently. Once a woman becomes the single head of her own family (having been married or not), she may leave the status in one of three ways: she may move in with a relative or other head of household, she may marry or remarry, or her child may move out. Although only a small number of mothers who have ever been married live with their parents, a larger number of never-married mothers do so. Eventually, the status of all women who are heads of mother-only families changes when their youngest child reaches age eighteen. The important point is that occupancy of the status is fluid and there are many routes of entry and exit.

The proportion of single women who head their own families at any time depends on the choices women make and the rates at which they enter and leave the various statuses described in figure 3. Similarly, changes in prevalence reflect changes in choices about statuses and rates of transition. An increase in the prevalence of formerly married women who head families may result from increases in initial marriage, increases in marital fertility, increases in divorce, increases in the propensity to establish independent households, or decreases in rates of remarriage among formerly married women who head their own families. Similarly, an increase in the prevalance of never-married mothers may result from decreases in marriage (before or after motherhood) or increases in out-of-wedlock births.

Components of Growth

To fully understand the trends in families headed by women during the past few decades, ideally we would want to examine changes in the rates at which women entered and left each of the statuses described in figure 3. Data on rates, however, are typically not available; in most cases we can only observe changes in the proportion of women who occupy each status at a particular time. Even this information is useful because it can indicate where the major increases have occurred and, when combined with limited data on rates, can suggest the behavioral changes underlying the growth in the number of mother-only families.

Several researchers have examined changes in the proportions of women in each status during the past several decades and have attempted to quantify the proportion of growth due to various factors such as marital disruption, out-of-wedlock births, and shifts in living arrangements. In an early analysis, Cutwright and Scanzoni found that change in living arrangements was the major factor in the overall increase between 1940 and 1970—accounting for more than 37 percent of the growth in families headed by formerly married mothers and for nearly 60 percent of the growth in families headed by never-married mothers.[8]

Looking at a different time period and a somewhat different sample, Ross and Sawhill found that marital disruption and the presence of children in disrupting households were the major components of growth of families headed by single women. These factors accounted for 46 percent of the growth of such families among whites and for 39 percent among blacks between 1960 and 1974. Out-of-wedlock births were less important overall, although among blacks they accounted for a substantial amount (21 percent) of the growth.[9]

In an attempt to reconcile the two sets of findings and to provide more complete information, we analyzed the major components of growth for three separate decades: the 1950s, 1960s, and 1970s. The analysis was based on the Public Use Samples of the U.S. decennial censuses.

Pattern for Whites. Table 3 shows that for whites the increase in mother-only families during each decade was due primarily to an increase in the prevalence of formerly married mothers. This factor accounted for approximately 45 percent of the growth in the 1950s and 1960s and for about 57 percent in the 1970s. In comparison, increases in never-married mothers accounted for less than 2 percent of the growth in the 1950s and for a little more than 7 and 8 percent during the 1960s and 1970s, respectively.

Although most of the overall increase since 1950 was due to an increase in formerly married mothers, the factors producing this growth changed significantly over time. Before 1960, growth was primarily the result of a larger proportion of women marrying and having children—a fact that increased the pool of women at risk of becoming formerly married mothers. After 1960 the marriage and fertility rates dropped; subsequent growth was due primarily

8. Phillips Cutwright and John Scanzoni, "Income Supplements and the American Family," *Studies in Public Welfare*, paper 12, prepared by Joint Economic Committee (Washington, D.C.: U.S. Government Printing Office, 1973), pp. 45-89. A revised and extended set of estimates is presented by Herbert L. Smith and Phillips Cutwright, "Components of Change in the Number of Female Family Heads Ages 15 to 44, an Update and Reanalysis: United States, 1940 to 1983," *Social Science Research*, vol. 14 (1985) pp. 226-50.

9. Heather Ross and Isabel Sawhill, *Time of Transition: The Growth of Families Headed by Women* (Washington, D.C.: Urban Institute, 1975).

TABLE 3

DECOMPOSITION OF GROWTH OF WHITE FAMILIES HEADED BY MOTHERS AGED
EIGHTEEN TO FIFTY-NINE, 1950–80
(*Percentage*)

Proportion of Growth in Families Headed by Mothers Due to a Change in	1950s	1960s	1970s
Proportion of formerly married women	45.1	45.5	56.5
Marriage rate	6.2	−7.4	−9.4
Marital birth rate	24.6	−7.4	−18.8
Marital disruption and remarriage rate	14.3	60.3	84.7
Proportion of never-married women	1.7	7.3	8.2
Marriage rate	0.4	0.7	2.1
Out-of-wedlock birth rate	1.3	6.6	6.1
Proportion of single mothers who head independent households	29.8	14.2	9.9
Size of population	12.5	24.3	29.4
Interaction (simultaneous change in two or more components)	11.9	8.7	−4.0

SOURCE: Sara McLanahan and Irwin Garfinkel, "A Decomposition of the Growth of Families Headed by Single Mothers, 1950–1980," Institute for Research on Poverty paper 811-86 (Madison Wisconsin: University of Wisconsin, 1986).

to increases in divorce rates and declines in remarriage. Some of the growth after 1960 was also due to an increase in never-married mothers.

An additional factor in each time period was increases in the propensity of single women with children to establish independent households. This type of change in living arrangements accounted for about 30 percent of the growth in the 1950s and for about 14 percent and 10 percent of the growth in the 1960s and 1970s.

The Pattern for Blacks. Perhaps the most striking feature in the pattern for blacks—and the factor most different from whites—is the extent to which, during the past two decades, growth in the population of never-married mothers has replaced growth in the population of formerly married mothers (table 4). Whereas more than 45 percent of the increase in families headed by single black women during the 1950s was due to increases in formerly married mothers, this component accounted for less than 30 percent of the growth in the 1960s and less than 3 percent in the 1970s.

The decline in the relative importance of formerly married mothers was offset by an increase in never-married mothers. The latter accounted for about 9 percent of the growth in the 1950s, 20 percent in the 1960s, and 23 percent in the 1970s. During the 1950s nearly all the increase in never-married mothers

TABLE 4

DECOMPOSITION OF GROWTH OF BLACK FAMILIES HEADED BY MOTHERS AGED
EIGHTEEN TO FIFTY-NINE, 1950–80
(*Percentage*)

Proportion of Growth in Families Headed by Mothers Due to a Change in	1950s	1960s	1970s
Proportion of formerly married women	45.4	28.4	2.9
Marriage rate	−2.2	−6.6	−17.1
Marital birth rate	28.8	11.4	−2.1
Marital disruption and remarriage rate	18.8	23.7	22.1
Proportion of never-married women	9.2	20.0	23.2
Marriage rate	1.1	4.5	12.7
Out-of-wedlock birth rate	8.1	15.5	10.5
Proportion of single mothers who head independent households	14.9	13.6	7.1
Size of population	11.9	20.2	44.0
Interaction (simultaneous change in two or more components)	18.6	17.8	23.1

SOURCE: Same as table 3.

was due to a rise in out-of-wedlock birth rates. Among blacks these rates peaked in the early 1960s and declined thereafter, first among older women and eventually among teenagers. After 1970, out-of-wedlock birth rates declined for all age groups. This suggests that the increase in never-married mothers after 1970 was due primarily to increases in the proportion of women at risk for a premarital birth (because of declines in marriage) rather than to changes in the fertility behavior of unmarried women. This point is important inasmuch as many observers continue to attribute the recent growth of never-married mothers among blacks to increases in the *rate* of out-of-wedlock pregnancies and births.

We conclude that the recent increase in families headed by unmarried women among blacks is due primarily to a decline in the propensity to marry on the part of young black men and women. In this sense the pattern for blacks and whites is similar: most of the growth in single parenthood is due to changes in marital behavior. The difference is that whites marry and increasingly divorce, whereas blacks are increasingly likely never to marry at all.

Causes of Growth

Why have marriage bonds become so fragile during the past two decades, and what lies behind the apparent rejection of initial marriage on the part of black men and women? The analysis of demographic components of change helps researchers identify specific behavioral changes affecting the formation of female-headed families. It is important also to understand why these behaviors changed. This section examines several possible explanations.

Changes in Welfare Benefits

Common sense and economic theory both suggest that increasing public benefits to mother-only families will contribute to the rising number of such families. Higher benefits increase the ability of women with children to establish themselves independently. Higher benefits increase the ability of an unwed pregnant woman to keep and rear a child rather than have an abortion or give the child up for adoption. Higher benefits increase the ability of a poor married woman with a child to afford a divorce and to be selective in her choice of a new mate. All these effects, other things equal, will tend to increase the number of mother-only families. Neither economic theory nor common sense, however, indicates how large any of the separate effects will be. The magnitudes can only be determined empirically.

Our analysis begins with a look at the time-series relations between government benefits and the prevalence of mother-only families. Figure 4 shows two trends for government benefits: expenditures per family in major federal programs for mother-only families, and AFDC plus food stamps guarantee levels for mother-only families with three children and no other income. Both trends are measured in constant 1983 dollars. The expenditures per family somewhat overstate the increase in benefits because some of the rise in expenditures is due to changes in the characteristics of the families (more never-married mothers, for example) and changes in the propensity of single women who head families to claim benefits. The AFDC-food stamp figure substantially understates the increase in benefits because it omits many benefits (such as Medicaid and public housing) to this group and because it omits the effects of legal and administrative liberalizations in eligibility. For example, the Supreme Court's 1969 decision that state residence requirements for AFDC eligibility were illegal led to increases in the proportion of families who were eligible for and participated in AFDC. On balance we believe the major program expenditures are a better reflection of benefit level changes because they are more inclusive of benefits and include the effects of eligibility changes.

FIGURE 4

TRENDS IN MOTHER-ONLY FAMILIES AND GOVERNMENT EXPENDITURES, 1940–84

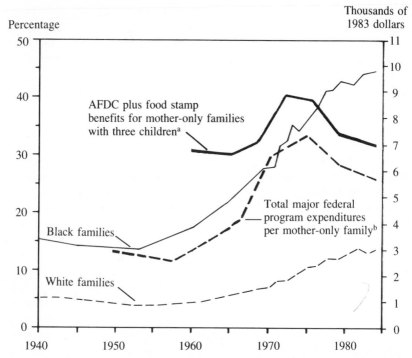

SOURCES: See figure 2 for the source of the rate of families headed by women. The number
           of families with a female head of household and children under age eighteen is
           divided by the total number of families with children under age eighteen.

    a.   "AFDC plus food stamps" is taken from the same sources as table 9. It is the combined
AFDC plus food stamp benefit levels for a family of four with no income (1983 dollars).

    b.   "Expenditure per family" is taken from the same sources as table 7 (1983 dollars).

The relation between the AFDC and food stamps guarantee levels and
the proportion of female-headed families, as reflected in figure 4, seems weak.
The relation between major federal program expenditures per mother-only
family and prevalence looks much stronger, except for the period from 1975
to 1985, when the number of mother-only families increased and benefits
declined. Statistical analyses confirm the impressions conveyed by figure 4.
The relation between expenditures per family and the number of mother-only
families is statistically significant, whereas the relation between the AFDC
plus food stamps guarantee and the number of female-headed families is not

statistically significant.[10] Because we believe that the trend in expenditures per family is a better measure of increases in generosity of government benefits than the trend in the AFDC and food stamp guarantee, we interpret the time-series evidence to be consistent with the hypothesis that the increases in government benefits did stimulate an increase in the prevalance of mother-only families.

Many studies have used cross-sectional data to examine the relation between generosity of welfare benefits and the prevalance of mother-only families. Nearly all rely on associations between the proportion of such families (or some aspect thereof, such as divorce rates) in a particular state (or metropolitan area) and the level of welfare benefits in that state. Some of the studies are based on associations between benefits and the various flows into and out of mother-only family status (divorce rates, illegitimacy rates); others are based on associations between benefits and the proportion of women who head such families.

The latter studies are less informative than the former because they fail to distinguish among the various flows. In particular, studies based on the proportion of women do not distinguish between the effect of welfare on the incidence or prevalence of single parenthood and the effect of welfare on whether the single mothers live with their parental families or not. Presumably, we care less about the latter, even if it has adverse effects, than we do about the effects of welfare on divorce, out-of-wedlock births, and remarriage. The association between benefit levels and proportions of mother-only families also reflects migration effects. These women are more likely to come into, and less likely to leave, high-benefit states. Consequently, an association across states between welfare generosity and the proportion of single mothers who head families may simply be due to the effect of welfare on the mobility of these women. It is also possible that states with large proportions of families headed by single women have higher welfare benefits because of the political power of large numbers.

For all these reasons, it is not surprising that studies which examine the effects of welfare benefits on the proportions of mother-only families find

---

10. We also conducted a crude multiple regression analysis in which the proportion of all mother-only families was the dependent variable, and the independent variables included expenditures per female-headed family, unemployment rates or employment rates of males, wage rates of males and females, and the female labor force participation rate. The data covered the years 1950, 1960, and 1968 through 1984. Separate regressions by race were estimated. The statistical significance of the expenditure per female-headed family variable was sensitive to the inclusion of some variants of the other independent variables and to the inclusion of a time trend. Until a more refined analysis is completed, we hesitate to rely heavily on these results, which is why they are not reported in the text.

significant effects. Studies by Honig, by Ross and Sawhill, and most recently, by Danziger and colleagues find that benefit levels are associated with single female family headship, although their estimates of the magnitude of the effects vary widely.[11]

Research on flows, in contrast, do not find effects on divorce or illegitimacy, but suggest that the primary effects of welfare are on living arrangements and rates of remarriage. Cutwright and Madras, for example, have shown that welfare benefit levels are associated with the proportion of unmarried mothers who have their own living units but not with the percentage of women who are divorced or separated.[12] A recent study by Ellwood and Bane confirms these findings. After examining the effect of welfare benefit levels on living arrangements, marital breakup, and out-of-wedlock births, they concluded that the major consequence of welfare is that it allows the woman with children to establish an independent residence rather than having to live with her parental family.[13]

Studies based on longitudinal data also find that welfare has a minimal effect on the incidence of divorce and separation. Numerous researchers report no effects on divorce and separation. A few report small or mixed effects. Hoffman and Holmes, for example, find that low-income families are more likely to split up if they live in high-benefit states; Cherlin finds a small effect for young white women but no effect for older whites; and Moore and Waite report a small effect with one data set and no effect with another.[14]

Much the same pattern is found for out-of-wedlock births: the relation between welfare benefit levels and illegitimacy is weak to nonexistent. Studies by Ellwood and Bane, Cutwright, Fechter and Greenfield, Winegarden, and

---

11. Marjorie Honig, "The Impact of AFDC Income, Recipient Rates, and Family Dissolution," *Journal of Human Resources*, vol. 9 (1973), pp. 303-22; Ross and Sawhill, *Time of Transition*; and Sheldon Danziger et al., "Work and Welfare as Determinants of Female Poverty and Household Headship," *Quarterly Journal of Economics* (August 1982), pp. 519-34.

12. Phillips Cutwright and Patrick Madras, "AFDC and the Marital and Family Status of Ever-Married Women Ages 15-44: United States, 1950-1970," *Sociology and Social Research*, vol. 60 (1976), pp. 314-27; and David Ellwood and Mary Jo Bane, "The Impact of AFDC on Family Structure and Living Arrangements," report to U.S. Department of Health and Human Services, 1984.

13. Ellwood and Bane, "The Impact of AFDC."

14. Saul Hoffman and John Holmes, "Husbands, Wives and Divorce," in G. J. Duncan and J. Morgan, eds., *Five Thousand American Families*, vol. 4 (Ann Arbor, Michigan: University of Michigan, Institute for Social Research, 1976); Andrew Cherlin, "Social and Economic Determinants of Marital Separation" (Ph.D. dissertation, University of California at Los Angeles, 1976); and Kristin A. Moore and Linda J. Waite, "Marital Dissolution, Early Motherhood and Early Marriage," *Social Forces*, vol. 60 (September 1976), pp. 20-40.

Moore and Caldwell report no effect.[15] Moore and Caldwell, however, find that pregnant teenagers in high-benefit states are less likely to have an abortion than their counterparts in low-benefit states. A study of a sample of 300 pregnant teenagers in California by Leibowitz, Eisen, and Chow reports that those on welfare are less likely to have an abortion, give their child up for adoption, or marry the child's father than are those not on welfare. But this study does not establish causation, which could just as easily go the other way. That is, those who plan to keep the child and not marry may be more likely to go on welfare. Somewhat more convincing is the response of 18 percent of a sample of never-married welfare mothers in New York City— a high-benefit jurisdiction—who claim that the availability of welfare influenced their decision to forgo marriage to the fathers of their children.[16]

Several studies suggest convincingly that welfare does reduce the likelihood of remarriage. Hutchens finds that benefit levels were related to remarriage rates, with high benefits discouraging remarriage.[17] Ellwood and Bane do not look directly at remarriage, but their results provide indirect evidence of a remarriage effect. For example, they find that welfare is related to the proportion of never-married mothers and the proportion of divorced and separated mothers, but not the out-of-wedlock birthrates and not the rates for divorce or separation. If welfare levels are not affecting the inflow but

---

15. Ellwood and Bane, "The Impact of AFDC"; Phillips Cutwright, "Illegitimacy and Income Supplements," *Studies in Public Welfare*, paper 12, prepared for the Joint Economic Committee (Washington, D.C.: U.S. Government Printing Office, 1973), pp. 90-138; Alan Fechter and Stuart Greenfield, "Frequency, Duration and Probability of Marriage and Income," *Journal of Marriage and the Family* (May 1971), pp. 307-17; C. R. Winegarden, "The 'Welfare Explosion': Determinants of the Size and Recent Growth of the AFDC Population," *The American Journal of Economics and Sociology* (July 1973), pp. 245-56; and Kristin A. Moore and Stephen Caldwell, "The Effect of Government Policies on Out-of-Wedlock Sex and Pregnancy," *Family Planning Perspectives*, vol. 9 (July-August 1977), pp. 164-69.

16. Arleen Leibowitz, Marvin Eisen, and Winston K. Chow, "An Economic Model of Teenage Pregnancy Decision Making," *Demography*, vol. 23 (February 1986), pp. 67-77.

17. Robert M. Hutchens, "Welfare Remarriage and Marital Search," *American Economic Review*, vol. 69 (1979), pp. 369-79. Hutchens uses the AFDC guarantee of the state in which the individual resides. In contrast, Duncan and also Ross and Sawhill (*Time of Transition*) use the actual AFDC benefit received in 1967 to predict remarriage rates of female heads of household in 1968 over the next six and four years, respectively. Actual benefits received might be low in 1967 not because the state has low benefits but because the women under consideration only recently became a female head of household and received benefits only part of the year or because she worked. Finally, the woman may have received no welfare in 1967 but may have received it later. For all these reasons, actual benefits received is not as good a measure of the welfare benefit level as the guarantee that Hutchens uses. See Greg J. Duncan, "Unmarried Heads of Household and Remarriage," in Greg J. Duncan and James N. Morgan, eds., *Five Thousand Families*, vol. 4 (Ann Arbor, Michigan: University of Michigan, Institute for Social Research, 1976).

are related to the proportions of single mothers with children, those levels must be affecting the outflow, that is, the rate of remarriage.

The Seattle-Denver Experiment

The much-publicized results from the Seattle-Denver Income-Maintenance Experiment have been interpreted to show that the effect of welfare benefits on divorce is much greater than the foregoing summary indicates. The Seattle-Denver experiment was the fourth and largest income-maintenance experiment conducted by the federal government in the late 1960s and early 1970s to test the effects of a negative income tax on the work effort of beneficiaries. At the time of the experiment, as today, economists and others were concerned that limiting welfare benefits to single parents might be creating an incentive for two-parent families to divorce. They believed that extending benefits to intact families would do away with this incentive and reduce marital breakup.

The principal investigators have summarized their results by suggesting that the experiment increased divorce rates by more than 50 percent! These results, however, say nothing about the effects of raising or lowering the welfare benefits available to single mothers.[18] At most, they imply that extending welfare to intact families increases marital disruption for some reason other than increasing the economic independence of women. To understand why this is so, a brief description of the experimental design is necessary.

Low-income families in both Seattle and Denver were asked to participate in the experiment. If they agreed, they were then assigned on a stratified random basis to a control group or to one of several different experimental groups. Members of each group were eligible to receive benefits from a different negative income tax plan (NIT) if their income was low enough. Two-parent as well as single-parent families were eligible for NIT benefits if they were in the experimental groups. Finally—and this is critical—families in both the experimental and control groups retained whatever eligibility for welfare they would have had in the absence of the experiment. Many single women with children in the control group and some in the experimental group received welfare. Consequently, whatever effect the experiment had on behavior, it must be compared with a state of the world in which there is a welfare system. If divorce rates were

---

18. The SIME/DIME results have also been criticized for methodological shortcomings. See Glen Cain, "Comments on August 18th Version of Marital Stability Findings," chap. 3, SIME/DIME Final Report to Department of Health and Human Services, memorandum (Washington, D.C., September 2, 1981).

higher in the experimental groups than in the control group, this result was due to the characteristics of the experimental treatment other than an independence effect (that is, the availability of additional income to women who became single heads of households).[19]

If the experimental results do not represent an independence effect for women, what do they reveal about welfare and marital disruption? A possible answer comes from role theory, which argues that unsuccessful role performance leads to conflict between people who are filling reciprocal roles, in this case, the husband and the wife. According to this perspective, the welfare check serves as a public symbol of the husband's failure to successfully perform his breadwinner role, which in turn leads to an erosion of his respect and authority within the family. Bakke captures this effect in his description of families of the Great Depression in which fathers go on relief:

> Every goal he seeks to reach as a normal worker recedes further from realization when he turns to relief. Until that moment he could in a measure realize that even without current earnings the efforts he made in the past in the role of a "producer," a "good provider," a "good father," were still contributing to the support of his family. But now he has made a public declaration of his failure, and no rationalization can quite cover up the fact that a "reliefer" is not among the roles his associates respect.[20]

The role hypothesis is also consistent with another somewhat surprising finding of the Seattle-Denver experiment: that the marital disruption effect occurred among families receiving the lowest level of benefits. Those in the high-benefit experimental group did not have higher rates of disruption. Hannan and his colleagues argue that the difference in response between the two groups was due to the interaction of income and independence effects.[21] Increasing incomes has a stabilizing effect on marriage, whereas independence has a destabilizing effect. One could just as easily postulate a role effect rather than an independence effect. That is, receiving welfare has negative consequences for the marital relationship, but for the high-benefit groups the negative consequences are offset by the positive effect of income.

This explanation is supported by recent studies showing that many people who are eligible for welfare assistance do not apply for benefits. The Social Security Administration estimates that about half of the aged who are eligible

---

19. Marital disruption rates were higher in the low-benefit group and lower in the high-benefit group than among controls.

20. W. E. Bakke, *Citizens without Work* (New Haven, Connecticut: Yale University Press, 1940).

21. Michael T. Hannan, Nancy B. Tuma, and Lyle P. Groeneveld, "Income and Independence Effects on Marital Dissolution: Results from the Seattle and Denver Income-Maintenance Experiments," *American Journal of Sociology*, vol. 84 (1987), pp. 611-33.

for Supplemental Security Income do not apply for assistance; other research-ers have found that more than three-fifths of two-parent families who are eligible for food stamps do not apply. These findings suggest that for some families the costs associated with welfare stigma override the benefits of increased income.[22]

Estimates of the Welfare Effect.[23] The empirical studies reviewed above can be used to derive estimates of the effects of increases in government benefits on the prevalance of single mothers. By considering any single rep-utable study, it is possible to derive a wide range of estimates. Because some of the studies find no effect, a lower-bound estimate would be that the large increase in benefits between 1960 and 1975 had no effect on the prevlance. If we use the highest estimate in the literature—Honig's 1960 estimate for blacks (which is clearly too high because it includes the effects of welfare on living arrangements as well as on prevalence), an upper-bound estimate would be that the 1960-75 benefit increases led to an increase in prevalence of single motherhood among blacks of 42 percent. Neither the upper- nor the lower-bound estimates come close to the truth of the matter. But they do suggest how wide a range can be derived from the literature. In our view, the Ellwood and Bane and the Danziger and colleagues studies provide the most reliable sources from which to derive an estimate of the effect of in-creased government benefits on prevalence of families headed by women: the Ellwood-Bane study because it is comprehensive and distinguishes between

22. Jennifer Warlick, "Participation of the Aged in Supplementary Security Income," Discussion Paper 618-80 (University of Wisconsin-Madison, Institute for Research on Poverty, 1980); Richard D. Coe, "A Longitudinal Analysis of Nonparticipation in the Food Stamp Program by Eligible Households," Discussion Paper 773-85 (University of Wisconsin-Madison, Institute for Research on Poverty, 1985).

23. Honig's 1960 estimate is that a 10 percent increase in benefits would lead to a 3.9 percent increase in prevalence of female headship among blacks (see Honig, "The Impact of AFDC Income, Recipient Rates, and Family Dissolution"). According to the estimate in table 7 (chapter 4) benefits increased between 1960 and 1975 by 107 percent. Multiplying 3.9 percent by 10.7 yield an estimate of an increase in prevalence of 42 percent. Minarik and Goldfarb obtain a negative estimate of the effect of welfare benefits on prevalence. See Joseph Minarik and Robert Goldfarb, "AFDC Income, Recipient Rates, and Family Dissolution: A Comment," *Journal of Human Resources*, vol. 9 (Spring 1976), pp. 243-57. Honig's 1970 estimates are not significantly different from zero and the Cutwright and Scanzoni study also find no effect (Cutwright and Scanzoni, "Income Supplements"). Ellwood and Bane find that a $100 increase in benefits, which amounts to a 38 percent increase, would lead to a 5 percent increase in prevalence for both races combined (Bane and Ellwood, "Single Mothers"). Multiplying 5 percent by the ratio of 107 percent to 38 percent yields our estimate of the upper-bound increase of 14 percent. Danziger, et al., "Work and Welfare," estimate that eliminating AFDC could decrease female headship rates for whites and blacks respectively by 8.6 and 2.7 percent. Multiplying each figure by 107 percent and weighting each by the proportion of white and black families in the population yields an estimate of 9 percent.

effects on prevalence and effects on living arrangements; the Danziger study because of its care in modeling the effects of alternative opportunities. Using these studies, we estimate that the increase in government benefits led to a 9 to 14 percent increase in the prevalence of single motherhood from 1960 to 1975. The prevalence of single motherhood increased approximately 100 percent during this period. Thus, although increased government benefits may have led to a measurable rise in prevalence, they account for only one-tenth to one-seventh of the total growth in mother-headed families.

That the increase in government benefits played only a small role in the overall growth in families headed by single mothers does not mean that the effects of benefits on single-mother headship should be ignored. It seems reasonable to assume that welfare benefits played little or no role in the marital decisions of those in the top half of the income distribution. If so, welfare played a bigger role in the decisions of the poorer half of the income distribution. Thus if the growth in benefits accounted for 14 percent of the total growth in single-mother headship, it could possibly account for 30 percent of the growth within the bottom part of the income distribution. Moreover, as documented in chapter 2, girls who grow up in families headed by single women are more likely to become single parents themselves. The effects therefore can mushroom over time. Finally, the effects on living arrangements are a cause for concern because there is some evidence that children in families headed by single mothers, which also include other adults, do better than children in families in which the mother is the only adult.

Changes in Women's Employment

Many people believe that the recent growth of families headed by single mothers is due to increases in the labor force participation of women. In general, economic theory holds that increases in economic opportunities for women outside marriage will increase the proportion of women who are not married. In particular, Becker, an economist, has shown that marriage is more beneficial to both parties when there is a high degree of role specialization in the family, with women specializing in housework and men in work in the marketplace.[24] The traditional sociologists have also argued that a gender-based division of labor is functional for the family and for marital stability. According to Parsons, gender-role segregation takes advantage of the "nat-

---

24. Gary S. Becker, "A Theory of Marriage: Part I," *Journal of Political Economy*, vol. 81 (1973), pp. 813-46, and "A Theory of Marriage: Part II," *Journal of Political Economy*, vol. 82 (1974), pp. 511-26; and Gary S. Becker, Elizabeth M. Landes, and Robert T. Michael, "An Economic Analysis of Marital Instability," *Journal of Political Economy*, vol. 85 (1977), pp. 1149-87.

ural'' proclivities of men and women and reduces competition for status between husbands and wives. Following Parsons, family sociologists have stressed the psychological consequences of changes in women's employment for marital conflict and satisfaction.[25]

Changes in wives' employment may increase marital conflict in one of several ways. In traditional marriages, in which both partners believe that the woman's place is in the home, conflict may arise when the wife is forced to work to supplement the family income. Her working may reflect the couple's decision or an individual decision; in either case, it is inconsistent with the values of both partners and implies that the husband is not successfully performing the obligations of his role. In such situations, the conflict is actually due to the husband's behavior (nonperformance) rather than to the wife's working, which merely symbolizes the inadequacy of the male breadwinner. Although this type of conflict over roles is not new—wives have often had to work to make ends meet—increases in job competition among men and increases in women's employment during the past few decades suggest that this conflict may be more common today than it was in the past.

Conflict about a wife's working may also arise when her new earnings alter the power relationships within the marriage. Studies on marital power and decision making have shown that working wives have more power vis-à-vis their husbands than wives who are full-time homemakers. In many cases, the material advantages gained from the increased family income may be offset by the psychological costs for the husband, who loses authority and power within the family or marriage. Even when both partners agree that the wife should enter the labor force, shifts in power relationships may lead to marital conflict, especially among more traditional couples.

Finally, conflict may occur in families in which the partners do not agree about how much the husband should be helping with household chores and child care. When the wife is employed and also does most of the household work, she may become resentful. Conflict may also result when the husband is helping against his will.

Empirical Studies. Numerous researchers have examined the relation between women's employment and the growth of mother-only families. The empirical evidence is quite consistent across a variety of studies, including analyses of time-series and cross-sectional aggregate data as well as analyses of longitudinal data on individuals. Many people have noted that the explosion of divorce and decline in marriage that took place in the 1960s and 1970s

---

25. Talcot Parsons and Robert Bales, eds., *Family, Socialization and Interaction Process* (Glencoe, Illinois: The Free Press, 1955).

followed quite closely the rise in labor force participation of married women with children. This pattern holds for within-group differences as well: the biggest increases in divorce occurred among mothers of young children who also had the largest increases in labor force participation. Figure 5 reports the changes in labor force participation rates and divorce rates for the 1948-84 period.

Although the two trends mirror one another between 1960 and 1980, this similarity does not mean that women's employment was the cause of increases in marital disruption. First, it is clear from figure 5 that the labor

FIGURE 5

MARITAL DISSOLUTION AND LABOR FORCE PARTICIPATION OF MARRIED WOMEN, 1948–84

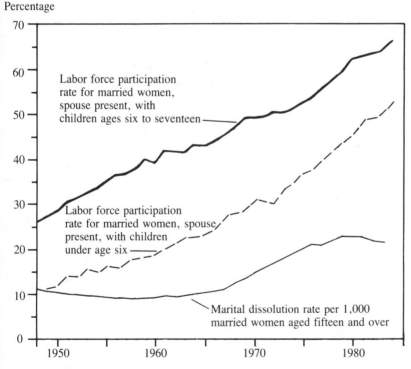

SOURCES: Labor force participation rate is from U.S. Department of Labor, *Handbook of Labor Statistics*, bulletin 2217 (Washington, D.C.: U.S. Government Printing Office, June 1985), p. 123. The marital dissolution rate is from U.S. Department of Health and Human Services, National Center for Health Statistics, *Monthly Vital Statistics Report*, Supplement, no. 9 (Hyattsville, Maryland: HHS, December 26, 1985), p. 5.

force participation of married women was increasing rapidly in the 1950s (when divorce increased very little) as well as in the 1960s. In fact, the increase in labor force participation among married women with children over age six was even greater during the 1950s than during the 1960s. Second, when interpreting a time-series correlation, reverse causality is always possible, as is the existence of a third variable causing both trends. For example, some have argued that married women were working because marriages were less stable.

To address the question of whether increased women's employment caused increased single female headship, researchers have used other measures of economic independence, such as area-wide employment opportunities for men and women. Preston and Richards examined the 100 largest metropolitan areas in the United States in 1960 and found that job opportunities, female earnings, and the local unemployment rate were all good predictors of the marital status of women in the population.[26] Communities in which opportunities for women were high relative to opportunities for men had a higher proportion of women who were not married than did other communities. The strongest predictor of marital status was the "femaleness" of the industrial sector, that is, the number of jobs for women relative to the number of jobs for men in the area. These researchers concluded that changes in job opportunities for men and women in the 1960s could account for about half of the decline in marriage or half of the increase in single women during this period.[27]

Although this study is not subject to the causality problems that have been described above—few would argue that singleness was a cause of job opportunity—the findings also are open to alternative interpretations. For example, single women may migrate to areas that offer more opportunity for them whereas men may be more likely to leave such areas, in which case the positive association between jobs and marital status is not necessarily the effect of opportunity on marriage.

Another way to look at the question is to observe married women over time to see if employed mothers are more likely to divorce and less likely to remarry than unemployed mothers. Several studies based on longitudinal data have found that married women who are in the labor force or who have higher earnings potential are more likely to divorce than more dependent women.

---

26. Sam H. Preston and Alan T. Richards, "The Influence of Women's Work Opportunities on Marriage Rates," *Demography*, vol. 12 (1975), pp. 209-22.

27. Lynn White has replicated the Preston and Richards's study for blacks and whites and reports that female headship is not related to work opportunities for black women. See Lynn White, "A Note on Racial Differences in the Effect of Female Economic Opportunity on Marriage Rates," *Demography*, vol. 8 (1981), pp. 349-54.

Using data on married couples from the Michigan PSID study, Ross and Sawhill found, when they controlled for husband's income along with other factors, that an increase of $1,000 in the wife's earnings was associated with a 7 percent increase in separation rates.[28] In a similar study based on the National Longitudinal Survey data (NLS), Cherlin found that the ratio of the wife's earnings capacity to the husband's earnings was a strong predictor of marital disruption.[29] Although one cannot be certain that it is "economic independence" that leads to divorce, and not the anticipation of marital breakup that leads to working, this evidence from the longitudinal studies is consistent with the independence hypothesis. The fact that all three types of study (time-series, cross-sectional, and longitudinal) point in the direction predicted by theory, although still not conclusive, provides strong support for the hypothesis that increased women's economic independence resulted in increased divorce.

The Effect of Women's Employment on Marital Conflict. There is also empirical support for the hypothesis that a wife's employment is related to marital conflict and dissatisfaction. In a recent study, Booth and his colleagues found that wives' employment reduced spousal interactions, which increased disagreements and reduced marital happiness.[30] Each of these outcomes was related to increases in marital instability, as measured by thoughts of divorce.

Most of the empirical evidence in support of the role-conflict hypothesis comes from studies of psychological distress. Such studies do not measure marital conflict directly, but they show that in some cases a wife's employment is associated with her husband's distress. Several researchers have shown that husbands of employed wives have lower self-esteem and are more depressed than are husbands of full-time homemakers. In attempting to account for this relationship, Kessler and McRae found that increases in the husband's distress were not related to the earnings of the wife, which suggests that it is not simply shifts in economic power within the marriage that make the difference.[31] They also found that increases in housework and child care do not account for higher levels of a husband's distress. In fact, husbands who were helping with child care (but not housework in general) actually felt better than husbands who did not.

28. Ross and Sawhill, *Time of Transition.*
29. Andrew Cherlin, "Social and Economic Determinants."
30. Alan Booth et al., "Women, Outside Employment and Marital Instability," *American Journal of Sociology*, vol. 90 (November 1984), pp. 567-83.
31. Ron C. Kessler and James McRae, Jr., "The Effects of Wives' Employment on the Mental Health of Married Men and Women," *American Sociological Review*, vol. 47 (1982), pp. 216-27.

Ross and her colleagues have offered a solution to the puzzle.[32] They found that the negative effects of a wife's working were limited to couples who believed that the wife should be at home. In these families, both husbands and wives reported unusually high levels of depression, with husbands reporting even more distress than wives. This suggests that the negative consequences of wives' employment are concentrated among couples with traditional values who find it necessary for the wife to work.

Changes in Male Employment Patterns

Another explanation for the rapid increase of families headed by women during the past few decades focuses on declines in employment opportunities for men. Decreases in male employment (just like increases in female employment) are viewed as reducing the benefits of marriage (or the costs of remaining single) for both men and women. They are also thought to increase marital conflict among couples in which the husband is unemployed. Those who stress the change in male employment generally focus on black families rather than on white families. Race, in this case, is used primarily as a surrogate measure of social class.

Moynihan's Hypothesis. The most widely discussed hypothesis concerning male employment comes from Senator Daniel Patrick Moynihan, who argued in the early 1960s that unemployment among black men was causing a breakdown of the black family and that government should take a more active role in providing jobs for these men. Figure 6 shows Moynihan's correlation between nonwhite male unemployment and the percentage of nonwhite women who are separated from their husbands. The relation is, to say the least, remarkably close.[33]

Since Moynihan's report on the black family was published in 1965, unemployment has risen further for black and also white men (see table 5). The data shown in table 5 for blacks (nonwhites until 1970) are astounding: between 1955 and 1965 unemployment rates averaged over 10 percent, and since the mid-1970s they have been increasing steadily. If we focus on young black men, the picture is even bleaker. With the exception of the Vietnam War period, unemployment has increased steadily since 1955 and for those

---

32. Catherine Ross, John Mirowsky, and John Huber, "Marriage Patterns and Depression," *American Sociological Review*, vol. 48 (1983), pp. 809-23.

33. Daniel P. Moynihan, "The Negro Family: The Case for National Action" (Washington, D.C.: U.S. Department of Labor, Office of Policy Planning and Research, 1965). Moynihan focuses exclusively on separated women. If we look at both divorce and separation, the connection with unemployment is not nearly so strong.

FIGURE 6

MOYNIHAN RESULTS: UNEMPLOYMENT RATE FOR NONWHITE MEN COMPARED WITH
PERCENTAGE NONWHITE, MARRIED WOMEN SEPARATED FROM THEIR HUSBANDS,
1951–63

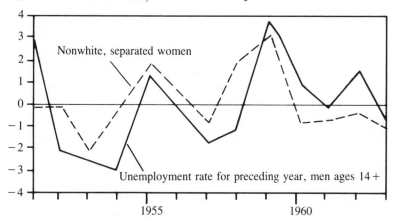

SOURCE: Reprinted with permission of Daniel P. Moynihan, "The Negro Family: The Case
for National Action" (Washington, D.C.: U.S. Department of Labor, Office of Policy
Planning and Research, 1965).

TABLE 5

MALE UNEMPLOYMENT RATES BY RACE AND AGE, 1954–84

Year or Period	Whites			Nonwhites			Blacks		
	16 and Over (Total)	16–19	16–24	16 and Over (Total)	16–19	16–24	16 and Over (Total)	16–19	16–24
1954	4.8	13.4	11.3	10.3	n.a.	15.8	n.a.	n.a.	n.a.
1955–59	4.3	12.6	9.8	10.0	n.a.	16.6	n.a.	n.a.	n.a.
1960–64	4.8	14.8	10.9	10.8	n.a.	18.3	n.a.	n.a.	n.a.
1965–69	2.8	10.8	7.3	6.1	n.a.	14.1	n.a.	n.a.	n.a.
1970–74	4.3	13.8	10.3	8.4	n.a.	19.6	9.0	30.9	20.7
1975–79	5.6	15.6	12.0	12.0	n.a.	25.3	13.0	37.1	27.3
1980–81	6.3	17.1	13.4	13.7	n.a.	27.4	15.1	39.1	29.8
1982–84	7.3	18.6	n.a.	n.a.	n.a.	n.a.	17.4	43.7	n.a.

SOURCES: U.S. Department of Labor, Bureau of Labor Statistics; labor force statistics derived from the *Current Population Survey: A Databook*, vol. 1 (Washington, D.C.: U.S. Government Printing Office, 1982), pp. 502–40. For 1982–84 and ages 16–19, see U.S. Department of Labor, Bureau of Labor Statistics, *Employment and Earnings* (Washington, D.C.: U.S. Government Printing Office, December 1984), p. 273.

n.a.   Not available.

aged sixteen to twenty-four has been more than 20 percent during the 1970s and since.

Moynihan's figures compared trends in male unemployment rates to trends in separation for blacks. Unemployment also can be expected to affect marriage and divorce rates, and all three affect family headship (see table 6 for marriage and divorce rates). Figure 7 shows the relation between the rates of male unemployment from 1950 to 1968 and the rate of family headship by single mothers from 1949 to 1968 for both races combined. The association is not nearly as close as Moynihan's. The biggest discrepancy appears in the mid-1960s, when male unemployment declined and headship rates of single mothers continued to accelerate. As noted above, however, this discrepancy coincides with the Vietnam War when unemployment and marriage both might have been low for the same reason: men were overseas. Also, because it was a prosperous time, single women with children were more likely to live independently.

Figure 8 shows the same relations during the 1968-84 period for whites and blacks separately. The upper curves represent the trends for blacks and the lower curves, the trends for whites. Although there appears to be some relationship for blacks, it is difficult to discern any relationship for whites. Nevertheless, in a recently published article, South finds that when he controls

TABLE 6

TRENDS IN RATES OF MARRIAGE, DIVORCE, ILLEGITIMACY, AND REMARRIAGE, 1940–80

Race and Period	Marital Disruption Rate[a]		Marriage Rate[b]		Illegitimacy Rate[c] Women Ages 15–44	
	Divorce or Separation	Widowhood	Following Divorce or Separation	For Previously Never Married	Nonwhites	Blacks
Whites						
1940–45	4.5	26.6	126.5	2.8	n.a.	3.6
1945–50	4.3	25.8	101.6	8.5	n.a.	6.1
1950–55	4.7	24.8	81.6	8.4	n.a.	7.9
1955–60	5.5	24.1	92.2	5.6	n.a.	8.7
1960–65	6.9	23.7	59.0	7.1	n.a.	10.4
1965–70	10.1	25.0	69.8	10.3	n.a.	12.7
1970–75	14.0	24.9	67.1	9.1	n.a.	12.3
1975–80	20.5	24.1	67.4	6.7	n.a.	13.8

TABLE 6 (Continued)

Race and Period	Marital Disruption Rate[a]		Marriage Rate[b]		Illegitimacy Rate[c]	
	Divorce or Separation	Widowhood	Following Divorce or Separation	For Previously Never Married	Women Ages 15–44	
					Nonwhites	Blacks
Blacks						
1940–45	10.8	33.5	173.1	13.4	35.6	n.a.
1945–50	11.4	29.7	50.7	4.0	71.2	n.a.
1950–55	10.2	28.9	63.4	9.2	87.2	n.a.
1955–60	14.1	28.1	78.6	5.2	95.2	n.a.
1960–65	15.3	28.1	70.7	7.5	98.1	n.a.
1965–70	22.8	29.4	36.9	9.0	89.6	n.a.
1970–75	24.6	31.5	47.6	6.3	71.5	90.2
1975–80	37.6	30.9	33.4	3.9	77.6	82.6

SOURCES: Divorce and marriage rates are taken from Thomas Espenshade, "Black-White Differences in Marriage, Separation, Divorce, and Re-marriage," report (Washington, D.C.: Urban Institute, 1985). Illegitimacy rates are taken from U.S. Department of Health and Human Services, Vital and Health Statistics, "Trends and Differentials in Births to Unmarried Women: United States, 1970–76," series Z1, number 36 (Hyattsville, Maryland: HHS, National Center of Health Statistics, May 1980).

a. The marital disruption rate is based on the number of disruptions per 1,000 divorced and 1,000 widowed persons in a stationary population.

b. The marriage rate is based on the number of remarriages following divorce (and the number of marriages for previously never-married women) per 1,000 persons.

c. The illegitimacy rate is based on the number of live births per 1,000 unmarried women ages fifteen through forty-four.

FIGURE 7

TRENDS IN MALE UNEMPLOYMENT AND FAMILY HEADSHIP BY SINGLE WOMEN,
1950–68

SOURCES: Unemployment rate is for all civilian workers, aged sixteen and over, from *Economic Report of the President, February 1985*, table B-33. The rate for families headed by single women for 1956–68 is from *Current Population Reports*, series P-20, for each respective year. The number of families headed by single women with children under age eighteen is divided by the total number of families with children under age eighteen. The 1950 rate for such families is taken from the U.S. Bureau of the Census, "General Characteristics of Families" (Washington, D.C.: U.S. Government Printing Office, 1950), table 4.

FIGURE 8

TRENDS IN MALE UNEMPLOYMENT AND FAMILY HEADSHIP BY SINGLE WOMEN, BY
RACE, 1968–84[a]

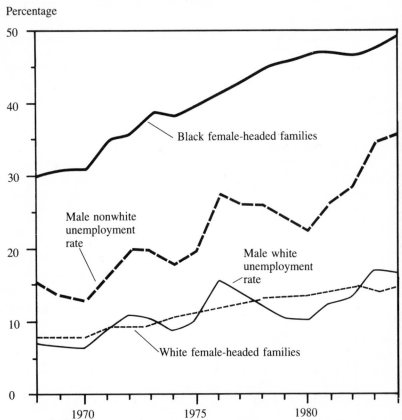

SOURCES: See figure 2 for the source of the rate of families headed by single women. The
number of families with a female head of household and children under age eighteen
is divided by the total number of families with children under age eighteen. The
unemployment rates for all civilian workers, aged sixteen and over, are from *Economic Report of the President, February 1985*; table B-33.

a. To bring the trend lines for each race together (but not on top of each other), we
multiplied the unemployment rates by 2.0.

The unemployment rates are lagged by one year. (For instance, the 1983 nonwhite unemployment rate of 17.8 is multiplied by 2.0 and then shown as the 35.6 in 1984.)

for other changes over time, unemployment rates during the post-World War II period have a strong effect on divorce rates.[34]

Although the time-series relation between family headship by single mothers and male unemployment rates is consistent with the hypothesis that increases in black male unemployment help account for increases in black female family headship, the strongest evidence for an effect of male unemployment comes from micro-level analyses of longitudinal and cross-sectional surveys. Using data from the Michigan PSID study, Hoffman and Holmes and Ross and Sawhill find that the probability of marital disruption is greater for families in which the husband has experienced unemployment. Cohen finds the same phenomenon for whites but no effect for blacks. Using NLS data, Cherlin finds that less-than-full-time work as well as low wages for the husband increased the probability of marital disruption.[35]

A problem with all these studies is the possibility that some other unmeasured factor (such as alcoholism) may be leading to the observed relation by affecting both unemployment (or low wages) and divorce. Presumably, however, there is little chance that such an omitted variable would be correlated with aggregate variations in unemployment rates across cities. Using the NLS data, Caldwell finds that young women who live in areas with high unemployment are more likely than others to experience divorce. Similarly, Honig finds that higher unemployment rates and lower male earnings were significantly associated with higher rates of mother-only families for both blacks and whites in 1960, but not in 1970. Using the same data as Honig but a slightly different set of variables, Minarik and Goldfarb report that male wage rates but not unemployment were associated with female household headship. Finally, Ross and Sawhill, using data on low-income areas in forty-one cities in 1970 and a somewhat different unemployment variable, find a strong relation between male unemployment and female family headship for whites but not for blacks.[36]

---

34. Scott J. South, "Economic Conditions and the Divorce Rate: A Time Series Analysis of the Postwar United States," *Journal of Marriage and the Family*, vol. 47 (1985), pp. 31-42.

35. Hoffman and Holmes, "Husbands, Wives and Divorce"; Ross and Sawhill, *Time of Transition*; Alan Cohen, "Economics, Marital Instability and Race," (Ph.D. dissertation, University of Wisconsin, 1979); and Cherlin, "Social and Economic Determinants."

36. K. A. Moore, et al., "The Consequences of Early Childbearing: An Analysis of Selected Parental Outcomes Using Results from the National Longitudinal Survey of Young Women," report to the National Institute of Child Health and Development (Washington, D.C: Urban Institute, 1978); Honig, "The Impact of AFDC Income, Recipient Rates, and Family Dissolution," pp. 303-22; Minarik and Goldfarb, "AFDC Income, Recipient Rates and Family Dissolution: A Comment"; and Ross and Sawhill, *Time of Transition*.

Wilson's Hypothesis. Wilson and his colleagues have proposed a more recent version of the male employment argument.[37] Like Moynihan, they focus on black families as an indicator of poor families and attribute the recent growth of families headed by single mothers to increased joblessness among black men. Their indicator of male opportunity is somewhat broader than male unemployment and measures the number of employed men per 100 women of similar age in the population. This ratio is viewed as a measure of "the pool of marriageable men" in the population and takes into account not only male unemployment but also the high mortality and incarceration rates for black men—and the fact that many are likely to be out of the labor force entirely.

Wilson and his colleagues point out that declines in marriageable black men between 1960 and 1980 were greatest in the North Central and Northeast regions of the country, which also showed the greatest increase in the number of mother-only families. The South had a somewhat lower decline and experienced a lower growth in such families. The West, which accounts for only 9 percent of the total black population, did not fit the pattern. The marriageable pool of men in the West remained fairly constant, whereas mother-only families increased substantially. The researchers attribute this anomaly to the fact that black single mothers who head families in the West are more likely to be middle class and to behave more like whites than are blacks in other parts of the country. Thus they should be expected to be like whites in responding more to increases in opportunities for women than to declines in opportunities for men.

Wilson and his colleagues note that declines in employment among blacks were due initially to a shift in unskilled jobs from South to North and later to a loss of jobs in central cities in the North where blacks are highly concentrated. Jobs for unskilled workers in cities such as New York, Philadelphia, and Baltimore declined by more than 30 percent during the 1970s, whereas jobs for skilled workers increased from 21 to 38 percent. Ironically, the shift to higher-paying jobs in the central cities worked to the disadvantage of black

---

37. W. J. Wilson and K. M. Neckerman, "Poverty and Family Structure: The Widening Gap between Evidence and Public Policy Issues," Paper prepared for the conference entitled Poverty and Policy: Retrospect and Prospects, Williamsburg, Virginia, December 6-9, 1984; and R. Aponte, K. Neckerman, and W. J. Wilson, "Race, Family Structure and Social Policy," Working Paper 7 (University of Chicago, Project on the Federal Social Role, 1985). For a discussion of the effects of the sex ratio on family structure, see W. Darity, Jr., and S. L. Myers, Jr., "Changes in Black Family Structure: Implications for Welfare Dependency," American Economic Association (May 1983, *Papers and Proceedings*), pp. 59-64.

men who lacked at least a high school education.[38] Because mother-only families are much more common among black women with little education than among middle-class women, the researchers conclude that the loss of jobs in the central cities is a major factor in the increase of families headed by single mothers.

Psychological Costs of Joblessness. Male joblessness, like the other factors that have been discussed, has psychological as well as economic costs that undermine the stability of marriage and encourage the growth of mother-only family headship. Changes in family relationships as a result of unemployment were first documented by Bakke and Komarovsky in their research on the Great Depression.[39] We quoted from Bakke earlier in the chapter. We quote here from Komarovsky, describing the shift in respect and authority that results from the father's unemployment:

> Mr. Brady says that while the children don't blame him for his unemployment, he is sure that they don't think as much about the old man as they used to. It's only natural. When a father cannot support his family, supply them with clothing and good food, the children are bound to lose respect (p. 98).

More recently, Liebow has presented a vivid picture of how unemployment or underemployment undermined marital relationships and attitudes toward marriage among the men who hang out at "Talley's Corner."[40] Faced with few opportunities for occupational stability or mobility, Liebow's street men appear to reject the values of family responsibility and commitment in order to disguise their failure as breadwinners.

Quantitative research reinforces these findings in several areas. Several researchers have shown that unemployment lowers psychological well-being.[41] Using the Michigan PSID data, Cohn found that male heads of households who lost their jobs experienced a decline in self-esteem, especially if the husband assumed some of the wife's obligations, for example, spending more time doing housework. Other studies have shown that unemployment is as-

---

38. John Kasarda, "Urban Change and Minority Opportunities," in Paul E. Peterson, ed., *The New Urban Reality* (Washington, D.C.: Brookings Institution, 1985).

39. Mira Komarovsky, *The Unemployed Man and His Family* (New York: Octagon Books, 1940); and Bakke, *Citizens without Work*.

40. Elliot Liebow, *Talley's Corner* (Boston, Massachusetts: Little, Brown and Co., 1967).

41. R. Catalano and C. D. Dooley, "Economic Predictions of Depressed Mood and Stressful Life Events in a Metropolitan Community," *Journal of Health and Social Behavior*, vol. 18 (1977), pp. 292-307; Susan Gore, "The Influence of Social Support and Related Variables in Ameliorating the Consequences of Job Loss" (Ph.D. dissertation, University of Pennsylvania, 1973); Richard Cohn, "The Effects of Employment Status Change on Self Attitudes," *Social Psychology*, vol. 41 (1978), pp. 81-93; and G. W. Comstock and K. J. Helsing, "Symptoms of Depression in Two Communities," *Psychological Medicine*, vol. 6 (1976), pp. 551-63.

sociated with marital unhappiness, marital conflict, and even family violence.[42]

Changes in Social Norms and Sexual Mores

The last explanation for the increase in mother-only families examines changes in attitudes and values as the critical determinants. At its most general level, this argument attributes changes in social norms during the past century to an overall decline in the functional importance of the family and to an increasing emphasis on individual rights and fulfillment. In particular, it claims that norms about the acceptability of divorce and single parenthood have changed among men as well as women and that these changes have led to increases in marital disruption and family headship by single women.

Changes in Male Attitudes and Values. In her book *The Hearts of Men*, Ehrenrich focuses specifically on changes in male attitudes and values.[43] According to the author, the increase in female-headed families is the result of a "male revolt" against traditional family values—a revolt that began in the 1950s along with the initiation of *Playboy* magazine, the development of pop psychology, and a new concern for self-fulfillment and consumerism. Ehrenrich claims that the antiwar and counterculture movements of the 1960s fueled the revolt and generated widespread acceptance of the new male role. For Ehrenrich, the leaders of the revolt are white male professionals who shifted their support from the breadwinner ethic in the 1950s to the liberated male image in the 1960s and 1970s.

The author's argument has several weaknesses. First, her focus on middle-class men ignores the groups in which the increase of families headed by single mothers has been greatest: the poor and racial minorities. Second, her description is inconsistent with other research on the attitudes and marriage behavior of white men, who appear to be better off than women when married (they report high levels of happiness and psychological well-being) and worse off when divorced.[44] Furthermore, most middle-class males remarry very quickly after divorce and widowhood, which suggests that marriage is their preferred state.

---

42. Murray A. Straus, Richard Gelles, and Suzanne Steinmetz, *Behind Closed Doors* (New York: Anchor Books, 1981).

43. Barbara Ehrenrich, *The Hearts of Men* (Garden City, New York: Anchor Press/Doubleday, 1983).

44. Walter Gone, "The Relationship between Sex Roles, Marital Status, and Mental Illness," *Social Forces*, vol. 51 (1972) pp. 34-44. Gone reviewed more than twenty-two studies of mental illness and found that in seventeen of seventeen studies married men had lower rates of mental illness than married women and in seventeen of twenty-two studies formerly married men had higher rates than formerly married women.

Despite its limitations, the Ehrenrich argument provides an interesting counterbalance to theories that focus exclusively on changes in women's independence. Moreover, her analysis does offer a possible explanation for why many middle-class fathers are so reluctant to provide child support commensurate with their economic status. Indeed, their behavior suggests that although marriage may be the preferred state, their sense of obligation to offspring is weak. It is unfortunate that we have no data on whether noncustodial fathers today pay child support more or less regularly than they did before Ehrenrich's postulated "male revolt," so this hypothesis cannot be tested empirically.

The Relationship between Changes in Values and Divorce. Unlike Ehrenrich's thesis, a good deal of other evidence on attitudes toward divorce suggests that changes in values do occur, but that they follow rather than cause changes in behavior. In his book on marriage and divorce, for example, Cherlin notes that attitudes about divorce apparently changed very little until the late 1960s (see his findings in figures 9 and 10), but changed a great deal between 1968 and 1978.[45] In both 1945 and 1966 the most common response (34-35 percent) to the question of whether divorce laws were too strict or not strict enough was "not strict enough." Thereafter attitudes changed substantially. In 1968, 60 percent of the people interviewed thought that divorce should be more difficult to obtain. By 1974 and 1978 only about 42 percent thought so. Cherlin concludes that changes in attitudes could not have caused the initial increase in divorce.

Even if changes in attitudes cannot account for the long-term rise in divorce during the twentieth century or for the acceleration of the trend in the 1960s, there are two reasons to think that values may have played an important role in sustaining the trend. First, as single parenthood has become more common and more acceptable, the stigma associated with the status probably declined. Thus parents who might have stayed together in the past for the sake of social approval have become more free to divorce and establish separate households. Second, as the risk of marital disruption increases, young mothers are more likely to make career choices that enhance their economic independence and reduce their dependence; such choices, in turn, make it easier to divorce in the event that the marriage is unsatisfactory.

Sexual Permissiveness and Premarital Births. Some people attribute the increase in mother-only families to changing social norms about premarital sexuality, out-of-wedlock births, and the acceptability of single motherhood

---

45. Andrew Cherlin, *Marriage, Divorce, Remarriage* (Cambridge, Massachusetts: Harvard University Press, 1982).

FIGURE 9

ATTITUDES ABOUT DIVORCE LAWS, 1945–65[a]

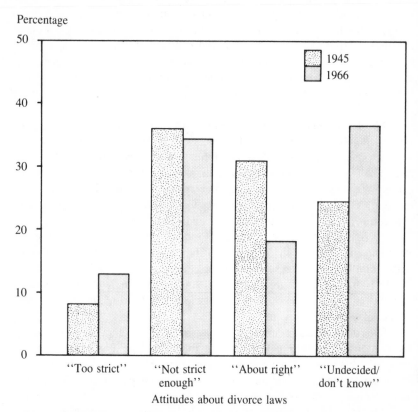

Attitudes about divorce laws

SOURCE: Reprinted by permission from Andrew Cherlin, *Marriage, Divorce, Remarriage* (Cambridge, Massachusetts: Harvard University Press, 1982), p. 47.

a.   Attitudes toward divorce laws, 1945 and 1966 (1945: "Do you think the divorce laws in your state are now too strict or not strict enough?" 1966: "Generally speaking, would you say divorce laws in this state are too strict or not strict enough?"). Based on American Institute of Public Opinion, Study 341 (1945) and 723 (1966). The 1945 data were published in "The Quarter's Polls," *Public Opinion Quarterly*, vol. 9 (Summer 1945), p. 233. The 1966 data were published in Gallup Opinion Index, report no. 9 (February 1966), p. 21.

FIGURE 10

ATTITUDES ABOUT DIFFICULTY OF OBTAINING DIVORCE, 1968–78[a]

Percentage

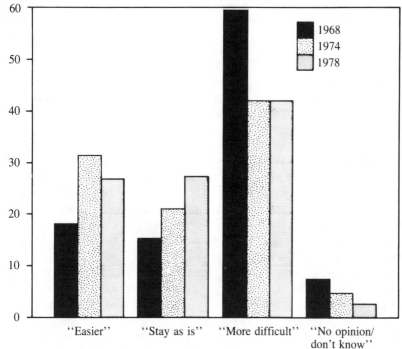

Attitudes about obtaining a divorce

SOURCE: Reprinted by permission of Cherlin, *Marriage, Divorce, Remarriage*, p. 48.

a.   Attitudes toward divorce, 1968, 1974, and 1978: "Should divorce in this country be easier or more difficult to obtain than it is now?" Data for 1968 from American Institute for Public Opinion, Study 764, data published in Gallup Opinion Index, report no. 41, November 1968; for 1974 and 1978, National Opinion Research Center, General Social Surveys.

for never-married women. This argument is most often used to account for high rates of illegitimacy and single motherhood in low-income communities, but it has also been used to describe similar behavior among celebrities.[46] According to this view, the stigma previously associated with premarital sexuality and out-of-wedlock births has all but disappeared in some segments of society, and single motherhood has increasingly become an acceptable alternative family form.

Changes in values may affect the growth of families headed by never-married women in two ways: through changes in sexual permissiveness, which increase the proportion of women who are at risk for an out-of-wedlock birth, and through changes in the acceptability of single motherhood, which increase the likelihood that an unmarried women who becomes pregnant will bear and raise her child alone.

The empirical evidence on norms governing premarital sexual activity is limited before the 1970s, and most of it is based on studies of college students, who may be very different from the general population. Thus any conclusions about changing norms and behavior must be viewed with some caution. Two surveys carried out by the National Opinion Research Center, however, indicate that the proportion of adults who believed in total sexual abstinence before marriage dropped from 80 percent in 1963 to only 30 percent in 1975.[47] The shift in attitudes was even greater among college students. The proportion of students who believed in total sexual abstinence for unmarried women fell from about 55 percent in 1967 to about 11 percent in the early 1970s. During the same period the proportion who believed that it was all right for a young women to engage in sex without love jumped from 5 percent to about 24 percent.[48] Taken together, these studies indicate that a rather dramatic change in attitudes occurred during the late 1960s and early 1970s.

Information on changes in behavior is consistent with the research on attitudes. Studies of premarital sexual activity indicate that about 20 percent of women reported having had sex before marriage in surveys conducted in

---

46. Charles Murray, "White Welfare Families, 'White Trash,' " *National Review* (March 28, 1986), pp. 30-34.

47. National Opinion Research Center, "Cumulative Codebook for the 1972-1977 General Social Surveys" (Chicago, Illinois: University of Chicago, NORC, 1977); and Ira Reiss, *The Social Context of Premarital Sexual Permissiveness* (New York: Holt, Rinehart and Winston, 1967).

48. J. Gagnon and W. Simon, *Sexual Conduct: The Social Sources of Human Sexuality* (Chicago, Illinois: Aldine Publishing Co., 1973); and John Delamater and Patricia Mac-Corquodale, *Premarital Sexuality* (Madison, Wisconsin: University of Wisconsin Press, 1979).

the 1940s and early 1950s.[49] By 1967 the proportion had jumped to 32 percent, and by 1973 it had increased to 60 percent.[50] Moreover, the change in behavior appears to have continued during the 1970s among younger age groups. In their study based on a nationally representative sample of adolescent women (ages fifteen to nineteen), Zelnick, Kantner, and Ford found that the proportion of teenage women who were sexually active before marriage increased by 41 percent among whites and by 18 percent among blacks between 1971 and 1976.[51]

The empirical studies indicate that the change in sexual norms occurred about the same time as the change in behavior. Moreover, since sexual activity has continued to increase among teenage women during the 1970s, we conclude that norms have probably played a causal role in the increase in risk of pregnancy among unmarried women. It is not clear just how large the role is. We must remember that the never-married component represents only a small portion of the growth of mother-only families among whites, even during the past decade, and therefore changes in sexual norms and behavior cannot account for very much of the overall trend.

Among blacks, never-married mothers represent a much larger proportion of all mother-only families, but there are other reasons for doubting that changes in sexual norms have been the most important factor for this group. First, the increase in sexual behavior during the 1970s was much smaller among blacks, 18 percent as compared with 41 percent. Second, the Zelnick, Kantner, and Ford research indicates that the increase in sexual activity did not result in an increase in pregnancies among young black women, at least not during the 1970s.[52] Increases in premarital sex were offset by greater use of contraceptives so that the incidence of pregnancy remained fairly constant during this period.

What about the changes in the acceptability of out-of-wedlock births? Has the stigma associated with illegitimacy declined during the past few decades, and can this account for the increase in families headed by single

---

49. A. C. Kinsey, W. B. Pomeroy, and C. E. Martin, *Sexual Behavior in the Human Male* (Philadelphia, Pennsylvania: W. B. Saunders, 1948); A. C. Kinsey, W. B. Pomeroy, C. E. Martin, and P. H. Gebhard, *Sexual Behavior in the Human Female* (Philadelphia, Pennsylvania: W. B. Saunders, 1953); and W. Ehrmann, *Premarital Dating Behavior* (New York: Holt, Rinehart and Winston, 1959).

50. Gagnon and Simon, *Sexual Conduct: The Social Sources of Human Sexuality*; and Delamater and MacCorquodale, *Premarital Sexuality*.

51. Melvin Zelnick, John Kantner, and Kathleen Ford, *Sex and Pregnancy in Adolescents* (Beverly Hills, California: Sage Publications, 1981).

52. Ibid.

mothers? The Zelnick, Kantner, and Ford study described above found some increases in social tolerance between 1971 and 1976, as reported by young black and white adolescents. When asked about their perceptions of social condemnation toward unwed mothers, less than 2.6 percent of whites and 8.6 percent of blacks reported no condemnation at all in 1971. By 1976, the numbers had increased to 4.8 and 13.6, respectively. Although the direction of the trend is toward more tolerance, these figures demonstrate that most young women do not see widespread approval of premarital births.[53]

Interestingly, neighborhood norms about single motherhood appear to be more tolerant among blacks and more polarized among whites than societal norms. When asked about neighbors' attitudes toward unwed mothers, a higher percentage of white adolescents reported both "no condemnation" and "very strong condemnation" than was reported for the question on societal norms. This disparity suggests that there is a good deal of conflict within the white community, with some neighborhoods being perceived as more tolerant and others more traditional. Black adolescents, on the other hand, reported more tolerance at both ends of the scale (a lower percentage reported strong condemnation and a higher percentage repored no condemnation). These findings are consistent with the notion that the black community is more tolerant about births for unwed mothers than society at large. On balance, however, the empirical evidence indicates that there continues to be a good deal of stigma associated with premarital births as perceived by young adolescent women, regardless of race.

The Value of Children. Before concluding our discussion of social norms and attitudes, we should note one more value that appears to play an important role in the recent growth of never-married mothers. This is the value of children. In our previous discussion, we have attempted to explain why *changes* in values might be related to the growth of mother-only families. In the following discussion we argue that growth may result from the fact that certain values remain constant while other factors change.

In their study of the costs and benefits of children, Blake and Pinal found that most adults view children as a valuable social investment. When asked whether children were a hedge against loneliness in old age, whether they provided a goal in life, and whether they provided a sense of having achieved adulthood, an overwhelming proportion of respondents (nearly 75 percent) answered positively to all three questions. Blake and Pinal note that there is more consensus in this set of questions than on any other in their study and

---

53. Ibid.

that the highest (most positive) scores were reported by the least educated respondents.[54]

The finding that children are a valued asset in and of themselves may help explain why young unmarried women continue to become mothers, even though their behavior appears to be irrational from an economic point of view. While having a child out-of-wedlock undoubtedly reduces long-term economic well-being, the decisions of young women must be viewed in a context that compares single motherhood with other options. As Blake and Pinal note, "People are most likely to see reproduction as being socially instrumental when their alternative means for achieving social goals are the most limited."[55] The fact that children have a social value makes it easier to understand why some young women with minimal education and few employment opportunities continue to become mothers even though their prospects for finding a "marriageable male" are rather bleak.

It also suggests that plans for reducing the prevalence of never-married mothers must consider the economic opportunities of young unmarried women as well as young men. Until now, researchers concerned with the growth of female-headed families have focused on the high unemployment or nonemployment of young black men. In a recent study of young black women, however, Jones found that a large proportion of this group are "inactive," that is, they are not enrolled in school, are not working, and are not mothers. Presumably this group is at high risk for becoming single mothers, but as of now we do not know how such an event may alter the life changes of these women.[56]

---

54. Judith Blake and Jorge H. del Pinal, "The Childlessness Option: Recent American Views of Nonparenthood," in Gerry Hendershot and Paul Placek, eds., *Predicting Fertility: Demographic Studies of Birth Expectations* (Lexington, Massachusetts: Lexington Books, 1981), pp. 235-64. The Blake and Pinal research is based on a national sample of adults taken from a Gallup Poll in 1978.

55. Blake and Pinal, "The Childlessness Option," p. 249.

56. Elizabeth Jones, "Women, Race and Work: A Study of Transitions to Adulthood," Ph.D. dissertation (Evanston, Illinois: Northwestern University, 1986).

CHAPTER 4

A REVIEW OF AMERICAN WELFARE POLICY: COLONIAL ERA TO 1980

Given that current public income transfer policy leaves such a large proportion of mother-only families both poor and highly dependent on the government, and may contribute somewhat to the prevalence of families headed by women, this chapter addresses the question, how did the nation arrive at such a policy? By examining what is common about current and previous policy and what is different, we may gain some insight into whether we can strike a better balance between improving the lot of mother-only families and removing incentives for their growth and dependence.

Our findings may be summarized briefly. During the course of more than three centuries many American practices have changed, but four important ones are constants: first, from colonial days through the present, Americans have always charged their government with the responsibility of aiding the poor. Only once in U.S. history—in the late nineteenth century, when millions of poor Catholic immigrants poured into the country sparking nativism, bigotry, and the temporary ascendance of Social Darwinism—was the principle of public provision seriously challenged in practice. That challenge, however, was rebuffed.

Second, the commitment to publicly aid the poor has been accompanied throughout American history by attempts to ensure that public provision did not lead to overdependence on government. In a country that prides itself on adherence to self-reliance and independence, any other position would be hard to imagine. The most important American political leaders—from Benjamin Franklin to Franklin D. Roosevelt, who created the modern welfare state in America, and Lyndon Johnson, who expanded it—have feared that public aid, if not properly tailored, might unduly encourage dependence on government.

Third, U.S. public aid policy has always distinguished among groups of the poor and treated them differently. The most important distinction has been between those expected to work and those not expected to work. This has implications for policy toward single mothers because the policy on whether they have been expected to work or not has changed over time. In the aftermath of President Johnson's War on Poverty (1965-70) the traditional practice of categorization was briefly challenged by some of the proponents of a negative income tax (NIT), who advocated equal treatment of all categories of the poor and replacement of all other income support programs with the NIT. That challenge was also rejected.

Fourth, and most generally, aid programs in America have always reflected and reinforced community values. One such value is compassion, which is reflected in the constant public provision of aid. Another is the value of self-reliance, which has been demonstrated in the ongoing concern about avoiding undue dependence on government. Still another is equality of opportunity, which has been inherent in American leadership in providing free public education. Finally, a less admirable value, racial and ethnic prejudice, has been reflected in the discriminatory provision of benefits to minority groups.

Of the many changes in policy, we focus on three. The first is that the level of benefits provided to poor mother-only families has increased steadily in the three centuries of America's history. By current American standards, the level of aid in the past was meager—a meagerness that has led many historians to characterize the poor law as stingy and mean spirited.[1] No doubt during six hundred years in Great Britain and more than half that many in America, there are ample examples of stinginess and meanness. But there are

---

1. See, for example, June Axinn and Herman Levin, *Social Welfare: A History of the American Response to Need* (New York: Harper and Row, 1975); and Samuel Mencher, *Poor Law to Poverty Programs* (Pittsburgh: University of Pittsburgh Press, 1967). For a somewhat different perspective, see Michael B. Katz, *Poverty and Policy in American History* (New York: Academic Press, 1983); and James F. Patterson, *America's Struggle against Poverty, 1900-1980* (Cambridge, Massachusetts: Harvard University Press, 1981).

Other historians have argued that public aid policy is nothing more than a tool of the elites for the regulation of labor (see Frances F. Piven and Richard A. Cloward, *Regulating the Poor: The Functions of Public Welfare*, New York: Pantheon, 1971). However, we do not equate constant concern about the effects of aid on welfare dependence with the proposition that public aid to the poor serves no other purpose than regulating the labor of the poor. Any sensible community that is committed to providing public aid to the poor will be concerned about the effects of such provision on the dependence of the poor on help from the government. Furthermore, this is not a class issue, in which the interest of the capitalist economic elite differs from that of the lower, or working, classes. However defined, it is in the interest of the working class as well as of the capitalist class to minimize the dependence of the poor on relief. Public policies that pursue long-run equality of opportunity rather than short-run relief of distress and thereby minimize dependence on government further the interest of capital and labor, because they promote efficiency and mobility. For a discussion of the historical validity of the Piven-Cloward thesis see Walter I. Trattner, ed., *Social Welfare or Social Control* (Knoxville, Tennessee: University of Tennessee Press, 1983).

also ample examples of generosity. The historical evidence suggests that the level of aid has depended more on the income of the population than on their degree of generosity or quality of spirit. Over the years, even the effects of religious and racial prejudice—the most quantifiable measure of meanness— have diminished over time, while the effects of income have grown.

The gradual growth in expenditures on the poor has fluctuated over time and across towns and cities, colonies and states. Examples of extreme bursts of stinginess and generosity, however, illustrate our second point about change: during some periods, priority has been given to reducing dependence, while in other periods, priority has been given to reducing economic insecurity. Throughout, however, there is strong statistical evidence that differences in income explain much of the variation in the generosity of aid over time and across states.

Finally, although able-bodied men always have been expected to work, the expectations with regard to poor single mothers who head families have changed. Until the early twentieth century, these women were expected to work. For the next half-century, however, the stated objective of government policy was to provide enough aid to enable them to imitate the then current middle-class ideal of the mother who refrained from work in the marketplace and stayed home to rear the children. Not until the late 1960s, however, was sufficient aid provided to make the objective achievable, and by that time middle-class ideals and practice had changed. And expectations about the activities of poor single mothers who headed families had begun to revert to those of the nineteenth century.

Our discussion of policies toward mother-only families is divided into five periods: (1) colonial times to the nineteenth century, (2) the nineteenth century, (3) the Progressive era, 1900-17, (4) the New Deal and the Social Security Act, and (5) the post-New Deal and post-World War II era. Because knowledge of more recent developments is more complete, and also because these developments are more relevant to an evaluation of the Reagan admin- istration's policies and of alternatives to these policies, we devote increasing attention to each successive historical period.

To understand the history of public aid policy to mother-only families, it often is necessary to consider the issue of aid to the poor in general and, in some cases, to consider broader social policy developments such as free public education.

Colonial Times to the Nineteenth Century

From their earliest beginnings, Americans provided a publicly funded "safety net" to assure a minimal standard of living to destitute mothers who headed families with children. Along with numerous other British laws and customs, the early colonists brought with them the British poor law, which embodied the principle that it was the responsibility of the government to aid the poor.[2] As feudalism gave way to capitalism in all Western European nations, the state supplanted the church in bearing the responsibility to aid the poor. In England, this development began in 1349 with the Statute of Laborers, which prohibited private almsgiving to the able-bodied, and culminated in 1601 with the enactment of the famous Elizabethan poor law.

The Commitment to Public Provision of Aid

The strength of the principle of public provision for the poor in Great Britain is illustrated by the position of Adam Smith, the father of laissez-faire. In *Wealth of Nations*, Smith's major discussion of the poor law comes in the context of a broader discussion of laws that restrict the mobility of labor.[3] After the monasteries closed and several alternatives of providing for the poor were tried and failed, the crown required local parishes to provide public aid to their residents. Because relief for the poor was funded locally, each parish had an incentive to avoid allowing poor laborers to relocate within their jurisdiction. Apparently when unscrupulous officials in some districts tried to get poor dependents in their districts to move to other districts, Parliament imposed restrictions on the movement of laborers from one parish to another. What is most striking about Smith's account and the lesson he draws from it is that the law of settlement, not the poor law, was the problem. As a consequence, Smith quite sensibly recommended elimination of the former but said nothing about the latter. Even the apostle of laissez-faire took it for granted that aid for the poor was a public responsibility.

By current standards, the level of aid provided under the American poor laws was quite meager, but in many American towns, shortly after the American Revolution, expenditures on public assistance for the poor was one of

---

2. For a description of the British poor law and its evolution, see Karl de Schweinitz, *England's Road to Social Security* (Philadelphia, Pennsylvania: University of Pennsylvania Press, 1943). For historical accounts of the development of assistance policy in the United States, see Axinn and Levin, *Social Welfare*; Mencher, *Poor Law*; Katz, *Poverty and Policy*; and Patterson, *America's Struggle*.

3. Adam Smith, *The Wealth of Nations* (New York: Random House, 1965), pp. 135-40.

the largest items in the budget.[4] The provision was still meager, however, because the community's income was meager.[5]

The Concern about Dependence

Throughout the history of the United States there has been concern that generosity toward the poor would increase their numbers. As Benjamin Franklin said of Britain's poor law:

> The day you passed that Act you took away from before their eyes the greatest of all inducements to industry, frugality and sobriety, by giving them a dependence on somewhat else than a careful accumulation during youth and health for support in age and sickness . . . . I think the best way of doing good to the poor is not making them easy in poverty, but leading or driving them out of poverty . . . . There is no country in the world where so many provisions are established for them, so many hospitals to receive them when they are sick or lame founded on voluntary charities; so many almshouses for the aged of both sexes, together with a solemn general law made by the rich to subject their estates to a heavy tax for the support of the poor. In short, you offered a premium for the encouragement of idleness, and you should not wonder that it has had its effect in the increase of poverty.[6]

The fear that generosity would increase dependence not only limited the level of benefits in colonial times but also affected the manner in which aid was given. Entering a workhouse, poorhouse, or almshouse was often a condition of aid. Even when relief was given in one's own home, receipt was often discouraged; for example, a 1718 Pennsylvania statute referred to recipients as paupers and required them to wear a "P" on their sleeves.[7]

Most female heads of families were widows. Divorce, separation, and out-of-wedlock births were strongly discouraged by law and custom and were relatively uncommon by current standards.

Within the poor law, widows and their children were treated better than other families headed by single women and the rest of the poor. Widows with children were frequently given relief in their own homes rather than being

---

4. See Raymond A. Mohl, "Poverty in Early America, a Reappraisal," *New York History*, vol. 50 (January 1969), pp. 5-27; and Carl Bridenbaugh, *Cities in Revolt* (New York: Knapf, 1955), pp. 319-25.

5. See the discussion by Lebergott below in this chapter and in note 8 for evidence of the effects of income on benefits over time. There is a vast literature on the determinants of state welfare expenditures. Some measure of average income in the state is invariably one of the key determinants of state generosity. For one of the best studies and numerous citations, see Larry Orr, "Income Transfers as a Public Good: An Application to AFDC," *American Economic Review*, vol. 66 (June 1976), pp. 359-71.

6. Quoted in Mencher, *Poor Law*, p. 96.

7. Axinn and Levin, *Social Welfare*, p. 14.

required to board with another family or enter the poorhouse. This differential treatment was a consequence of two factors. First, because widowhood was an involuntary state, there was no concern that aiding widows would increase their numbers. Second, the widows who were treated the best were those whose husbands had contributed most obviously to the community good (that is, men who had died in the service of their country). Separate, nonwelfare cash-benefit pension programs for war widows were developed. By the outbreak of the American Revolution, most of the colonies (as opposed to local governments) had assumed responsibility for aiding veterans and their widows. After the Revolution, all the states enacted legislation to provide pensions for disabled veterans and their widows and children.

Despite these pensions, women who had children but no husbands were expected to work. Widowhood was a respectable status. Even so, widows with children were expected to take in wash, become seamstresses, or take in boarders. Indeed, poor children were expected to work from the colonial era through the nineteenth century. One common method of aiding children was to indenture or apprentice them.

Developments during the Nineteenth Century

As incomes increased during the nineteenth century, public provision for the poor gradually became more generous. Lebergott found that the level of aid to the poor increased from $59 per person per year in 1850 to $125 per person per year in 1903. The increase was greater than the cost of living but about equal to the increase in real wages during that period.[8] Benefits did not, however, expand steadily. A few of the most important milestones of this period are summarized in the sections that follow.

The Attempt to Restrict Relief outside the Poorhouse

In the early 1800s a movement developed in most American states to provide aid only within the poorhouse; a parallel movement developed in Great Britain. Such a movement had occurred previously from time to time in both places, but this time it was fueled by the arguments of Malthus. For a brief period, Malthus, who argued that population growth inevitably outstripped food growth, became the most influential of the British political economists. In his view, aiding the poor simply compounded the population-

---

8. See Stanley Lebergott, *The American Economy: Income, Wealth, and Want*, especially chapter 5, "A Century of Guaranteed Income in the United States," (Princeton, New Jersey: Princeton University Press, 1976), pp. 53-67.

food problem (the view that earned economics its reputation as the dismal science).[9] Although the followers of Malthus never succeeded in abolishing public aid, they did succeed in severely limiting relief. In Britain, the movement led to enactment of the landmark 1834 reform of the poor law, under which willingness to enter the poorhouse became the test of need for relief. In principle, except for poorhouse relief, aid was abolished; in practice, many parishes continued to grant what was called "outdoor relief," especially to widows with children. During the next half-century several other similar attempts to abolish outdoor relief in Britain occurred—suggesting that such relief in fact remained common throughout the period. Similar legislation in Massachusetts and New York and a host of other states also failed to eliminate outdoor relief, although such legislation did lead to restrictions on it.

These restrictions spurred a movement to create special institutions for children, on the argument that the poorhouse was an unfit environment for children. In the second quarter of the nineteenth century religious and ethnic groups in the United States did found special institutions for children, most of them orphanages. The children who were cared for included "half-orphans" (as children from poor mother-only families were called) and even some from poor two-parent families.

Free Public Education

During the second quarter of the nineteenth century the free public education movement also developed. Free public education was of great importance to the poor in general and to mother-only families in particular because it offered their children the opportunity, through education, to earn their way out of poverty. It also removed an important rationale for putting children in the poorhouse or orphanages, where education typically was provided. Finally, of special importance to single mothers heading families, free public education provided free child care.

The United States led the world in the development of free public education.[10] As early as 1803, when Ohio was admitted to the Union, the federal government donated one section of each township to the state's education fund. During the Jacksonian era (1828-36), the free public education movement flourished. By 1848, when Marx and Engels issued their famous Manifesto of the Communist Party, calling for, among other things, free public

---

9. Thomas Robert Malthus, *On Population*, (New York: Random House, 1960).

10. See Arnold J. Heidemheimer with John Layson, "Social Policy Development in Europe and America: A Longer View on Selectivity and Income Testing," in Irwin Garfinkel, ed., *Income-Testing Transfer Programs: The Case For and Against* (New York: Academic Press, 1982), pp. 141-63.

education, most American states were already providing it at the elementary school level.

That the United States led the world in the development of free public education is at least in part due to the high value that Americans have historically accorded to equality of opportunity. Two of the most noted foreign observers of the United States, writing more than a century apart—Tocqueville in the early nineteenth century and Myrdal in the 1940s—commented on the strength of the American commitment to the value of equality of opportunity.[11] The generous land policy of the United States throughout most of the nineteenth century was also due in part to the value placed on equality of opportunity.

Civil War Pensions

In 1862 the U.S. Congress enacted the first federal income transfer program in the history of the United States. It was a program of federal pensions for Union men disabled in the war and pensions for widows and children of Union men killed in action. Eligibility did not depend on income. This program was substantially liberalized in 1890 to provide pensions to disabled and retired Union veterans regardless of whether their disability occurred during service, and also pensions to widows and children of deceased Union veterans regardless of whether the men died while in the service. Orloff estimates that nearly half of native, male Northerners had received these pensions by 1900.[12] The federal Civil War pension program thus was a precursor of the twentieth-century Old Age and Survivors' Insurance program.

The exclusion of Southern veterans from eligibility for Civil War pensions is a stark example of how public aid policy has always reinforced community values. As already explained, war widows have generally been treated better than other widows as a reward for the patriotic sacrifice of their husbands. From the point of view of the Northern victors of the Civil War, however, the Southerners who fought in the war had not performed a civic duty and thus were not to be rewarded.

The Attempt to Eliminate Public Aid

Toward the end of the nineteenth century the principle of public responsibility for the poor was seriously challenged in practice for the first and

---

11. See Alexis de Tocqueville, *Democracy in America* (New York: Anchor/Doubleday, 1969); and Gunnar Myrdal, *An American Dilemma* (New York: Random House, 1972).

12. See Ann Shola Orloff, "The Politics of Pensions: A Comparative Analysis of the Origins of Pensions, and Old Age Insurance in Canada, Great Britain and the United States, 1980-1930's" (unpublished Ph.D. dissertation, Princeton University, Department of Sociology, 1985), pp. 70-71.

only time in America's history. In the era when the United States was be-coming an industrial giant, wealth and immigration increased rapidly. Native Protestant Americans felt threatened by masses of poor Catholic immigrants. Bigotry increased. For a time it appeared that a class society based on reli-gion—well-to-do native Protestants versus poor immigrant Catholics—might emerge. These native Protestant Americans flirted with the Social Darwinist idea that the survival-of-the-fittest doctrine should be applied to all social and economic life. According to these Social Darwinists, government aid to the poor was an interference with natural law, although private philanthropy was deemed appropriate.

From this environment emerged the Charity Organization Society (COS), which established the first organization of professional social workers. The first COS workers and leaders were the mothers in the well-to-do Protestant families who volunteered their time to help the poor. They called themselves friendly visitors and practiced what they referred to as "scientific philan-thropy," by which they meant the provision of intensive services to poor families to help them achieve economic independence. COS members were so influenced by Social Darwinism and were so militantly committed to independence that they opposed public provision of aid to the poor (even though many of their relatives, quite paradoxically, were receiving Civil War pensions). For a short time, in some towns and cities, public aid could not be dispensed without the approval of the local COS, and in some places COS members actually became the administrators of public aid. Despite its great influence, the COS failed to eliminate public provision of aid. However, largely as a consequence of COS influence, it was common practice by the late nineteenth century to provide nonpension aid to the children of single mothers only if the children were placed in an institution for children. These single mothers were still predominantly widows, but they were widows of immigrants and Southern men. The rationale was twofold: to expose the children to the wholesome values imparted by these institutions and to allow the mother to work.

In summary, the nineteenth century began and ended with attempts to severely restrict aid to the poor. Despite these efforts, the level of benefits provided to the poor increased as the standard of living of the people increased. By midcentury every state in the country provided free public education for its citizens. The Civil War pension program, enacted and liberalized by the politically ascendant Republican party, was the first federal income transfer program and provided relatively generous aid to the widowed families of Northern soldiers. But even as Civil War pensions were being liberalized at the end of the century, poor law aid was being restricted, and the indigent widows of immigrants and Southern men who sought public aid were frequently told by administrators that they could receive such aid only if they placed their children in an institution.

The Progressive Era

The Progressive era (1900-17) emerged as the political response to Social Darwinism. Republicans and Democrats alike emphatically rejected the idea that government had no responsibility for ameliorating social ills. The leading Republican Progressives were Presidents Theodore Roosevelt and William Howard Taft and Wisconsin's Governor Robert La Follette. The leading Democratic Progressive was President Woodrow Wilson. Between 1905, when Wisconsin enacted the first workmen's compensation law, and 1917, when the United States entered World War I, one state after another enacted workmen's compensation laws, industrial and labor legislation, income taxes, and pensions for widows regardless of the cause of their husband's death.

Workmen's Compensation

The workmen's compensation laws and later the widows' pension laws were both viewed by their advocates as extensions of the principles embodied in veterans' pension programs. They were also viewed as a method of reducing the reliance of the poor on poor law aid. Just as the whole community benefited from the sacrifices of servicemen in war and thereby had an obligation to support the veterans and their families, the whole community was benefiting from the sacrifices of the new and growing industrial working class. The American economy during the late nineteenth and early twentieth centuries was burgeoning. The growing ranks of industrial workers were fueling that growth—often at the expense of loss of limbs and even life.

A group of economists and legal scholars at the University of Wisconsin argued that a sensible and equitable resolution to this problem was for the community to compensate the injured or deceased workmen and their families. Proponents of this argument convinced a great many influential Wisconsin residents of its wisdom, including La Follette, who championed the first workmen's compensation law in the United States.[13] Other states soon fol-

---

13. Of course, Germany, the country from which a large proportion of Wisconsin residents had migrated, had enacted a similar law in the late 1880s. The conservative chancellor Bismarck had been the champion of workmen's compensation and old age insurance in Germany. By compensating the working-class victims of the emerging capitalist system in Germany, Bismarck was able to steal the thunder of the German socialist party founded by Marx. In view of the fact that the German socialist party was the strongest in Europe, growing fast, and committed to revolution, this was no mean feat.

lowed Wisconsin's lead and, by the outbreak of the Great Depression, all but a few states had enacted workmen's compensation laws.

Workmen's compensation programs, the first social insurance programs enacted in most other countries as well as in the United States, were important to working-class widows and their children. If the fathers were killed in an industrial accident, whether or not it could be blamed on the employer or company for which the father worked, the widow and children were entitled to a pension; they need not be reduced to the level of paupers and be dependent on poor law aid. The amount of the pension, unlike the earlier Civil War pensions, depended on how much the father had earned, so earnings were rewarded.

Mothers' Pensions

Widows', or mothers', pension programs, like workmen's compensation, were designed to enable widows and their children to avoid becoming dependent on poor law aid.[14] A number of juvenile court judges began to believe that, in the absence of any alternative means of economic support for the children of destitute widows, the judges were being forced to choose between placing the children in an institution and condemning them to poverty. So the judges pushed for pension programs for widows with children.

Although the COS remained vehemently opposed, juvenile court judges and other Progressives had allies in the social work profession in their campaign for widows' or mothers' pensions. Public welfare workers and a new group of settlement-house workers—such as Jane Addams—were key advocates. Many of these workers, like the original COS workers, were affluent, native, Protestant volunteers. But they were younger and had been taught by thinkers who had thoroughly rejected the arguments of the Social Darwinists. This generation of social workers believed in the potential positive effects of government programs to reduce poverty and economic insecurity. They had immense influence with the leading Progressive politicians—particularly Theodore Roosevelt.

In 1909 Roosevelt convened the White House Conference on the Care of Dependent Children. The participants agreed that "Home life is the highest and finest product of civilization. It is the great molding force of mind and character."[15] Consequently, they recommended that financial support be provided to children in their own homes. Between 1910 and 1920, forty states

---

14. If all widowhood were attributable to death of the breadwinner on the job, there would have been no need for widows' pensions as well as for workmen's compensation programs.

15. Quoted in Winifred Bell, *Aid to Dependent Children* (New York: Columbia University Press, 1965), p. 5.

plus the territories of Alaska and Hawaii enacted mothers' pension laws.[16] By the onset of the Great Depression, only two states had failed to enact such legislation.

The principles underlying this movement were clearly articulated in a 1913 New York commission report:

1. The mother is the best guardian of her children.

2. Poverty is too big a problem for private philanthropy.

3. No woman, save in exceptional circumstances, can be both the homemaker and the breadwinner of her family.

4. Preventive work, to be successful, must concern itself with the child and the home.

5. Normal family life is the foundation of the state, and its conservation an inherent duty of government.[17]

The first mothers' pension law in Illinois contained a broad definition of dependent children that also encompassed deserted families and unwed mothers. This law provoked such a storm of controversy that most of the other early laws restricted aid to widows or to families in which the father was disabled. Even by 1934, only three states had expanded their laws to specifically include never-married mothers, although in eight other states the law was broad enough to include them.[18] Children of deserted mothers could be aided in thirty-six states. Children of divorcees could be aided in twenty-one states. As of 1931, however, 82 percent of those aided were widows.

Equally important, virtually every state required that aid be provided only to children living in "suitable homes."[19] In all states there was much local discretion in determining what was suitable, and the definition of suitable varied. Many states required that religion be fostered. Delaware required that the child's school record be satisfactory. Massachusetts and Michigan specified that no male boarder could live in the home. Social workers were given the responsibility of investigating each case to ascertain the suitability of the mother.

---

16. For a description of the development of mothers' pensions and other aid to mother-only families with children, see Emma Octavina Lundberg, *Unto the Least of These*, (New York: Appleton-Century Company, 1974). See also Bell, *Aid to Dependent Children*; Mark Leff, "Consensus for Reform: The Mothers' Pension Movement in the Progressive Era," *Social Service Review*, vol. 47, no. 3 (September 1973), pp. 391-417; and Helen Slessarev, "From Mothers' Pensions to Aid to Dependent Children: The Legalization of Women's Traditional Role as Childrearer," unpublished document, University of Chicago, Winter 1983.

17. Quoted in Lundberg, *Unto the Least of These*, p. 130.

18. Slessarev, "From Mothers' Pensions."

19. See Bell *Aid to Dependent Children*; and Slessarey, "From Mothers' Pensions."

Local discretion meant that programs would reflect local community values and, in view of the prevailing norms, discrimination was the almost inevitable result.[20] Although families headed by women were disproportionately black, in 1931 only 3 percent of the caseload was black. Some idea of the amount of racial discrimination is given by the fact that nearly half of blacks receiving aid were from Ohio and Pennsylvania. In Houston, Texas, where blacks made up one-fifth of the population, no blacks received mothers' pensions. In North Carolina, the only Southern state with more than a scattered program, only one black family received aid.

Although many more poor families headed by white mothers were aided by mothers' pensions, it was still only a small minority of the total in need.[21] The state laws permitted but did not require localities to provide such pensions, and only fourteen states helped to finance the cost of the pensions. Only slightly more than half of the jurisdictions authorized to grant aid as of 1931 were doing so. Poor rural counties were least likely to have a program. The program was almost nonexistent in the South. The Depression exacerbated the difficulty.

In principle, the mothers' pension movement represents a clear reversal of previous expectations that poor mothers should work. But in practice the benefits were never high enough to keep most beneficiaries from working in the marketplace. In a 1928 federal survey of mothers receiving pensions, more than half reported working during the month they had received the pension.[22] (In view of the fact that the mothers' pensions were income tested, it is likely that this is an underestimate of the extent to which respondents were working.)

The New Deal and the Social Security Act

Except for brief periods at the beginning and end of the decade, the 1920s were prosperous. Indeed, by the end of the decade, Americans were so optimistic about the economy that they fueled what Morison has termed "the greatest orgy of speculation and over-optimism since the South Sea Bubble of 1720."[23]

---

20. See Bell, *Aid to Dependent Children.*
21. See Bell, *Aid to Dependent Children*; and Slessarev, "From Mothers' Pensions."
22. Survey cited in Bell, *Aid to Dependent Children,* p. 16.
23. See Samuel Eliot Morison, *The Oxford History of the American People,* vol. 3, (New York: Mentor, 1965), p. 281.

The prosperity of the 1920s was accompanied by a return to a more laissez-faire government philosophy. The reforms of the Progressive era were not repealed, and the popularity of the reforms most relevant to this story—workmen's compensation and mothers' pensions—continued to grow. But no major new reforms were initiated. It was as if all the creative energy with which the century began had been spent.

Then came the stock market crash in October 1929 and The Great Depression of the 1930s. So many people were unemployed and unemployment lasted for so long—an average of 18 percent of the labor force was unemployed from 1930 thru 1940—that virtually everyone in the country either knew someone who had suffered from the Depression or were themselves affected. Under these circumstances, it was difficult to blame the poor for their impoverished conditions. Undoubtedly the Depression also convinced many people that the chances of becoming poor were higher than they had previously thought. Finally, so many people who had been accustomed to being self-reliant and independent could no longer manage without help that the general faith in self-reliance was shaken. President Herbert Hoover became identified with the position that the government should let the Depression take its natural course—while the Depression kept worsening—and was soundly defeated in the election of 1932 by Franklin D. Roosevelt. F.D.R. was not only related to Theodore Roosevelt by blood, but also inherited the Progressive faith that judicious government action could make a capitalist economic system function better than no government action at all.

The Expansion of Benefits

Within the first hundred days of taking office, President Roosevelt proposed and Congress enacted thirteen major pieces of legislation, including the Federal Emergency Relief Act (FERA), the first federal cash relief program. The Roosevelt administration preferred work relief to cash relief, however, and soon, with congressional approval, replaced FERA with the Works Projects Administration and the Civil Works Administration.

The new president was also committed to a more comprehensive and permanent approach to the problem of economic insecurity. In 1934 he appointed the Committee on Economic Security to design and draft permanent legislation to deal with this problem. Edwin Witte, a Wisconsin economist and legal scholar, chaired the committee. Witte's mentor John R. Commons had helped La Follette draft the first workmen's compensation law; Witte had helped to draft one of the first two state unemployment insurance laws in 1932. (The other was a New York law enacted when Franklin Roosevelt was governor.) Witte and the other architects of the Social Security Act—Frances

Perkins, Harry Hopkins, Katherine Lenroot and, of course, Roosevelt himself—were heirs of the traditions and experiences of the Progressive era. They had not only contemplated the appropriate government response to the problems of economic insecurity created by a dynamic capitalist economic system, but already had practical experience with designing and running some state programs to combat economic insecurity. Within six months, the committee had drafted a report and designed legislative proposals that were to be the first steps toward achieving economic security for all Americans. The historic report said, in part:

> A program of economic security, as we vision it, must have as its primary aim the assurance of an adequate income to each human being in childhood, youth, middle age, or old age—in sickness or in health. It must provide safeguards against all of the hazards leading to destitution and dependency. A piecemeal approach is dictated by practical considerations, but the broad objectives should never be forgotten. Whatever measures are deemed immediately expedient should be so designed that they can be embodied in the complete program which we must have ere long.[24]

The designers of the Social Security Act did not believe in treating all groups the same. As the committee report put it: "The measures we suggest all seek to segregate more clearly distinguishable large groups among those now on relief or on the verge of relief and to apply such differential treatment to each group as will give it the greatest practical degree of economic security."[25]

The 1935 Social Security Act created five new federal income support programs. Two were social insurance programs: Old Age Insurance and Unemployment Insurance. Three were welfare programs: Aid to the Blind, Old Age Assistance, and Aid to Dependent Children. Old Age Insurance was federally financed and administered; Unemployment Insurance was funded and administered by the states; and the three welfare programs were funded jointly by federal and state governments and administered by states and localities.

The Aid to Dependent Children program was the most important for mother-only families. It was patterned after the mothers' pension programs of the individual states. The Committee on Economic Security clearly stated the common philosophical underpinnings of the two programs with respect to mothers' working. Aid to Dependent Children benefits were "designed to release from the wage earning role the person whose natural function is to

---

24. *The Report of the Committee on Economic Security of 1935*, 50th Anniversary Edition, National Conference on Social Welfare, 1985, p. 3.

25. Ibid., p. 7.

give her children the physical and affectionate guardianship necessary, not alone to keep them from falling into social misfortune, but more affirmatively to rear them into citizens capable of contributing to society."[26]

In several respects, however, Aid to Dependent Children went beyond the mothers' pension programs. First, the definition of dependent children explicitly included children of divorced, separated, and never-married mothers as well as the children of widows. This definition was a compromise between the positions of those who advocated coverage of all needy children regardless of the parental status of the children—that is, including children in two-parent families—and those who advocated limiting eligibility to the children of widows.[27] But most states incorporated "suitable home" provisions in their statutes. As with mothers' pensions, many jurisdictions used these provisions to deny benefits to children born out of wedlock and to blacks.[28] Still, between 1937 and 1940 the proportion of beneficiaries of Aid to Dependent Children who were black ranged between 14 percent and 17 percent—in contrast to the 3 percent of mothers' pension beneficiaries who were black.[29]

Second, to receive federal aid, the states were required to have statewide programs, establish a single state agency to supervise the program, make payments in cash, and allow any recipient whose claim was denied a fair hearing to appeal the denial. These provisions made benefits more like a right or entitlement than was the case under the mothers' pension programs.

Third, benefits were somewhat higher in Aid to Dependent Children than in the mothers' pension programs.[30] Perhaps even more important, the number of families being aided jumped from 227,000 receiving mothers' pensions in 1935 to 527,000 receiving ADC in 1937.[31]

In addition to creating the five programs under the 1935 Social Security Act, the architects envisaged establishing a permanent work relief program, a national health insurance program, Survivors' Insurance, and a disability insurance program. Because the president feared that including the work relief program might threaten the entire bill, he submitted that measure as a separate piece of legislation and Congress did not pass it. Health insurance legislation was so controversial that Roosevelt never even proposed it; he only created a committee to study it. Disability assistance and insurance were not introduced until the 1950s. Survivors' Insurance was proposed and enacted into

26. Ibid., p. 34.
27. See Bell, *Aid to Dependent Children*.
28. See Myrdal, *An American Dilemma*, vol. 1, p. 360.
29. See Slessarev, "From Mothers' Pensions," p. 29
30. Ibid., p. 18. Slessarev's figures are unreliable, because they are crudely averaged and contradict earlier evidence of decreases in average mothers' pension grants.
31. Ibid., p. 18.

law by Congress in 1939. The enactment of Survivors' Insurance once again placed widows in their traditional preferred position. Most widows with children would receive benefits much higher than the ADC benefits if their husbands had earned a sufficient amount of credits.

The Social Security Act led to an immediate, notable increase in the economic status of the aged, the unemployed, and families headed by single mothers. Even more important, as the architects of the act had foreseen, the programs created by the act were expanded and liberalized over the next forty years so that the economic status of these groups was substantially improved.

The Continuing Concern about Dependence

The dramatic improvement in the economic status of vulnerable groups achieved by the Social Security Act should not obscure the fact that the basic design of the act reinforced both the central role of work in American society and the commitment to self-reliance. Although the act also shifted existing compromises on the work issue—by permitting some groups in special circumstances to work less—the shift was not fundamental. The architects of the act consciously sought to reinforce work and self-reliance.

The Old Age Insurance program, for example, was designed to remove the aged from the labor market; benefits were available only if the beneficiary was retired. But coverage under Old Age Insurance depended on the degree of participation in the labor force, and benefits were related to the workers' previous earnings. People who had not participated in the labor force or had participated to a minimal extent were thus not eligible. Better records in the labor market were rewarded by better benefits in retirement.

The Unemployment Insurance program also provided benefits to persons without jobs, but again strong previous participation in the labor force was a prerequisite for coverage. As in Old Age Insurance, higher previous earnings led to higher unemployment benefits. Also, the Unemployment Insurance benefits were designed to be short term, and beneficiaries were required to accept suitable employment offers. Finally, the states were given the responsibility for financing Unemployment Insurance benefits, establishing benefit levels, and administering the Unemployment Insurance system, because the plan's designers sought to avoid undermining local labor markets. A uniform national benefit would have been too low (in terms of the cost of living and local labor markets) in some jurisdictions and too high in others.

The categorization of the relief programs reveals the same reinforcement of the work ethic. Because the aged, blind, and single mothers were not expected to work, the Aid to the Blind, Old Age Assistance, and Aid to Dependent Children programs provided cash aid without requiring the aged, blind, and mothers of dependent children to work. For able-bodied poor male heads of families, the architects preferred work relief to cash relief. The architects of the Social Security Act were so imbued with the work ethic that they not only believed that it would be better for the rest of society if work were reinforced; they also believed that people whom society expected to work would prefer to receive benefits in return for work rather than to accept charity. Equally important for the purposes of this discussion, the designers of the act preferred work to cash relief because they believed that cash relief was more likely to break up families. Anthropologists and sociologists who had studied relief practices in the Depression had observed that cash relief undermined the husband's critical role as breadwinner.[32] Cash relief was normally dispensed by a female caseworker and, more often than not, the transaction took place between two women; the men became bystanders. Work relief, in contrast, was designed to preserve the husband's role as breadwinner because he would at least bring home a paycheck.

The architects of the Social Security Act believed that it was the obligation of the government both to provide relief to people who needed it and to prevent as many people as possible from needing it. The assistance programs relieve poverty; the social insurance programs prevent poverty. Even for persons like widows and old people who were not expected to work, independence was to be achieved through social insurance benefits. The strong preference for preventing rather than relieving poverty is evident in the following excerpt from the report of the 1938 Advisory Council on Social Security:

> While public assistance is now being provided to a large number of dependent children in this country on a needs-test basis, the arguments for substituting benefits as a matter of right in the case of children are even more convincing than in the case of aged persons. A democratic society has an immeasurable stake in avoiding the growth of a habit of dependence among its youth. The method of survivors' insurance not only sustains the concept that a child is supported through the efforts of the parent but affords a vital sense of security to the family unit.[33]

Despite the fact that the architects of the Social Security Act provided federal cash relief on an unprecedented scale and enacted three new permanent federal cash relief programs, they remained uncomfortable with the widespread provision of cash relief even for persons not expected to work. Indeed,

---

32. W. E. Bakke, *Citizens without Work* (New Haven, Connecticut: Yale University Press, 1940); and Mira Komarovsky, *The Unemployed Man and His Family* (New York: Octagon Books, 1940).

33. *Final Report of the 1937-38 Advisory Council on Social Security*, in 50th Anniversary Edition of *The Report of the Committee on Economic Security*, pp. 17-18.

President Roosevelt referred to cash relief as a narcotic.[34] The Old Age and Survivors' Insurance programs could pay benefits only to persons who had earned them. In time this was expected to include almost everybody. Meanwhile, two groups were left out: those who were already beyond working age and poor, and poor single mothers with children. As Old Age and Survivors' Insurance matured, it was expected to reduce the numbers dependent on Old Age Assistance and Aid to Dependent Children to minuscule proportions. The elderly would become eligible through previous earnings. The single mothers would typically become eligible through the previous earnings of a spouse. There is some evidence, in fact, that the architects sought to prevent Old Age Assistance benefits from becoming too generous because they feared that the Old Age Insurance program would lose political support before it was given a fair chance to mature.[35]

The Post-New Deal and the Post-World War II Era

The Depression ended when the United States entered World War II. After the war the United States enjoyed another period of great prosperity. Demobilization did not lead, as many people had feared it might, to another Great Depression. Although there were recessions in 1955-56 and 1959-60, both were mild and short-lived compared with either the Great Depression of the 1930s or previous depressions in the 1870s and 1890s.

Just as World War I had marked the end of the Progressive era, World War II marked the end of the New Deal. President Harry S. Truman proposed a national health insurance program but was unable to gain the support of a majority in Congress. The result of this failure was to shift the debate in the 1950s and early 1960s from whether to have a universal national health insurance program to the issue of a health program for the elderly.[36]

Still, public benefit levels gradually increased. A federal disability assistance program was enacted in 1950 under President Truman, and a federal disability insurance program was enacted in 1956 under President Dwight D. Eisenhower. Similarly, Aid to Dependent Children benefits were increased and the commitment to enable poor female heads of families to stay home and rear their children was reinforced in 1950, when the Aid to Dependent Children program was

---

34. President Franklin D. Roosevelt, quoted in Josephine Brown, *Public Relief 1929-39* (New York: Henry Holt and Co., 1935).

35. See Jerry Cates, *Insuring Inequality: Administrative Leadership in Social Security, 1935-54* (Ann Arbor, Michigan: University of Michigan Press, 1983).

36. See Paul Starr, *The Social Transformation of American Medicine* (New York: Basic Books, 1982); and Theodore Marmor, *The Politics of Medicare* (Chicago, Illinois: Aldine Publishing Company, 1973).

amended to provide benefits to the custodial parent of the dependent child as well as to the child. (At the same time, the name of the program was changed from Aid to Dependent Children to Aid to Families with Dependent Children—AFDC.) By 1960 it was apparent that, despite the existence of Survivors' Insurance, AFDC was not withering away as had been planned. Divorce, separation, and out-of-wedlock births were increasing relative to widowhood. Consequently, Survivors' Insurance, which was providing increasingly good protection to widows and their children, was providing this protection to an increasingly smaller proportion of the population of needy children.

The Kennedy administration carried on the tradition of the original Social Security Act by seeking to reduce welfare dependence. However, the means employed reversed previous policy in two ways. The new intent was to decrease the number of female heads of families dependent on welfare by (1) encouraging them to work and (2) providing cash benefits to two-parent as well as separated families. In 1961 the states were given the option of extending eligibility for the AFDC program to children of unemployed parents. At least part of the rationale for extending eligibility for cash relief to able-bodied men was the hope of reducing family breakups and thereby reducing welfare rolls over the long term. This represented a departure from the New Deal conventional wisdom, when work relief was preferred to cash relief for able-bodied men because the latter policy was believed to be more likely to encourage dependence and to break up families.

In 1961 a city manager in Newburgh, New York, asserted that the welfare rolls were filled with loafers and cheats and initiated a thirteen point program that included a three-month limitation on all relief payments except to the aged and handicapped, and issuance of food, rent, and clothing vouchers instead of checks. The New York State Board of Social Welfare informed Newburgh that these proposals violated state and federal law. Overnight, the Newburgh controversy became a national issue. *The Wall Street Journal* editorialized, "It's a fine commentary on public morality in this country when a local community's effort to correct flagrant welfare abuses is declared illegal under both state and federal law."[37]

Against this background, in February 1962 President Kennedy delivered the first presidential message to Congress that focused solely on the subject of public welfare. He argued:

> Communities which have—for whatever motives—attempted to save money through ruthless and arbitrary cutbacks in their welfare rolls have found their efforts to little avail. The root problems remain.

---

37. "Newburgh," *Wall Street Journal*, July 10, 1961.

But communities which have tried the rehabilitative road—the road I have recommended today—have demonstrated what can be done with creative, thoughtfully conceived and properly managed programs of prevention and social rehabilitation. In those communities families have been restored to self-reliance and relief rolls have been reduced.[38]

As part of his message, President Kennedy asked Congress to amend the Social Security Act in ways designed to reduce welfare dependence. He asked for social services to "rehabilitate" welfare mothers, for the establishment of community work and training programs, for seed money for communities to initiate day care programs, and for a decrease in work disincentives. One amendment is worth additional comment. Before 1962 the welfare payments in most states were reduced by one dollar for each dollar earned by recipients. Because of expenses incurred in working—transportation, for example—many welfare recipients were worse off financially if they worked. The 1962 amendments required that the states deduct work-related expenses from earnings before reducing benefits.

Although this amendment ensured that welfare recipients who worked would not be worse off, it did not ensure that they would be better off. The day care provision included only $5 million of federal money. The federal government also provided only half of the administrative costs of the community work and training projects and none of the costs for supervision, materials, and training. In contrast, the government paid three-quarters of the costs of social services. Not surprisingly, states and localities expanded social services but not work and training programs.

Congress passed virtually all the amendments requested by the president. However, the 1962 amendments did not have the intended effects. Caseloads and costs continued to increase, but labor market work did not. Moreover, the growth in families headed by women began to accelerate. In consequence, as the next section details, attempts to cut AFDC caseloads and costs persisted even in the midst of the tremendous growth in other income-support programs generated by the War on Poverty.

The War on Poverty

Just as the Great Depression had accelerated developments in income-support policy in the 1930s, a combination of events led to a similar acceleration in the latter half of the 1960s. The post-World War II economic prosperity not only continued but in the 1960s reached new heights. The civil rights movement increased the awareness of Americans to social injustice in

---

38. See Message from President John F. Kennedy, quoted in Axinn and Levin, *Social Welfare*, p. 262.

the country and increased the political power of one of the poorest segments of American society. The assassination of President Kennedy created much sympathy for his legislative programs. Within this context, in March 1964 President Johnson declared his War on Poverty and ushered in the Great Society.

In the half decade that followed, income transfer expenditures on families headed by women jumped 61 percent (see table 7). Was this what President Johnson intended? The answer is clearly no.

TABLE 7

FEDERAL EXPENDITURES FOR SELECTED TRANSFERS TO MOTHER-ONLY FAMILIES
WITH CHILDREN, 1950–80
(Billions of 1983 Dollars unless Otherwise Indicated)

Item	1950	1955	1960	1965	1970	1975	1980
Expenditure per family (constant 1983 dollars)	2,786	2,568	3,243	4,113	6,630	7,402	6,404
Percentage change in per family expenditure over the previous 5-year period	. . .	−8	26	27	61	12	−13
Total expenditures	3.5	4.8	6.8	10.2	19.4	32.6	34.2
Welfare expenditures	1.8	2.3	3.3	5.8	13.8	23.5	25.4
Cash							
Total	1.7	1.9	2.7	4.8	8.9	12.8	11.4
AFDC[a]	1.7	1.9	2.7	4.8	8.9	12.2	10.8
Supplemental Security Income	n.a.	n.a.	n.a.	n.a.	n.a.	0.6	0.6
In-kind benefits							
Total	0.1	0.4	0.6	1.0	4.9	10.7	14.0
Food stamps	n.a.	n.a.	n.a.	0.1	0.7	3.8	5.2
Energy assistance	n.a.	n.a.	n.a.	n.a.	n.a.	n.a.	0.5
Medicaid[a]	n.a.	n.a.	n.a.	n.a.	3.0	4.7	5.5
Housing assistance	0.0	0.1	0.2	0.2	0.4	1.2	2.1
School lunch	0.1	0.3	0.4	0.7	0.8	1.0	0.7
Work-related program expenditures							
Total	n.a.	n.a.	n.a.	0.1	0.5	2.0	2.5
Employment and training	n.a.	n.a.	n.a.	0.0	0.2	0.7	1.4
Day care and Head Start	n.a.	n.a.	n.a.	0.1	0.3	1.3	1.1

TABLE 7 (continued)

Item	1950	1955	1960	1965	1970	1975	1980
Nonwelfare benefit expenditures							
Total	1.7	2.5	3.5	4.3	5.1	7.1	6.3
Survivors' Insurance	0.8	1.7	2.4	3.2	3.8	4.5	4.4
Unemployment Insurance	0.3	0.3	0.5	0.4	0.6	1.8	1.2
Veterans' benefits	0.6	0.5	0.6	0.7	0.7	0.8	0.7

SOURCES: The sources for expenditures are described in appendix A to this chapter. The expenditure per family was computed by dividing total expenditures by the total number of families with children under age eighteen headed by single women. Population data, for 1950, Bureau of the Census, *U.S. Census of the Population: General Characteristics of Families*, special report P-E, no. 2A (Washington, D.C.: U.S. Government Printing Office), table 4; for 1955, U.S. Bureau of the Census, "Household and Family Characteristics," *Current Population Reports*, series P-20, no. 67 (Washington, D.C.: U.S. Government Printing Office, 1955), table 4; for 1960 through 1975, U.S. Bureau of the Census, *Current Population Reports*, series P-20, no. 340 (Washington, D.C.: U.S. Government Printing Office, various years), table E; and for 1980, U.S. Bureau of the Census, *Current Population Reports*, series P-20, no. 366 (Washington, D.C.: U.S. Government Printing Office, 1980), table 1.

n.a. Not applicable.

a. Includes state and local as well as federal expenditures.

President Johnson stressed time and again that his objective was to provide a hand-up, not a hand-out.[39] The Economic Opportunity Act enacted by Congress in 1964 established the Office of Economic Opportunity, local Community Action programs, and a series of education and employment and training programs to assist the poor, such as Head Start, Job Corps, Neighborhood Youth Corps, Work Study, Upward Bound, and the Work Experience program for AFDC mothers. All these programs were intended to increase labor market skills of participants, and all provided a high proportion of their benefits to families headed by single mothers. The use of the term ''opportunity'' in the titles of both the act that created the War on Poverty and the office that administered it suggest that there was no change in the ideological or rhetorical attraction of independence as a social value. Furthermore, in his message to Congress in 1967 in support of his proposal to increase Old Age and Survivors' Insurance benefits by 13 percent—the second of five major benefit increases in the space of seven years—President Johnson argued that

---

39. See, for example, President Lyndon B. Johnson, ''Remarks upon Signing the Economic Opportunity Act, August 20, 1964,'' in *Public Papers of the Presidents of the United States* (Washington, D.C.: U.S. Government Printing Office, 1966), pp. 988-90. In these remarks President Johnson said, ''The days of the dole in our country are numbered.''

doing so would not only lift 1.4 million elderly people out of poverty but also would remove 200,000 of them from the welfare rolls.[40]

Despite President Johnson's intent to reduce the welfare rolls, the big increases in welfare recipients began under his administration. Ironically, the first large increase was a result of Johnson's attempt to reduce the dependence of the aged on a medical program restricted to the poor. President Kennedy had campaigned in the 1960 election for a national health insurance program to cover all the aged. In opposing the proposal of Vice President Richard M. Nixon for a medical assistance program for only the poor aged, President Kennedy argued that it was unjust to subject the aged to the indignities of the dole. Like so many of J.F.K.'s other proposals, however, Congress had not acted on it. Representative Wilbur Mills, the then powerful chairman of the House Ways and Means Committee, favored the health assistance or welfare approach. L.B.J., like J.F.K., favored the universal health insurance program for the aged of all income classes over the approach of health assistance for the poor. In return for Mills's support of a health insurance program for the aged (Medicare), President Johnson agreed to support a health assistance program for the poor (Medicaid).[41] Both were enacted in 1965. By 1980 Medicaid provided $5.5 billion in benefits to families headed by women (see table 7), about four-fifths of the amount spent on benefits in all federal programs in 1960.

Other Johnson administration initiatives contributed to the growth of welfare among single mothers. The food stamp program, which had begun on an experimental basis under President Roosevelt and was revived under President Kennedy, was expanded by President Johnson. Housing assistance programs were also expanded. Far more important than either, however, were the indirect effects of the War on Poverty that took place through increases in state AFDC benefit levels and percentages of applications accepted. Between 1965 and 1970 states increased AFDC benefit levels by 36 percent. This big increase in cash welfare benefits combined with Medicaid to make the welfare benefit package substantially more attractive to potential recipients. Moreover, lawyers working for the Legal Services program (Office of Economic Opportunity) successfully challenged the constitutionality of state laws that limited eligibility through residency requirements and "man in the house" rules. More generally, these lawyers and other Community Action employees from the Office of Economic Opportunity argued that welfare was

---

40. President Lyndon B. Johnson, "Special Message to the Congress Proposing Programs for Older Americans, January 23, 1967," in *Public Papers of the Presidents of the United States*, book 1 (Washington, D.C.: U.S. Government Printing Office, 1968), pp. 32-39.

41. See Marmor, *The Politics of Medicare*.

a right and became advocates for welfare recipients. Although state laws differed, rates of acceptance for participation in the AFDC program leapt dramatically: the proportion of eligible families headed by women who actually received benefits increased from around 60 percent to nearly 90 percent between 1967 and 1971.[42]

The Aftermath of the War on Poverty

The Ascendance of the Negative Income Tax. By the mid-1960s the negative income tax (NIT) was gaining ascendance among economists. The idea, first popularized by conservative economist Milton Friedman, was that just as the Internal Revenue Service collected taxes based on income and family size, it could pay out benefits (or negative taxes) based on income and family size to people with low-income.[43] The elegance and simplicity of the scheme appealed to economists of the left as well as those of the right. James Tobin and Robert Lampman, members of President Kennedy's Council of Economic Advisers, became its principal liberal academic advocates.[44]

Friedman advocated the NIT as a replacement for all public income transfer programs—the social insurance programs as well as the welfare programs. Tobin, in contrast, advocated the NIT only as a replacement for welfare programs.[45] Lampman did not even do that. He viewed it as a supplement to, rather than a substitute for, existing welfare programs, the only prominent advocate to do so.[46] As originally proposed by Lampman, the NIT would supplement the incomes of people who were expected to work; welfare would remain for people who were not expected to work. Not coincidentally, he was the only prominent NIT advocate who was also a specialist in income transfer programs and therefore knew much about the historical development and objectives of welfare programs. It is unfortunate that the subtleties and

---

42. See Barbara Bolland, "Participation in the Aid to Families with Dependent Children Program," in U.S. Congress, Joint Economic Committee, Subcommittee on Fiscal Policy, *Studies in Public Welfare—The Family Poverty and Welfare Programs*, paper 12, pt. 1. (Washington, D.C.: U.S. Government Printing Office 1973); and Richard Michel, "Participation Rates in the Aid to Families with Dependent Children Programs, Part 1: National Trends from 1967 to 1977," Working Paper 1387-02 (Washington, D.C.: Urban Institute, August 1980).

43. See Milton Freidman, *Capitalism and Freedom* (Chicago: University of Chicago Press, 1962).

44. See James Tobin, Joseph Pechman, and Peter Mieszkowski, "Is a Negative Income Tax Practical?" *Yale Law Journal*, vol. 77 (November 1967), pp. 1-27; and Robert Lampman, "Expanding the American System of Transfers To Do More for the Poor," in U.S. Congress, House, Joint Economic Committee (Washington, D.C.: U.S. Government Printing Office, 1968).

45. Indeed, Friedman questioned whether providing for the poor should even be a public responsibility. The NIT, for him, was simply the lesser of two evils. See Friedman, *Capitalism and Freedom*, pp. 177-95.

46. Lampman, "Expanding the American System of Transfers."

reservations of Lampman's analyses were lost amid economists' enthusiasm for the NIT. By the late 1960s a whole generation of economics students had been persuaded that if poverty was the problem, the NIT was the solution.

Friedman's endorsement of the NIT as a substitute for all other income transfer programs was quickly rejected in the political world. Senator Barry Goldwater, the Republican candidate for president in the 1964 election, briefly advocated replacing Social Security with an NIT, and the political reaction was devastating to his campaign. Despite the resounding defeat for the NIT as a replacement for social insurance programs, it had profound effects on welfare programs, although not in the way its academic proponents envisaged.

In the 1960s the contrast between the academic NIT proposals and actual welfare programs was stark. Welfare paid benefits only to certain categories of the poor. The NIT proposed to pay benefits to all those in need, regardless of the group or category to which they belonged. NIT advocates were particularly disturbed by the failure of the welfare system to aid the working poor. In response to the declaration of a War on Poverty, the Social Security Administration had developed a definition of and way of measuring poverty.[47] They discovered that about 40 percent of the poor lived in families headed by an able-bodied working-age man. In half these families, the head worked full-time year-round. Eliminating poverty required supplementing the incomes of the working poor. The fact that welfare programs did not aid the working poor not only limited their usefulness in combating poverty, but also, in the view of NIT advocates, led famiies to break up to qualify for welfare.

The reduction of benefits in welfare programs by the full amount of dollars earned provided no incentive for welfare recipients to work. The NIT schemes proposed by academic economists, in contrast, reduced benefits by no more than fifty cents for each dollar earned.

Benefits in welfare programs depended on numerous individual circumstances—payment of rent, the condition of the family's appliances, and even whether the caseworker believed the family needed a telephone. Thus the needs test in welfare programs was detailed, personally invasive, and stigmatizing. Benefits under the NIT, in contrast, were to depend only on income and family size and were to be administered impersonally by the Internal Revenue Service, in the same way that the income tax system was administered.

There was one critical feature that was common to most NIT proposals and all actual welfare programs: paying benefits to only those with low

---

47. Mollie Orshansky, "Who's Who among the Poor: A Demographic View," *Social Security Bulletin*, vol. 28 (1965), pp. 3-22.

income.[48] As the NIT ideal began to influence the shape of welfare programs, it became harder to distinguish between negative income tax and welfare programs. The NIT ideal quickly made its way into government; in those days, when economists talked everyone listened. We were in the midst of the longest economic boom in our history; it appeared that Keynesian economics had at last tamed the business cycle. Nearly every government agency and commission, including the Office of Economic Opportunity (OEO), avidly sought to hire economists. By 1966 the OEO was lobbying the president to propose an NIT.[49] President Johnson, who adhered to the vision of the architects of the Social Security Act, resisted but agreed to allow the agency to mount a social experiment to test the NIT concept.

The first effect of the NIT idea on practical policy came in 1967. To encourage work and reduce dependence on welfare, Congress amended the AFDC program to allow beneficiaries to keep a small part of their earnings— the first thirty dollars earned each month plus one of every three dollars earned in excess of thirty dollars. If the 1962 amendments had given social workers their opportunity to reduce dependence through a social service strategy, economists were now being given their chance to reduce welfare dependence through a work-incentives, NIT type of strategy. The amendments included a provision that ignored a portion of earnings in calculating benefits. This was to provide a positive incentive to work by increasing the amount of income a beneficiary could have and still be eligible for welfare. Some research suggests that this provision expanded welfare caseloads by more families than it induced to work their way off the rolls, although other research comes to the opposite conclusion.[50]

In 1968 President Johnson appointed a Commission on Income Maintenance to make recommendations on reforming the nation's income maintenance system. It was the first such presidential commission since the Economic

---

48. One notable exception is Earl Rolph, "The Case for a Negative Income Tax Device," *Industrial Relations*, vol. 6 (1967), pp. 155–65.

49. See *National Anti-Poverty Plan: FY1968-FY1972*, (Washington, D.C.: Office of Economic Opportunity, Executive Office of the President, June 1966).

50. See Gary Louis Appel, *Effects of Financial Incentive on AFDC Employment—Michigan's Experience Between July 1969 and July 1970* (Minneapolis, Minnesota: Institute for Interdisciplinary Studies, 1972). On the other hand, the following studies suggest that the work-incentive provision may have reduced caseloads: Michael Wiseman, "Work Incentives and Welfare Turnover," unpublished document (Berkeley, California University of California, Department of Economics, October 13, 1983); and Vernon K. Smith, *Welfare Work Incentives: The Earnings Exemption and Its Impact upon AFDC Employment, Earnings and Program Costs*, Studies in Welfare Policy, no. 2 (Lansing, Michigan: State of Michigan Department of Social Services, 1974).

Security Committee appointed by Roosevelt. The commission concluded its deliberation in 1969, after President Nixon had assumed office. It found that existing welfare programs were inadequate, inequitable, and inefficient. Its most serious criticism was that no program supplemented the incomes of working poor, and it repeated the view that failure to aid the working poor not only precluded the elimination of poverty but also led to family breakup. To address these problems, the president's commission advocated the adoption of an NIT.[51]

President Nixon was favorably disposed toward accepting the commission's recommendation of a NIT.[52] When he assumed office in 1969 the national impetus to reduce poverty was still strong. Because he had always preferred public programs that aid only the poor—recall his support for a health assistance program for the aged poor in the 1960 election—he was attracted to the feature of the NIT proposed by the commission that limited benefits to those with low income. In the first televised presidential speech to the American people ever devoted entirely to welfare reform, President Nixon argued that the best way to stem the growth in welfare expenditures for families headed by single mothers was to extend eligibility for cash assistance to two-parent families. Of AFDC he said, "It breaks up homes. It often penalizes work. It robs recipients of dignity. And, it grows."[53] He proposed to scrap AFDC and replace it with a Family Assistance Program. This program was a variant of a negative income tax for all families with children. Like other NIT proposals, it extended aid to two-parent as well as mother-only families and provided a federal minimum benefit. Due to the extension of eligibility to intact as well as split families, the Family Assistance Program, if enacted, would have doubled welfare caseloads. The Nixon administration claimed (dubiously) that this program would ultimately reduce caseloads and costs.[54]

---

51. When President Nixon proposed the Family Assistance Program in 1969, the only people who had any experience with administering a negative income tax were whose who were operating the NIT experiments. Not surprisingly, they, along with welfare administrators, were the key consultants on how to operate the program.

52. For an account of the origins and fate of the Family Assistance Plan, see Daniel Patrick Moynihan, *The Politics of a Guaranteed Income* (New York: Vintage Books, 1973); and Vincent J. Burke and Vee Burke, *Nixon's Good Deed* (New York: Columbia University Press, 1974).

53. "Reform in Welfare," Message from President Richard M. Nixon, August 11, 1969, in Axinn and Levin, *Social Welfare*, pp. 290-98.

54. The Family Assistance Plan would have increased caseloads by 14 million and costs by $4 billion in its first year of operation, but the administration argued that, if benefit levels were held constant, costs and caseloads would decrease over time as earnings increased due to economic growth. This projected decrease was contrasted with an extrapolation of current growth rates in AFDC caseloads and costs—growth rates that had resulted in part from increases in benefit levels and from increases in female headship.

Although the Family Assistance Program passed the House twice, in 1970 and again in 1971, it failed twice to pass the Senate. In each case, what killed the program was the revelation that even though the program reduced benefits by only 50 percent as earnings increased, by the time food stamps were taken into account, the total rate of benefit reduction was much closer to 70 percent.[55] And, when Medicaid was taken into account, benefits in many cases would be reduced by more than a dollar for each dollar earned. This, of course, was already the case for AFDC beneficiaries. For families headed by single mothers the Family Assistance Program version of the NIT offered little more in the way of work incentives than the reformed AFDC program, which had a 66 percent benefit reduction rate. For two-parent families the Family Assistance Program was even worse; for them the program clearly constituted a reduction in the incentive to work.

The eventual policy outcome of the effort to replace welfare with an NIT was to add a welfare-like variant of an NIT to the array of welfare programs already in existence. As an outgrowth of the debate over the Family Assistance Program in Congress plus the national concern prompted both by a moving CBS television documentary "Hunger in America" and by congressional hearings on the topic conducted by Senator George McGovern, the food stamp program was converted and expanded into a national NIT for all poor Americans paid in food stamps. In 1971 and again in 1973 the food stamp program, which had been unavailable in many jurisdictions, was amended to provide benefits nationally to all who met eligibility standards; to mandate provision in all areas of the country as of July 1, 1974; and to automatically tie future benefits to increases in the cost of food. By 1980 the federal government was spending $5.2 billion on food stamps for mother-only families (see table 7), an amount nearly equal in real terms to three-quarters of all federal transfers to such families in 1960.

The expansion of the food stamp program placated the constituency that had favored the NIT because food stamps were one pragmatic way of reducing poverty. But this did nothing to ameliorate the concerns of people who had favored the NIT as a way of increasing work by, and reducing the dependence of, single women with children.

The Shift toward Enforcing Work Requirements. Continuing concern about work incentives led, in 1972, to another amendment to the AFDC program. This one required AFDC mothers with no children under age six to register for work. This was the first time in the thirty-five-year history of

---

55. See Burke and Burke, *Nixon's Good Deed*; and Moynihan, *The Politics of a Guaranteed Income*.

AFDC and the thirty-year history of mothers' pensions that benefits were predicated on any kind of work requirement. In practice, this work requirement was never effectively enforced. The principal reason is that there were always more AFDC recipients who wanted to avail themselves of the services offered by the work registration program than there were funds available to finance these services.

By the mid-1970s politicians on both ends of the political spectrum were advocating policies that included work in the marketplace for single women with no preschool-age children. There was still some division on whether work should be encouraged or required, but there were few advocates of the Progressive and New Deal views that women who head families should be provided with sufficient income to stay home and rear their children.

As the Comprehensive Employment and Training Act (CETA) evolved into a major public service employment program late in the 1970s, the jobs it provided became targeted increasingly on disadvantaged workers, including single women with children. Furthermore, the Ford and Carter administrations funded several large-scale demonstration and experimental work programs— the two most notable being the Supported Work Demonstration and Employment Opportunity Pilot Projects—which were designed to reduce welfare dependence.[56]

The Supported Work Demonstration was a controlled experiment conducted in thirteen cities from 1975 to 1979. The program provided subsidized employment opportunities from twelve to eighteen months to reformed addicts and offenders, delinquent youth, and—most important for our purposes— women on AFDC for thirty of the previous thirty-six months with no pre-school-age children. The work experience was provided in an atmosphere designed to be supportive and closely supervised. The Employment Opportunity Pilot Projects were conducted in fifteen cities from 1979 to 1981. This demonstration program was designed to test the feasibility of a guaranteed jobs program by providing a minimum-wage job to the principal earner in a family with children (although it turned out to be mainly a job search).

---

56. For descriptions and evaluations of these programs, see Manpower Demonstration Research Corporation, *The Final Report. Summary and Findings of the National Supported Work Demonstration* (Cambridge, Massachusetts: Ballinger, 1980); and Stanley H. Masters and Rebecca A. Maynard, *The Impact of Supported Work on Long-Term Recipients of AFDC Benefits*, vol. 3 of the *The Final Report: Summary and Findings of the National Suggested Work Demonstration* (New York: Manpower Demonstration Research Corporation, February 1981); and John Bishop, et al., "A Research Design To Study the Labour Market Effects of the Employment Opportunity Pilot Projects," in Ernst W. Stromsdorfer and George Farkas, eds., *Evaluation Studies Review Annual*, vol. 5 (Beverly Hills: Sage Publications, 1980), pp. 759-800.

Three possible explanations can be offered for the change in attitudes about whether welfare mothers should work. Two of these focus on the changing characteristics of poor single women with children—first from predominantly white to about 50 percent black, second from predominantly widowed to predominantly divorced, separated, or never married. Although both these changes in characteristics have no doubt contributed to the change in attitudes, we do not believe they are the important explanation. We believe the fundamental explanation is the revolutionary increase in married mothers' labor force participation—most of which took place in the 1960s and 1970s.

Thus the War on Poverty and its aftermath were accompanied by a shift from the Progressive and New Deal era policy of seeking to keep poor single women with children at home to a policy of encouraging work and perhaps even requiring work as a condition of aid to such women. Correspondingly, the already strong political pressure to reduce welfare rolls increased. Because this policy shift toward enforcing work and reducing welfare dependence was accompanied by increases in the generosity of welfare benefits, however, the nature of the shift was obscured. Once the enthusiasm for reducing poverty that had been generated by President Johnson's campaign had dissipated, however, the nature of the shift in policy became increasingly clear.

President Ford shared the goal of reducing welfare dependence, but unlike President Nixon, rejected the strategy of expanding welfare eligibility to achieve that end. When the then Secretary of Health, Education, and Welfare, Caspar Weinberger, proposed that the Ford administration support a purer NIT version of the Family Assistance Plan, President Ford refused.

President Carter, like President Nixon before him, proposed a major expansion of welfare assistance to poor families. Like the Family Assistance Plan, President Carter's Program for Better Jobs and Income (PBJI) proposed a national minimum benefit for families with children and included two-parent families. But unlike the Family Assistance Plan, PBJI included a major guaranteed jobs program from the outset. It also would have required single mothers without preschool-age children to work. For mothers with children aged seven to thirteen, the work requirement was to apply only if child care was available. Unlike the Nixon, Johnson, Kennedy, and Roosevelt administrations, the Carter administration made no claim that PBJI would reduce welfare rolls in the long run. The PBJI proposal did not come close to passing in either house of Congress. One reason for the failure of this program was that welfare rolls were projected to increase rather than decrease. Another was that the Seattle-Denver income-maintenance experiment described earlier in this chapter appeared to show that extending cash relief to two-parent families broke up more families than confining cash relief to single-parent families.[57] The rejection of PBJI signaled the end of the nation's experiment of expanding welfare to reduce poverty. Indeed, by 1980 it appeared that the national will to reduce poverty by any means had disappeared.

Why was the War on Poverty conducted in a manner that reduced the work effort of single mothers and increased their welfare dependence when a consensus was emerging to increase work and reduce welfare dependence among these women? The answer begins with a comparison between the 1930s and the 1960s. Since the Social Security Act was enacted in the midst of the greatest depression this country had ever suffered, the architects of the act therefore had to be extremely careful in their efforts to provide help. The country could ill afford mistakes. The War on Poverty, in contrast, took place during the most prolonged economic boom in the nation's history. In 1965 the country could afford to try many approaches, discard those that did not work, and build on those that did work. Indeed, President Johnson made it quite clear that this was to be his policy. Roosevelt, as governor of New York in the 1930s, had helped to pioneer unemployment insurance and work relief and therefore held views in accordance with those of the academics and administrators who designed the Social Security Act. By contrast, Johnson was a product of the New Deal, adhered to the vision of the architects of the Social Security Act, and resisted the idea of a negative income tax. The boom time made it possible to try many approaches. The absence of a coherent policy did not ensure a contradictory policy with regard to work and welfare dependence, but it facilitated it. Within this environment, the heavy reliance on welfare to reduce poverty among families headed by women with children was in part accidental (for example, the effect of President Johnson's political deal on the Medicaid coverage issue); in part the indirect, unintended consequences of other policy choices (for example, the effect of the Community Action and Legal Services programs on participation rates in AFDC); and in part the byproduct of the temporary victory of the NIT concept in the world of policy ideas.

Enforcement of Child Support: Faint Beginnings of a New Approach. By 1975 Congress took a different tack. Senator Russell Long persuaded his colleagues to enact legislation to reduce welfare cost and caseloads by strengthening the collection of private child support due to children on

---

57. M. T. Hannan, S. E. Beaver, and N. B. Tuma, "Income Maintenance Effects on the Making and Breaking of Marriages: Preliminary Analysis of the First Eighteen Months of the Denver Income Maintenance Experiment," Research Memorandum draft (Menlo Park, California: SRI International, 1974); and Michael T. Hannan, Nancy Brandon Tuma, and Lyle P. Groeneveld, "Income and Marital Events: Evidence from an Income Maintenance Experiment," American Journal of Sociology, vol. 82 (1977), pp. 1186-1211.

welfare. This was the addition of Part D to Title IV of the Social Security Act, which established the child support program. Federal interest in child support enforcement was not entirely new but had been growing along with increases in AFDC cases. In 1950, for example, Congress had enacted legislation that required state welfare agencies to notify law enforcement officials when a child receiving AFDC benefits had been deserted or abandoned. The 1962 Social Security amendments also included a provision for federal aid to localities in locating absent parents. Other legislation, enacted in 1965 and 1967, required states to enforce child support and establish paternity. It also allowed them to request the addresses of absent parents from the Internal Revenue Service and the Department of Health, Education, and Welfare. The 1975 legislation was the most significant step. Responsibility for administering the child support enforcement program rests with the states, although the federal government pays 75 percent of the cost of establishing paternity, locating absent fathers, and collecting child support. Use of Internal Revenue Service data to collect child support that was owed to AFDC beneficiaries was authorized by the 1975 law and, in 1980, was extended to non-AFDC families. Little additional child support had been collected from the fathers of AFDC children and, therefore, little reduction in welfare dependence had been achieved by 1980. But, as the next chapter notes, these reforms of the child support system set the stage for a different approach to aiding families headed by women.

Appendix A

Additional Sources of Data: Benefits Available for Mother-Only Families

Total benefits for each year in table 7 were computed as the sum of the individual program expenditures for mother-only families with children. The proportion of the individual program budgets expended on such families is given in table 8. The sources for the individual program expenditures are these:

The Medicaid expenditures were inflated to 1983 dollars by the consumer price index for medical care. The consumer price indexes were taken from *Economic Report of the President, February 1986*, p. 279.

TABLE 8

Estimated Proportion of Selected Program Budgets Allocated to Mother-Only Families with Children under Age Eighteen

Income-Tested Programs	1979 Income Survey Development Program (Wave 2)[a]	1980 Current Population Survey[b]	1983 Current Population Survey[b]	Other
Cash				
AFDC	0.72	0.74	0.72	n.a.
Supplemental Security				
Income	0.08	n.a.	n.a.	n.a.
In-kind benefits				
Food stamps	0.47	0.49	0.48	n.a.
Energy assistance	n.a.	0.24	n.a.	n.a.
Medicaid	0.18	n.a.	n.a.	n.a.
Housing assistance	0.32	n.a.	n.a.	n.a.
School lunch	n.a.	0.43	n.a.	n.a.
Job-related[c]				
Training and				
employment	n.a.	n.a.	n.a.	0.16
Public Service				
Employment	n.a.	n.a.	n.a.	0.19
Day care	n.a.	n.a.	n.a.	0.96
Head Start	n.a.	n.a.	n.a.	0.38

TABLE 8 (*Continued*)

Income-Tested Programs	1979 Income Survey Development Program (Wave 2)[a]	1980 Current Population Survey[b]	1983 Current Population Survey[b]	Other
Nonincome-tested				
Old Age, Survivors,				
and Disability Insurance	0.03	n.a.	n.a.	n.a.
Unemployment Insurance	0.05	0.05	0.04	n.a.
Veterans' benefits[d]	0.05	n.a.	n.a.	n.a.

SOURCES: U.S. Congress, House, *Background Materials and Data or Programs within the Jurisdiction of the Committee on Ways and Means* (Washington, D.C.: U.S. Government Printing Office, February 21, 1984). The Head Start ratio is based in the proportion of recipient families headed by women in 1970. Source: Sar Levitan and Karen Cleary Alderman, *Child Care and ABC's Too* (Baltimore, Maryland: Johns Hopkins University Press, 1975), table 12, p. 87.

n.a. Not available.

a. To calculate the proportion of program benefits going to female heads of families we used aggregate reported transfer income from the second set of interviews, or Wave 2, from the 1979 Income Survey Development Program. The proportion is simply the ratio of benefits reported by these women to all benefits reported. These are the primary proportions used in computing tables 7 and 11 in the text.

b. The proportions, computed as outlined in note a, are shown here for comparison purposes with two exceptions. First, the energy assistance ratio is used for computing the text tables because this was not available in the data from the Income Survey Development Program. Second, the school lunch ratio, also used to compute text tables 7 and 11, is the ratio of the recipients and not benefits. In the case of table 7, the school lunch ratio is used as a proxy for child nutrition programs.

c. The training and employment and the Public Service Employment ratios are computed using recipients rather than benefits. The ratio for the training and employment programs is computed from the selected characteristics of enrollees 1969 and 1970; *Statistical Abstracts of the United States, 1971*; and the CETA Supplemental Management Information System Tables by Initial Program Assignment—New Enrollees during October 1980–September 1981. The data source for the Public Service Employment ratio is the CETA Supplemental MIS Tables by Initial Program Assignment—New Enrollees during October 1980–September 1981. The day care ratio is based on the proportion of Title XX day care expenditures in fiscal year 1979 to expenditures on AFDC and income eligibles (those who do not receive AFDC). Assumes that 100 percent of the groups are female heads of households.

d. Veterans' benefits include compensation (not an income-tested program) and pensions (an income-tested program).

Welfare expenditures are as follows. Data on AFDC benefit expenditures for 1950 through 1965 are from U.S. Bureau of the Census, *Social Security Bulletin, Annual Statistical Supplement, 1982*, table 192. For benefit years 1970 through 1980, the source of federal expenditure is U.S. Bureau of the Census, *Statistical Abstract of the United States, 1982/1983*, table 515. Supplemental Security Income federal benefit expenditures are from *Statistical*

Abstract of the United States, 1982/1983, table 515. Federal benefit expenditures for food stamps are from *Statistical Abstract of the United States, 1982/1983*, table 515. Federal benefit expenditures for low-income energy assistance are from *Statistical Abstract of the United States, 1982/1983*, table 517. Medicaid benefit expenditures are from *Statistical Abstract of the United States, 1982/1983*, table 515. Federal benefit expenditures for housing assistance, 1950-60, are from *Statistical Abstract of the United States, 1970*, table 415; 1965-80 expenditures are from *Statistical Abstract of the United States, 1982/1983*, table 515. Federal benefit expenditures for the school lunch program, 1950-80, are from *Statistical Abstract of the United States, 1970*, table 121; 1965-80 expenditures are from the *Statistical Abstract of the United States, 1982/1983*, table 20.6.

Job-related expenditures are as follows. Employment and training figures are from *Statistical Abstract of the United States, 1980*, table 294. Day care expenditures are from *Background Material and Data on Programs within the Jurisdiction of the Committee on Ways and Means*, U.S. House of Representatives, February 21, 1984. Computations were based on expenditure in fiscal year 1979 and assume that 100 percent of the AFDC eligibles and income eligibles are not mother-only families with children. Head Start expenditures are from *Statistical Abstract of the United States, 1984*, table 660.

Nonwelfare benefit expenditures are as follows. The ratio of Social Insurance benefits paid to mother-only families with children to total Survivors' Insurance benefits is clearly not a constant over time. There was no Disability Insurance program until 1956. Early retirement provisions and practices have changed over time. And, the proportion of children eligible for Survivors' Insurance benefits has changed over time. Because of these changes and because these benefits are such a small proportion of total Social Insurance benefits, using the 1979 ratio to estimate the changes in Survivors' Insurance benefits over time would lead to large errors.

Survivors' Insurance expenditures are from the Social Security Bulletin, *Annual Statistical Supplement, 1982*, tables 92, 93, and 102. Table 92 provides data on benefits paid to children less than age eighteen of deceased workers for each year from 1940 through 1980. Table 93 provides data on the number of children of deceased male and deceased female workers. The ratio of the children of deceased male workers to total children is used to multiply the amounts figure from table 92 to arrive at a total for child survivors living with their mothers. Table 102 provides data on the amount of survivors' benefits paid to widowed mothers and fathers. Beginning in 1975 surviving fathers became eligible for benefits. For 1975 and 1980 therefore, the amounts from table 102 were multiplied by the ratios in table 93 to derive an estimate of survivors' payments to mothers. Finally, the benefits to children that result from the calculations described in this paragraph include benefits paid to remarried mothers. To estimate what proportion was received by female-headed families we multiply total Social Insurance benefits in 1980 times the proportion in table 8 of Old Age, Survivors, and Diability Insurance benefits paid to female-headed families. We then divide the resulting figure by the 1980 estimate of total Survivors' Insurance benefits paid to widows and their children. The resulting ratio is assumed to be constant over time and is used to derive estimates for the other years. Assuming the ratio is constant assumes that the proportion of widows receiving Survivors' Insurance who remarry has been constant over time. While this is also almost certainly not true, data by Espenshade on remarriage rates of widows in general suggest that the assumption may not be invalid. See Thomas J. Espenshade, "The Recent Decline of American Marriage: Blacks and Whites in Comparative Perspective" working paper (Washington, D.C.: Urban Institute, December 1984), table 7. Unemployment Insurance expenditure data are from *Social Security Bulletin, Annual Statistical Supplement*, 1982, table 2. Federal expenditures for veterans' benefits are from *Social Security Bulletin, Annual Statistical Supplement, 1982*, table 2. This program area includes both veterans' compensation and a non-income-tested program.

A Comparison between Estimates of the Increase in Benefit Generosity, 1960-80

The first row in table 9 presents the time series from 1960 through 1980 from the House Ways and Means Committee study on the real value of AFDC plus food stamp benefits for a family of four with no other income—what economists refer to as the guarantee benefit level. The second row presents the percentage increase in benefit guarantees for each of the four-year periods. Note that the AFDC and food stamp guarantee is somewhat higher in 1980 than 1960, but not much—$7,486 compared with $6,715. Benefits increased respectively by 8 percent and 25 percent in two of the periods, 1964-68 and 1968-72, but they decreased in the other three periods by a total of 21 percent. Thus the total increase over the 1960-80 period was only 12 percent. This conveys a picture dramatically different from that shown in the time series in table 7 (in the text) on expenditures per mother-only families with children. Between 1960 and 1980, expenditures for such families increased by 97 percent.

The major difference between the two measures of the generosity of benefits is that the AFDC plus food stamp guarantee fails to take account of increases in Medicaid, housing assistance, energy assistance, school lunches, and employment and training benefits. Medicaid, which is the most serious single omission, accounts for nearly half of the total omitted benefits. The third row in table 9, therefore, simply adds the market value of Medicaid to the value of the AFDC and food stamp guarantee.

The fourth row in table 9, however, conveys the same qualitative picture as table 7 in the text. Benefit levels continued to grow until the mid-1970s; the small 9 percent cuts in benefit levels in the first and last periods are dwarfed by the 53 percent increase in the four middle periods. In this case, the benefit increases are nearly six times as much as the decreases. That is somewhat smaller than the more than six to one ratio in the text, but much closer to the text than the first and second rows of table 9 in quantitative terms and exactly the same as the text in qualitative terms.

TABLE 9

A COMPARISON OF TIME TRENDS FOR DIFFERENT MEASURES OF THE GENEROSITY OF
WELFARE BENEFITS
(*1983 Dollars*)

Source of Guarantee Benefits	1960	1964	1968	1972	1976	1980
AFDC + food stamps[a]	6,715	6,604	7,129	8,894	8,743	7,486
Percentage increase	. . .	−2	8	25	−2	−17
AFDC + food stamps + Medicaid[b] (market value)	6,715	6,604	8,186	10,267	10,652	9,923
Percentage increase	. . .	−2	24	25	4	−7
AFDC + food stamps + Medicaid[c] (0.28 of market value)	. . .	6,604	7,425	9,278	9,278	8,168
Percentage increase	. . .	−2	12	25	0	−12

a. Row 1 is taken directly from U.S. Congress, House, *Background Material and Data on Programs within the Jurisdiction of the Committee on Ways and Means* (Washington, D.C.: U.S. Government Printing Office, February 22, 1985), table 15, "Combined AFDC and Food Stamp Benefit Levels for a Family of Four with No Income," p. 532.

b. To obtain the estimates for the values of Medicaid, we used the amount of Medicaid for a family of a single parent and three children from the figures reported for 1979 in U.S. Department of Commerce, Bureau of the Census, "Estimates of Poverty, Including the Value of Non-Cash Benefit: 1983" Technical Paper 52 (Washington, D.C.: U.S. Government Printing Office, 1983), table B-8, p. B-9. For 1979, this came to $1,637 per year. This is a nominal dollar figure. Therefore the 1979 estimate was inflated by the Consumer Price Index for medical care to 1983 dollars yielding $2,240. This estimate for Medicaid was added to the AFDC plus food stamps estimates for 1980 and 1984 to obtain an upper-bound estimate of the AFDC plus food stamps + Medicaid guarantees in 1980 of $9,923. To obtain estimates for 1968, 1972, and 1976, we simply multiplied the ratios of 1976, 1972, and 1968 total Medicaid expenditures by 1980 total Medicaid expenditures.

c. To obtain lower-bound estimates for 1980 and 1984, the above Medicaid estimates derived in note b were discounted by the largest estimate of the appropriate discount reported by Timothy Smeeding for valuing selected in-kind transfer benefits and measuring their effect on poverty. This value is 0.28. See U.S. Department of Commerce, Bureau of the Census, "Alternative Methods," Technical Paper 50 (Washington, D.C.: U.S. Government Printing Office, March 1982), table 4, p. 37.

The fifth and sixth rows, which value Medicaid benefits at only 28 percent of their cost, paint an intermediate picture, but one that is still closer to the picture conveyed in the text than to the picture conveyed by the House Report. In this case, the 37 percent increase from 1960 to 1972 still dwarfs the cuts of 2 and 12 percent. But now the increases are only 2.5 times the decrease rather than nearly 6 times, as in the fourth row.

We believe that valuing Medicaid at 100 percent rather than only 28 percent (let alone zero) gives a truer picture of the trend in the value of government benefits to mother-only families with children. Twenty-eight percent is the lowest value of all those used by Smeeding for discounting the value of Medicaid. Furthermore, ancedotal evidence from AFDC caseworkers, newspaper accounts, and stories from recipients all testify to the large value recipients place on Medicaid. Finally, even if Medicaid were worth only 28 percent on the dollar for recipients, public housing, Head Start, day care services, school lunches, and public employment and training programs are certainly worth more than nothing per dollar spent. Taken together these programs spend as much as Medicaid on mother-only families with children. Thus together these programs would add back at least another 28 cents that would put the value of all benefits much closer to the fourth row than the sixth row. Consequently, we conclude that the value of benefits to a four-person family with no other income increased by at least six times more between 1964 and 1976 than it decreased during the beginning and ending periods.

A second way in which the two estimates of benefit generosity differ is that we measure average benefits received by all mother-only families with children, whereas the committee report measures only the welfare benefits that families with no other income are entitled to. Part of the increase in our estimates is attributable to both increased availability of benefits and to higher participation rates among single women with children eligible for welfare programs. Which approach is more theoretically correct depends on the question being addressed. Our measure reflects in economic terms the effects of noneconomic increases in benefit generosity. For example, the elimination of the "man-in-the-house rule" in the AFDC program increased the number of such women who could claim AFDC without fear of being declared ineligible because there was a man in their life and home. Our measure reflects this liberalization of welfare, the committee report's does not. Our measure also incorporates increases in participation due to liberalized acceptance rates of AFDC applications. Between 1964 and 1971, acceptance rates increased from 62 to 74 percent.[58] From a theoretical perspective it is appropriate to include both these effects.

Conversely, our measure also incorporates increased participation in AFDC which was induced by increased benefits, whereas the committee report does not. The latter is preferable on this account. Furthermore, to the extent

---

58. Heather L. Ross and Isabel V. Sawhill, *Time of Transition: The Growth of Families Headed by Women* (Washington, D.C.: Urban Institute, 1975), p. 105.

that the composition of the population of mother-only families with children shifted toward those who were more likely to receive transfers, our measure also reflects this shift, which again ideally it should not. On balance, we believe that our more inclusive measure is superior for most theoretical questions.

The third and fourth rows of table 9, unlike table 7, do not take account of increases in the availability of benefits to families with no other income or of increases in benefits to families with other income. Table 7 takes account of both. We strongly suspect that further research will show that most of the remaining difference between the third and fourth rows of table 9 and table 7 will be attributable to those omissions rather than to an overcounting bias in table 7.

CHAPTER 5

THE REAGAN POLICY INITIATIVES AND ESTIMATES OF THEIR EFFECTS

How much has the Reagan administration altered previous resolutions to the policy dilemma of whether to give priority to increasing the economic well-being of families headed by women or to reducing their prevalence and dependence on welfare? This is a difficult question because the overall picture is inevitably obscured by our proximity to the proposals, political battles, and outcomes that will determine the existence and magnitude of any alterations. Moreover, political partisans on both sides have incentives to exaggerate and minimize the extent of changes proposed and achieved. In this chapter we try to stand back, to the extent possible, and analyze policy changes during the first six years of the Reagan administration. Our intent is to set the stage for the analysis of policy alternatives at the end of the book.

The discussion begins with an examination of current federal policy regarding mother-only families with children. We describe the objectives, proposals, and legislative outcomes of three policies developed under the Reagan administration: (1) the 1981 budget cuts that mark the first explicit attempt by the federal government in the twentieth century to actually reduce public benefits to these families, (2) the shift from work incentives toward work requirements for those receiving welfare benefits, and (3) the expansion of federal efforts to strengthen the public enforcement of private child support obligations. In some instances these policies represent an extension or expansion of previous programs; in others they reflect a sharp break with the past.

In the first section of this chapter we review the policies of the Reagan administration pertaining to mother-only families. The next three sections develop estimates of the effects of the three shifts in income transfer policy. In each of these three sections the effects on the economic well-being, the welfare dependence, and the prevalence of families headed by single mothers are examined. We find the following.

The 1981 cuts in public benefits moderately reduced the incomes of most families headed by single mothers who received AFDC and substantially decreased the incomes of the few employed recipients who received welfare. The cuts appear to have reduced dependence modestly and prevalence hardly at all. We conclude that further large reductions in benefits would substantially decrease economic well-being, moderately to substantially decrease dependence, but result in only a small decrease in prevalence.

To date, states have only begun small-scale implementation of the work programs, so changes in work requirements have had little effect. To implement work programs on a large scale would require a large initial investment of additional resources. Some people maintain that such a policy is not technically, economically, or politically feasible. We do not share this view. We believe that such an investment is feasible and that the positive effects on the economic well-being and dependence (and perhaps even prevalence) of families headed by single women are potentially large.

It is too early to detect the effects of the 1984 milestone legislation, the Child Support Enforcement Amendments. They will range from small to quite large depending upon how effectively the law is implemented. If implemented effectively, there are good reasons to believe that economic well-being will increase and both dependence and prevalence will decline.

In the fourth section of this chapter, we look at two other policies that are not part of income transfer policy but could have profound consequences for mother-only families: macroeconomic policy and antiabortion policy. We conclude that the extraordinary high unemployment rates of the early 1980s resulted in a small short-term decrease in the incomes of single women with children, a small short-term increase in welfare dependence, and most important, a moderate increase in prevalence. Continued high unemployment will result in the further deterioration of two-parent families. We argue that a stronger antiabortion policy adds the risk of increasing the prevalence of mother-only families, so substantially as to dwarf the effects of most other policies on prevalence.

In the last section of this chapter, the effects of these five policy shifts are added together to develop a scorecard for the Reagan administration's achievements in the areas of reducing economic insecurity, decreasing dependence on government, and reducing the prevalence of families headed by women. From that analysis, the irony emerges that, despite the priority given by the Reagan administration to reducing the prevalence of female headship—as opposed to increasing the economic well-being of female-headed families—

the actual policies that emerged may increase both economic well-being and increase the prevalence of female headship.

Objectives, Proposals, and Legislative Outcomes

Reducing Public Benefits

The real value of AFDC benefits declined throughout the 1970s, not because of explicit cuts, but because state legislatures failed to increase AFDC benefit levels to keep pace with inflation. In the 1980s, however, President Reagan actively sought to cut benefits.

In the 1980 presidential campaign, Ronald Reagan argued that large government benefits and the accompanying high taxes were undermining economic incentives and strangling growth. He campaigned on a platform to reduce federal domestic expenditures and taxes and increase military expenditures. Once elected, he proposed legislation to carry out each of these objectives and persuaded Congress to pass most of his proposals. In this context, cuts in benefits to families headed by single women may appear to be nothing more than part of a much larger effort to reduce government spending. The desire to cut government spending in general, however, was only one of two reasons for the cuts in benefits to families headed by single women.

The other reason is implied by this excerpt from one of President Reagan's radio addresses: "But there is no question that many well-intentioned Great Society-type programs contributed to family breakups, welfare dependency, and a large increase in births out-of-wedlock."[1] In this address the president did not single out any particular program, but conservative intellectuals such as George Gilder and Charles Murray have clearly stated their belief that AFDC and the accompanying cash and in-kind benefit programs are the culprits.[2] Gilder advocates substantial reductions in AFDC, food stamp benefits, and Medicaid; Murray proposes elimination of these benefits.

President Reagan has proposed large cuts in welfare benefits to poor single women who head families. His most radical proposal was for the federal government to drop the AFDC and food stamp programs; the states would

---

1. December 3, 1983, radio address as reported in the *Wisconsin State Journal*, December 4, 1983, p. 2.

2. George Gilder, *Wealth and Poverty* (New York: Basic Books, 1981); and Charles Murray, *Losing Ground: American Social Policy, 1950-1980.* (New York: Basic Books, 1984).

be free to provide these benefits if they so chose. As part of the same proposal, the federal government would take full responsibility for financing the Medicaid program. This proposal is radical in the sense that it would dramatically reverse a fifty-year trend in the United States of increasing federal responsibility for assuring a minimum standard of living for all citizens. It is also radical because it would almost certainly have led to substantial cuts in benefit levels for families headed by single mothers.

Under current law, the federal government subsidizes state expenditures for both AFDC and Medicaid. For each dollar a state spends on AFDC and Medicaid benefits, the federal government pays on average somewhat more than fifty cents of the cost. This arrangement encourages states to spend more on AFDC and Medicaid than they would if they had to pay full costs. The end of federal financing of AFDC and food stamps would almost certainly have resulted in reductions in total benefits both for this reason and also because state governments, unlike the federal government, have an incentive to keep benefits low to discourage the in-migration and encourage the out-migration of potential beneficiaries.

Three studies suggest that benefits to mother-only families under the so-called AFDC, food stamps/Medicaid swap might have been reduced by between 11 to 56 percent.[3] We believe that the higher figure is nearer the truth because it is based on the only study that includes the effect of interstate competition on benefit levels.

Congress never seriously considered this proposal; but President Reagan also proposed a series of specific budget cuts (in 1981, 1982, and 1984) in benefits to mother-only families, some of which were passed by Congress. The president proposed to cut benefits in AFDC, food stamps, Medicaid, and public housing that would have amounted by fiscal 1985 to 29, 52, 16, and 20 percent, respectively. Congress actually cut these programs by 14, 14, 3, and 11 percent.[4] The president's proposal to cut the program for Women, Infants, and Children (WIC, a supplemental food program) and Supplemental Security Income programs by 64 percent and 3 percent, respectively, did not pass. Congress increased benefits in each by 9 percent.

---

3. See L. Orr, "Income Transfers as a Public Good: An Application to AFDC," *American Economic Review* vol. 66 (June 1976), pp. 359-71; Robert A. Moffitt, "The Effects of Grants-in-Aid on State and Local Expenditures! The Case of AFDC," unpublished document, University of Wisconsin-Madison, Institute for Research on Poverty, November 1982; and Edward M. Gramlich, "An Econometric Examination of the New Federalism," *Brookings Papers on Economic Activity* vol. 2 (1982), pp. 327-60.

4. D. Lee Bawden and John L. Palmer, "Social Policy: Challenging the Welfare State," in John L. Palmer and Isabel F. Sawhill, eds., *The Reagan Record* (Cambridge, Massachusetts: Ballinger Publishing Company, 1984), table 6.1, pp. 185-86.

Most cuts that were adopted were targeted at the least needy among the poor.[5] Welfare benefits to working mothers were cut substantially. The work incentive provision in AFDC that ignored the first $30 of earnings plus $1 of every $3 in excess of $30 per month was reduced from eight to four months. Individually determined work-related expense deductions with no maximum were replaced by standard deductions of $50 a month for part-time work and $75 per month for full-time work. Furthermore, families with gross incomes in excess of 150 percent of the state's need standard—the level of income for determining initial eligibility—were made ineligible for benefits. (Once families begin receiving AFDC, their total income can exceed the state's need standard.) As part of the 1984 legislation in which some benefit cuts were restored, work incentives were liberalized somewhat—the $30 set-aside was extended from four to twelve months; the $75 a month deduction for work-related expenses was applied to part-time as well as full-time work; and the eligibility level for people already on welfare was increased from 150 to 185 percent of the state's need standard.

Such targeting had the obvious virtue of minimizing the resulting hardship, but there was an additional rationale. The Reagan administration rejected the welfare incentives strategy of reducing long-run welfare dependence.[6] Rather than encouraging work and remarriage by extending welfare eligibility to those who worked and remarried, the administration sought to reduce dependence and prevalence directly by reducing the attractiveness of welfare for them. Furthermore, as is described in the next section, the administration sought to reinforce the objectives of its benefit cuts through specific work requirements.

---

5. See table 11 in text. Of the $4.6 billion in cuts, $1.3 billion came in work-related programs and another $200 million in Unemployment Insurance. As described in the text discussion, most of the $1.2 billion cut in AFDC was for employed recipients. In the child nutrition programs, which include the national school breakfast, summer feeding, and child care feeding programs, most of the savings came from the reductions in the family income levels that determine eligibility and benefits and from the reductions in federal subsidy rates. These cuts most heavily affected people with the most income, which means, for female-headed families, *employed mothers*. Although most of the savings in the food stamp program came from a delay in benefit increases, some savings also resulted from eliminating eligibility for households with gross monthly incomes of more than 130 percent of the poverty level. If we assume that $1 billion of the AFDC cuts, $300 million of the child nutrition cuts employed and $200 million of the food stamp cuts were absorbed by low-income, female heads of families, and if we add those figures to the $1.5 billion cut in work-related and Unemployment Insurance programs, low-income employed women who head families with children absorbed about $3 billion of the $4.6 billion benefit cuts, or nearly two-thirds of the total.

6. For a discussion of the rationale for the Reagan administration's abandonment of the incentives strategy, see Blanche Bernstein, "Welfare Dependency" in D. Lee Bawden, ed., *The Social Contract Revisited* (Washington, D.C.: Urban Institute Press, 1984), pp. 125-52.

One benefit cut that was not targeted on the groups with other income is notable because it touches on the prevalence issue. AFDC eligibility of pregnant women not already on AFDC was delayed until the sixth month of pregnancy (formerly it was paid in the third month). It seems reasonable to assume that the supporters of this cut were concerned about AFDC benefits stimulating out-of-wedlock births more than they were concerned about economic hardship. It is important to note here that the largest benefit cuts were enacted as part of the Omnibus Budget and Reconciliation Act in 1981; much smaller benefit cuts were passed in 1982. And small increases that actually reversed some previous cuts followed in 1984. This pattern suggests that further substantial cuts in benefits are probably not politically feasible in the foreseeable future.

Strengthening Work Requirements

During the 1960s and 1970s, as we have emphasized repeatedly, there was an erosion in the early twentieth-century consensus that poor single mothers should not be employed. By 1980 a new consensus appeared to have emerged: poor single women with no preschool-age children should be employed.

Since 1972, as noted earlier, AFDC mothers with no children under age six have been required to register for work and training. Failure to register or, once enrolled, failure to accept available jobs or services needed to prepare these mothers for employment results in elimination of the benefit for the mother and payment of benefits for the children to a third party. Only a minority of AFDC recipients who registered, however, ever received services to help them find jobs.

The Reagan administration proposed that states require AFDC mothers to work for their relief checks in community work experience (workfare) programs. Congress passed legislation that permitted (although it did not require) states to substitute work relief for cash relief. Under workfare, the recipients work off their relief checks. The rate of pay is the minimum wage, and the hours are limited to the amount of the check divided by the minimum wage. Unlike the Work Incentives Program, which exempts mothers with children under age six, workfare exempts only mothers with children under age three.

In addition to workfare, Reagan proposed and Congress passed several other provisions to directly increase work. States may now require AFDC recipients to participate in a job-search program for up to eight weeks upon application and for an additional eight weeks for each year that benefits are received. States also are permitted to operate work supplementation (or grant diversion) programs in which federal funds that would ordinarily finance AFDC cash benefits may be used instead to subsidize a job for an AFDC recipient. Unlike workfare, work supplementation programs pay beneficiaries a wage and do not limit the number of hours they work so that their total income (earnings plus welfare grant) can exceed what they would have received in welfare alone.

As of September 1985, thirty-seven states have implemented one or more of these options. Twenty-three have workfare programs; twelve have job-search programs; and eleven have work supplementation programs.[7] So far, most of these programs are being operated on a demonstration basis in only a part of the state. In the few states with statewide programs, only a small proportion of the caseload is being served.[8]

The Reagan administration continues to push for mandatory work requirements. For fiscal 1986 it has proposed that unless at least 25 percent (75 percent after three years) of the eligible people in all states are involved in workfare, job search, or work supplementation programs, the state should face a financial penalty. At the same time, the administration proposes to cut federal funding for work programs. The proposals are still pending as this books goes to press.

Increasing Private Child Support

The Reagan administration was carried along by, and provided some leadership to, a large swing in the public's attitude toward the role of the federal government in the enforcement of private child support obligations. The underlying cause of this shift was the tremendous increase in the prevalence of mother-only families plus the growth in public expenditures on them. As noted in chapter 4, federal interest in enforcement for child support grew as the AFDC cases that were eligible for child support increased. It should come as no surprise, therefore, that both the Reagan administration and Congress sought to increase private child support as a method of reducing public child support.

The 1984 Child Support Enforcement Amendments went well beyond the objective of reducing welfare costs and caseloads. This significant child

---

7. See U.S. General Accounting Office, Report to the Chairman, Subcommittee on Intergovernmental Relations and Human Resources, House Committee on Government Operations, "Evidence Is Insufficient to Support the Administration's Proposed Changes to AFDC Work Programs," August 27, 1985.

8. U.S. Congress, House, Committee on Ways and Means, *Background Material and Data on Programs within the Jursidiction of the Committee on Ways and Means*, 99th Cong., 1st sess., February 22, 1985, tables 4 and 5, pp. 336-39.

support legislation applied not simply to parents whose children were receiving welfare but to all parents potentially liable for child support. The two most important provisions required all states to adopt an income-assignment law under which the child support obligation would be withheld from wages if the noncustodial payments were delinquent for one month, and to appoint state commissions to establish statewide standards for child support. In addition to these major provisions, for the first time the 1984 child support legislation gave states a financial incentive to increase child support collections from parents whose children were not on AFDC. Thus, in stark contrast to the budget cuts that restricted eligibility to the "truly needy" among the low-income families headed by women, the 1984 child support legislation extended child support services to people in all income classes.

The reason appears to be the emergence of a consensus that the child support system as a whole condones parental irresponsibility. A study conducted by the U.S. Bureau of the Census in 1979 found that only 59 percent of mothers with at least one child potentially eligible for support were awarded payments.[9] Of those awarded support, only 49 percent received the full amount due them, and 28 percent received nothing. Furthermore, the popular impression was that child support award levels and enforcement efforts were arbitrary and inequitable. This is confirmed by research findings that objective factors like the incomes of the parents and the number of children accounted for little of the variation in award levels.[10]

One weakness of the 1984 federal legislation is its failure to standardize the process for setting award levels. The child support standards to be developed by the state commissions were not to be binding upon local courts. Only a few states such as Delaware and Michigan have made extensive use of standards, and until the summer of 1984 when Minnesota was the first state to do so, no state had legislated a child support standard.

In separate legislative actions Congress approved two alternative ways to improve the economic status of mother-only families with children on AFDC by using at least some of the additional child support collections from the noncustodial spouse. First, as part of the 1984 legislation that increased AFDC benefits, Congress changed the way private child support payments were to be treated in the AFDC program. Previously each dollar received in

---

9. U.S. Bureau of the Census, *Child Support and Alimony: 1978, Current Population Reports Special Studies*, series P-23, no. 112 (Washington, D.C.: U.S. Government Printing Office, 1981).

10. Lucy Marsh Yee, "What Really Happens in Child Support Cases? An Empirical Study of Establishment and Enforcement of Child Support Orders in the Denver District Court," *Denver Law Journal* vol. 57 (1979), p. 1.

child support reduced the AFDC grant by one dollar. Beginning in October 1985, the first $50 per month of child support paid to AFDC families was to be ignored in calculating AFDC benefits. This provision was designed to increase the incomes of AFDC families and to create incentives both for custodial mothers to cooperate in identifying and locating noncustodial fathers, and for noncustodial fathers of AFDC children to pay child support.

Second, as part of the milestone 1984 Child Support Enforcement Amendments, Congress directed the secretary of the Department of Health and Human Services to authorize the state of Wisconsin to use federal funds that would otherwise have been spent on AFDC in Wisconsin to help fund a demonstration of a new child support assurance program. The demonstration is scheduled to commence in a few Wisconsin counties in July 1987 and is authorized to continue on a limited or statewide basis through 1993. Under the Wisconsin child support assurance program, the amount of child support owed is determined by a simple formula embodied in an administrative rule: 17 percent of the gross income of the noncustodial parent's income for one child, and 25, 29, 31, and 34 percent of gross income for two, three, four, and five or more children, respectively. The resulting child support obligation is withheld like income and payroll taxes from wages and other sources of income. These two provisions will become statewide law in July 1987. In four pilot counties, all children with a legal entitlement to child support are to receive either the amount paid by the noncustodial parent or an assured benefit, whichever is the largest. The assured benefit will be lower than the AFDC benefit—probably $3,000 per year for the first child—but unlike AFDC benefits, the assured benefit will not be reduced by a dollar for each dollar earned. In addition, the custodial parent will be entitled to receive approximately one dollar per hour worked in order to pay for child care and other work-related expenses. (Benefits are gradually reduced for families with incomes of more than half the average such that the state subsidy is confined to families with below-average income and most of the subsidy is focused on the poorest workers.) By providing benefits outside the welfare system that are not taken away when poor women go to work, the child support assurance program will supplement the earnings of poor women who have children and thereby lessen dependence on AFDC.

The Effects of the Reductions in Public Benefits

Evidence suggests, despite some uncertainties due to methodological and empirical difficulties, that the public benefit cuts during the Reagan administration reduced the incomes of poor mother-only families considerably in return for achieving modest reductions in dependence and trivial reductions in prevalence.

We begin our analysis by looking at the short-term trends in (1) income, as measured by the proportion of mother-only families who are poor, (2) prevalence, as measured by the proportion of all families with children that are mother-only families, and (3) welfare dependence, as measured by the proportion of mother-only families that receive AFDC benefits. These three measures are presented for the years 1975 through 1983 in table 10. The first

TABLE 10

SHORT-TERM TRENDS IN THE ECONOMIC WELL-BEING, PREVALENCE, AND WELFARE
DEPENDENCE OF MOTHER-ONLY FAMILIES WITH CHILDREN, 1975–83

Year	Economic Well-Being[a] (Percentage Poor)	Prevalence[b] (Percentage of Mother-Only Families with Children)	Welfare Dependence[c] (Percentage on Welfare)
1975	47.9	14.7	0.57
1976	47.3	15.3	0.56
1977	45.8	15.9	0.54
1978	45.8	17.1	0.49
1979	43.8	17.4	0.48
1980	46.7	17.5	0.50
1981	48.1	18.0	0.46
1982	51.6	18.9	0.44
1983	51.2	18.6	0.47

SOURCES: Economic well-being is from Christine Ross, "The Trend in Poverty, 1965–1983," paper prepared for the conference entitled Poverty and Policy: Retrospect and Prospects (sponsored by the Institute for Research on Poverty, held at Williamsburg, Virginia, December 6–8, 1984), table 8A. Prevalence is from U.S. Bureau of the Census, *Current Population Reports*, "Household and Family Characteristics," series P-20, nos. 291, 311, 326, 340, 352, 366, 371, 381, 388. Welfare dependence data for 1975–82 are from U.S. Department of Health and Human Services, *Social Security Bulletin, Annual Statistical Supplement, 1983*, p. 248; the data for 1983 are from U.S. Department of Health and Human Services, *Social Security Bulletin*, vol. 47, no. 12, p. 51. Because these data pertain to "all families" receiving AFDC, we multiplied by 0.72, that is, the proportion of families headed by women receiving Aid to Families with Dependent Children (AFDC) in 1979 (see chapter 4, table 8). The denominator (total number of female-headed families each year) was derived from U.S. Bureau of the Census, *Current Population Reports*, "Household and Family Characteristics," series P-20.

a. Proportion poor of families headed by single women with children under age eighteen.

b. Proportion of all families headed by single women with children under age eighteen. The trend in families headed by women is similar to the trend for all *households* headed by women except that in 1983 the number of families headed by women increased. This is because the Bureau of the Census improved its methods of identifying subfamilies within households. If the previous procedure of identification had been used, the number of families headed by single women with children would have declined between 1982 and 1983.

c. The proportion of households receiving AFDC.

column indicates that the proportion of mother-only families who were poor decreased steadily between 1975 and 1979; increased in 1980, the year before President Reagan took office; increased again in 1981 and 1982; and then decreased slightly in 1983. The second column shows that the proportion of mother-only families with children women increased steadily until 1978, flattened out somewhat between 1978 and 1980, began growing again in 1981 and 1982, and actually decreased in 1983. The third column demonstrates that the proportion of mother-only families receiving AFDC benefits declined more or less steadily until 1980 when they increased slightly, declined again in 1981 and 1982, and finally rose again in 1983.

By themselves these trends do not present a clear picture of the effects of the budget cuts. For example, the proportion of poor increased when the Reagan budget cuts took effect in 1982, but it also increased before they took effect in 1980 and 1981. Some of the increase in poverty in 1980 and 1981 was due to the fact that AFDC benefits did not keep pace with inflation, but the 1980-82 recession also increased poverty. Some of the change in prevalence and welfare dependence of mother-only families was due to benefit cuts. The next step is to use available data to estimate the separate effects of these benefit cuts on the economic well-being, prevalence, and welfare dependence of mother-only families.

Economic Well-Being

Table 11 presents estimates of the changes in federal and state expenditures for mother-only families with children in 1985 due to changes in major federal programs initiated by the Reagan administration and enacted by Congress in 1981 and 1982. The programs in table 11 correspond to those shown by expenditure in table 7 and are included only if they had expenditures of $500 million or more in 1980. Our estimates are derived from similar estimates by the Congressional Budget Office for all population groups.[11] The first and second columns of table 11 present, respectively, estimates of what the expenditures of each major program for families headed by women would have been in the absence of program changes initiated by the Reagan administration and the expenditures projected under current law. The third column shows the difference between the first two columns, which indicates the estimated magnitude of the budget cuts attributable to program changes initiated by

---

11. U.S. Congressional Budget Office, "Major Legislative Changes in Human Resources Program since January, 1981," staff memorandum, August 1983. To derive our estimates, we multiplied the Congressional Budget Office estimates of the effects on the budget for all beneficiaries by independent estimates of the proportion of benefits in each program that female-headed families receive. See table 8.

TABLE 11

FEDERAL EXPENDITURES FOR MOTHER-ONLY FAMILIES WITH CHILDREN IN 1985,
WITH AND WITHOUT REAGAN ADMINISTRATION PROGRAM CHANGES
(Billions of Dollars unless Otherwise Indicated)

Program	Estimated 1985 Expenditures under 1981 Law	Projected 1985 Expenditures under 1983 Law	Estimated Reduction in Budget	
			Billions of Dollars	Percentage
Total	38.2	33.8	4.4	12
Income-tested welfare programs				
Cash				
Total	9.6	8.5	1.1	12
AFDC[a]	8.9	7.7	1.2	10
Supplemental Security Income	0.7	0.8	0.1	9
In-kind benefits				
Total	19.5	17.9	1.6	11
Food stamps	6.0	5.4	0.6	12
Energy assistance	0.5	0.5	0.0	10
Medicaid[a]	8.0	7.8	0.2	3
Housing assistance	3.5	3.1	0.4	12
Child Nutrition	1.5	1.1	0.4	29
Work-related programs, total	3.0	1.7	1.3	46
Employment and training	1.4	0.4	1.0	71
Day care and Head Start	1.6	1.3	0.3	19
Nonincome-tested programs				
Cash				
Total	6.1	5.7	0.4	5
Survivors' Insurance	4.4	4.2	0.2	5
Unemployment Insurance	1.0	0.8	0.2	18
Veterans' benefits	0.7	0.7	0.0	1

SOURCES: The estimated expenditures under 1981 law were calculated using expenditure data from U.S. Congressional Budget Office, "Major Legislative Changes in Human Resources Program Since January 1981," staff memorandum, August 1983. Tables 5 to 9 of that document provide the 1983 projected expenditures, and table 4 provides the changes in outlays for 1983. With the exception of Survivors' Insurance, the proportion of each program budget expended on mother-only families with children was calculated by multiplying the total expenditure by the appropriate proportion found in table 8 in chapter 4. Expenditures for Survivors' Insurance in 1985 were estimated by multiplying the ratio of average monthly (OASI) benefits paid to children in 1985 and 1980 (taken from table M10 in *U.S. Department of Health and Human Services, Social Security Bulletin*, August 1985, vol. 48, no. 8, p. 62) times the 1980 estimate for Survivors' Insurance expenditures on mother-only families with children in table 7. See Appendix A in chapter 4 for sources and explanation of calculation.

a. Includes state and local as well as federal expenditures.

President Reagan. The last column divides the third column by the first column to obtain an estimate of the reductions in percentage terms.

Congress agreed to cuts that amounted to $4.4 billion in total expenditures for mother-only families in fiscal 1985 (total shown in third column)—a 12 percent reduction in benefits. For at least three reasons, however, this 12 percent reduction in benefits does not translate neatly into a 12 percent reduction in the economic well-being of low-income mother-only families. First, there is an element of adding apples and oranges. Losing one dollar's worth of Medicaid benefits is not exactly equivalent to losing one dollar's worth of AFDC cash benefits. Second, some beneficiaries are able to compensate for reduced benefits by working more. Third, the benefit cuts were not spread evenly. Low-income employed mothers were the hardest hit. Two independent studies suggest that those who were cut from the AFDC rolls suffered *net* income declines of about 20 percent in response to the benefit cuts.[12] Finally, to derive the estimates in table 11 we cannot be certain that the cuts in benefits in each program affected mother-only families in proportion to their share of benefits in the program in previous years (as we have assumed in making our calculations).

The larger picture is quite clear, even with these caveats. The benefit cuts initiated under the Reagan administration modestly reduced the average economic well-being of low-income mother-only families and substantially reduced the economic well-being of single mothers who both received AFDC and worked.

Prevalence

Our review of the studies on the effects of reduced benefits on mother-only families (see chapter 3) suggests that welfare has a relatively large effect on the living arrangements of single women with children; a smaller, but still considerable effect on remarriage rates; and very small effects, if any, on divorce, separation, and out-of-wedlock births.

The range of estimates in the literature, as discussed in chapter 3, is large. The most extreme estimate at one end of the range would lead us to conclude that a 12 percent cut in benefits would result in an increase in the proportion of families with children headed by single women. The most extreme estimate at the other end would lead us to conclude that a 12 percent

---

12. Steven Cole et al., "Poverty and Welfare Recipiency after OBRA: Some Preliminary Evidence from Wisconsin," unpublished document (Madison, Wisconsin: University of Wisconsin, Institute for Research on Poverty, October 1983); and U.S. General Accounting Office, "An Evaluation of the 1981 AFDC Changes: Initial Analyses" (Washington, D.C.: U.S. Government Printing Office, April 2, 1984).

cut would mean a 3.3 percent decrease.[13] In our judgment, neither extreme is reliable. We reject the study that predicts an increase in single parenthood because it is counter to theory and to common sense. We reject the estimated 3 percent decrease as an overestimate because it includes the effect of welfare cuts on single women with children who move in with their parental family. The two most careful and comprehensive studies suggest that a 12 percent cut in welfare benefits would reduce prevalence by 0.9 to 1.6 percent.[14] To obtain an idea of how small such an effect is, consider the data in table 10. A 1.6 percent reduction would have reduced the prevalence of mother-only families in 1983 from 18.6 percent to 18.3 percent. These estimates are very crude because they depend on the assumption that a cut in average benefit levels has the same effect as a cut of equal size targeted primarily at recipients who are employed—the case of Reagan administration cuts. We do not know whether this means that our estimates are too high or too low.

Welfare Dependence

We begin this section with an analysis of the effects on welfare dependence of the 1981 Omnibus Budget Reconciliation Act benefit cuts that reduced the work incentives in the AFDC program. These particular cuts have generated much controversy and have been studied rather thoroughly. Next, we consider the effects of further across-the-board cuts in benefits.

---

13. See Joseph Minarik and Robert Goldfarb, "AFDC Income, Recipient Rates, and Family Dissolution: A Comment," *Journal of Human Resources*, vol. 9 (Spring 1976), pp. 243-57; and Majorie Honig, "The Impact of Welfare Payments on Levels of Family Stability," in U.S. Congress, Joint Economic Committee, *Studies in Public Welfare*, paper 12, pt. 1 (Washington, D.C.: U.S. Government Printing Office, 1973). The negative estimate is derived from Minarik and Goldfarb. Honig finds that a 10 percent increase in benefits would increase the rate of white female family headship by 2.6 percent and the rate for blacks by 3.9 percent. Multiplying each figure by 1.2 (the ratio of 12 percent to 10 percent) and weighting the black and white responses by their proportions in the population (0.13 and 0.87, respectively) yields an estimated increase of 3.3 percent.

14. See Sheldon Danziger et al., "Work and Welfare as Determinants of Female Poverty and Household Headship," *Quarterly Journal of Economics* (August 1982), p. 532. They estimate that eliminating welfare altogether would reduce the rate of female family headship for blacks by 2.3 percent and the rate for whites by 8.3 percent. Multiplying each figure by 12 percent and weighting each by the proportions of white and black families in the population yield an estimate of 0.9 percent. Bane and Ellwood found that a $100 per month increase in AFDC benefits in 1975 would have led to a 5 percent increase in the number of families with children. See David Ellwood and Mary Jo Bane, "The Impact of AFDC on Family Structure and Living Arrangements," report to the U.S. Department of Health and Human Services (Washington, D.C.: U.S. Department of Health and Human Services, 1984), p. 5 of the executive summary. Because the median AFDC benefit in 1975 was $264 per month, a $100 increase constitutes a 38 percent increase. An increase of 12 percent, therefore, would increase the number of female-headed families with children by 1.6 percent.

The large body of research on the effects of the 1981 Budget Reconciliation Act cut makes it clear that they did reduce dependence on welfare. Most of the studies have examined the behavior of beneficiaries who were employed and had their benefits reduced or eliminated.[15] The studies are unanimous in showing that only a minority of recipients who were cut from the AFDC rolls returned. However, there are two problems with their approach. First, they do not take into account those who would have returned to the rolls even in the absence of the act. Second, they do not consider the effect on beneficiaries who were not working at the time the benefit cut occurred—a major omission since 85 percent of the beneficiaries were in fact not working.

Both of these problems have been tackled in the best study to date, conducted by Usher and Griffith of the Research Triangle Institute.[16] They developed a nationwide sample of AFDC cases (earners and nonearners) from the September 1981 caseload and then tracked the earnings and welfare participation of the sample through October 1982. Because the Budget Reconciliation Act cuts took effect in January 1982, this provides ten months of postimplementation data. They also developed an analogous sample of AFDC cases from the September 1980 caseload and tracked their earnings and welfare participation through October 1981. This provides the authors with a year of data before the implementation of the act, with which they can compare the experience of their other sample taken after the act was put into effect. Whereas only 28 percent of the September 1980 cases with earnings were off welfare a year later, 55 percent of the September 1981 cases with earnings were off welfare a year later. This provides fairly convincing support for the conclusion that the 1981 act reduced the rate of welfare dependence among workers. Equally important, there was no difference before and after the act in the proportions of *nonearners* who were working ten months later, which suggests

---

15. See Cole et al., "Poverty and Welfare Recipiency after OBRA"; U.S. Government Accounting Office, "An Evaluation of the 1981 AFCD Changes"; C.L. Usher and J.D. Griffith, "The 1981 AFDC Amendments and Caseload Dynamics," unpublished document, Research Triangle Park, North Carolina, October 22, 1983; City of New York, Human Resources Administration, "Effects of Federal Budget Cutbacks on Employed AFDC Parents," New York, October 1983; Tom Joe, Rosemary Sarri, and Mitchell Ginsberg, "Working Female-Headed Families in Poverty: Three Studies of Income Families Affected by the AFDC Policy Changes in 1981," unpublished document (Washington, D.C.: Center for the Study of Social Policy, March 1984); and Ira Muscovice and William Craig, "The Omnibus Budget Reconciliation Act and the Working Poor," vol. 58, *Social Service Review* (March 1984), pp. 49-62.

16. Usher and Griffith, "The 1981 AFDC Amendments." The study by the U.S. Government Accounting Office also replicated the methodology used by Research Triangle Park (RTI), that is, comparing AFDC and work status of a control group to AFDC and work status of a group affected by the Omnibus Budget Reconciliation Act in five different cities and found similar results.

that reducing the work incentives in AFDC did not reduce the number of mothers who work their way off the welfare rolls.

One problem with the Usher and Griffith study (and with all the others conducted to date) is that it was carried out such a short time after the changes took place. It may take longer than ten months for knowledge about legislative changes to diffuse and for people's behavior to adapt to changes in rules.[17] Another problem is that these results are inconsistent with the findings of studies of the 1967 changes, which indicated that the proportion of recipients who were employed increased when recipients were allowed to keep the first $30 per month plus one third of *all* additional earnings.[18] We cannot explain this inconsistency, but in view of the different time periods and methodologies, we are not inclined to take the results from the earlier period as refuting the evidence of the Budget Reconciliation Act. We conclude that the elimination of eligibility for many employed AFDC mothers did reduce the percentage of single female heads of families who were dependent on welfare at least over the first year.

We derived a crude estimate, based on the Usher and Griffith study, of the extent to which the 12 percent cuts in benefits reduced caseloads. The estimate is 9.5 percent.[19] Given their data and our methodology, 9.5 percent is probably an underestimate.[20] A study by the General Accounting Office, which estimated the effects of the 1981 Budget Reconciliation Act on caseloads with a time-series model that controls for unemployment, estimated the

---

17. For a discussion of other limitations, see Robert A. Moffitt, "Assessing the Effects of the 1981 Federal AFDC Legislation on the Work Effort of Welfare Recipients: A Framework for Analysis and the Evidence to Date," unpublished document (Madison, Wisconsin: University of Wisconsin, Institute for Research on Poverty, January 1984). Although Moffitt attacks the RTI study because it fails to account for the effects of the act's changes on nonrecipients, the RTI findings that caseloads were reduced would be reinforced if this group were included; the act made welfare less desirable.

18. Michael Wiseman, "Work Incentives and Welfare Turnover," unpublished document (Berkeley, California: University of California at Berkeley, Department of Economics, October 13, 1983); and Vernon K. Smith, *Welfare Work Incentives: The Earnings Exemption and Its Impact upon AFDC Employment, Earnings and Program Costs*, Studies in Welfare Policy, no. 2 (Lansing, Michigan: State of Michigan Department of Social Services, 1974).

19. According to their study, working cases of 1981 were 21 percent more likely to be closed a year later than were cases of 1980. The difference among nonworkers was 7 percent. Any difference among nonworkers may seem surprising. But in view of the facts that some nonworkers become workers and that they would be more likely to leave AFDC after rather than before the act's enactment in 1981, the results are not surprising. Averaging the large effect among the small group of workers with the smaller effect among the larger group of nonworkers yields an estimate for the entire AFDC caseload of a reduction due to the omnibus act of 9.5 percent.

20. The estimate is too low because unemployment was higher in 1982 than in 1981. As a consequence, the 1981 cases should have had more difficulty finding employment and achieving independence ten months later than the 1980 cases did.

caseload decline at 14 percent. We think it reasonable to conclude that the 12 percent benefit cuts reduced caseloads by more than 9.5 percent but less than 14.0 percent.

The potential effects on welfare dependence of further across-the-board cuts in AFDC benefits depend both on the magnitude of the cuts and the alternative opportunities of recipients. To see this point, consider the effects of completely eliminating welfare, which, of course, eliminates welfare dependence by definition. Because a 100 percent cut in benefits reduces dependence by 100 percent, it follows that a 10 percent cut on *average* will reduce dependence by 10 percent. However, the effect of a *first* cut of 10 percent may be much smaller than that. It depends on the alternatives that AFDC mothers face. If these alternatives are sufficiently limited, a 10 percent cut in benefits will reduce their standard of living by 10 percent but have little or no effect on caseloads. Additional 10 percent cuts, however, would make even poor alternatives look increasingly more attractive.

Evidence for the proposition that reductions in welfare dependence are likely to be somewhat proportional to reductions in benefits was provided in table 10. Note that between 1975 and 1983 when benefits declined by more than 20 percent (see tables 7 and 11), the proportion of mother-only families dependent on welfare declined from 57 to 47 percent or by nearly 18 percent.

The Feasibility and Effects of Enforcing Work Requirements

To date, the enforcement of work requirements has had little effect on the income, dependence, and prevalence of mother-only families. The reason is simple. As explained earlier, although a number of states have job-search, workfare, or work supplementation programs, the work requirements have been effectively enforced for only a small portion of the AFDC caseload.

Some experts believe that enforcing work requirements is not feasible.[21] Skepticism, however, is nearly always warranted when policies are dismissed on feasibility grounds. At the very least, the source of the infeasibility should be identified. Is it technical, economic, or political?

In this section we analyze the feasibility of effectively enforcing work requirements. We conclude that not only is it technically, economically, and

---

21. See U.S. Government Accounting Office, "Evidence Is Insufficient." For a skeptical analysis of the economic efficiency of job creation, see George Johnson, "Structural Unemployment Consequences of Job Creation Policies" and comment by Irwin Garfinkel in John L. Palmer, ed., *Creating Jobs: Public Service Employment and Wage Subsidies* (Washington, D.C.: Brookings Institution, 1978), pp. 123-52.

politically feasible to enforce work requirements, but also that doing so, at least for mothers with no preschool-age children, probably would be a good social investment in terms of the potentially large positive effects on the income, welfare dependence, and prevalence of mother-only families.

The Feasibility of Enforcing Work Requirements

People who argue that work requirements are not technically feasible suggest that, because the unemployment rate exceeds 7 percent, it is impossible to find or create enough jobs to enforce the work requirements test. Although it is true that willingness to work cannot be tested if there are no jobs, a number of states have already demonstrated their ability to find and create jobs. More important, if it was possible to create 3.5 million Works Progress Administration (WPA) jobs in the midst of the Great Depression, it must be technically possible to find or create a like number now. Finally, the few scholars who have taken seriously the question of whether there is sufficient work to do have come to the conclusion that there is more than enough.[22]

People who argue that work test enforcement is not economically feasible typically mean that it costs too much. The standard practice of economists when exploring costs is to compare costs to benefits. There have been numerous cost-benefit analyses of government work and training programs. These studies suggest that (1) in the short-run costs increase because the costs of nearly all these programs are higher than any short-run reduction in AFDC benefits, (2) in the long run, the benefits to society as a whole (both participants and nonparticipants) exceed the during-program costs, and (3) the division of the net gains to society between participants and nonparticipants depends on how welfare and the work programs are structured.

The short-run increase in costs comes about because the government must pay for the cost of finding or creating the jobs as well as any benefits to recipients while they are being trained or placed.[23] In many cases the wages paid for work-relief benefits add to a higher total than the cash-relief benefits they replace. In addition, one major cost of enforcing work among single mothers is child care costs, which either the government or the mother must absorb.

---

22. Alan Fechter, "Assessing Large-Scale Public Job Creation," Research and Development Monograph 67 (Washington, D.C.: U.S. Department of Labor, 1979).

23. See Irwin Garfinkel and John Palmer, "Issues, Evidence, and Implications," in Palmer, *Creating Jobs*.

The long-run social benefits of work and training programs for mother-only families nearly always exceed the social costs.[24] This is because the future increases in the earnings of participants (the principal social benefit of work and training programs) eventually more than offset the initial cost increase.[25] This difference due to the work program is generally large. In the Supported Work Demonstration—which is generally agreed to be the single best study from a scientific point of view[26] and is representative in terms of earnings gains of the estimates in other studies[27]—the present value of benefits exceeded the present value of costs by $8,000 per participant.[28]

There are three reasons why the estimated benefits from the programs that have been evaluated may overestimate the benefits from an ongoing national program. First, some of the earnings gains of beneficiaries of work programs come at the cost of displacing other workers. In the evaluation of the Supported Work Demonstration, the authors of the cost-benefit analysis showed that even if 75 percent of the earnings gains of participants was due to displacement of other workers and therefore was not counted, supported work would still have been a profitable investment.[29] Few economists believe that displacement effects are likely to be higher than that.

Second, with the exception of a few recent workfare programs, the work and training programs that have been evaluated have been voluntary. Even in the workfare programs, the extent to which participation has in fact been

---

24. See Lauri J. Bassi and Orley Ashenfelter, "The Effect of Direct Job Creation and Training Programs on Low Skilled Workers," in Sheldon H. Danziger and Daniel H. Weinberg, eds., *Fighting Poverty* (Cambridge, Massachusetts: Harvard University Press, 1986), pp. 133-51; Robinson G. Hollister, Jr., Peter Kemper, and Rebecca Maynard, *The National Supported Work Demonstration* (Madison, Wisconsin: University of Wisconsin Press, 1984); and Judith M. Gueron, *Work Initiatives for Welfare Recipients: Lessons from a Multi-State Experiment* (New York: Manpower Demonstration Research Corporation, March 1986).

25. For a discussion of cost-benefit analysis of these programs see Hollister, Kemper, and Maynard, *the National Supported Work Demonstration*.

26. Unlike most job training and employment programs, the Supported Work Demonstration was conducted as a formal experiment, with participants randomly assigned to experimental and control groups. Furthermore, the follow-up period in the experiment—three years—is much longer than normal.

27. Estimates vary on how much of the benefit goes to the participants in the form of increased earnings (see further discussion in text below). Bassi and Ashenfelter, "Effect of Direct Job Creation," find the earnings gain for women in these programs ranges from $600 to $1,200 per year. The earnings gain from the Supported Work Demonstration is about $900—the midpoint of this range.

28. Early cost-benefit analyses attempted to measure only social costs and benefits. They ignored transfers and taxes as representing merely a shift from one person to another within the society. For examples of different findings with respect to the distribution of benefits, see Gueron, *Work Initiatives*. For an excellent discussion and illustration of this issue, see Hollister, Kemper, and Maynard, *The National Supported Work Demonstration*.

29. Hollister, Kemper, and Maynard, *The National Supported Work Demonstration*, p. 267.

compulsory is unclear because of the small proportion of the caseload served in most of the programs. It seems likely that unwilling workers will be somewhat less productive than volunteers.

Third, and most important, virtually none of the participants in the work and training programs so far have had preschool-age children. Supported work, for example, limited eligibility to women with no children under age six. The child care costs for preschool-age children are substantially higher than those for school-age children.

It is possible that the benefits of creating jobs for AFDC mothers with preschool-age children will still exceed the costs, but we have no good evidence on the matter. Prudence as well as scientific curiosity suggest evaluation on a demonstration basis before proceeding to extend the work requirement to parents with preschool-age children.

We now come to the question of political feasibility. Several major reasons are typically given for believing that political constraints will prevent the country from embarking on a massive job-creation program to enforce work requirements in AFDC. The first is that the country has never accepted such a policy. Recall that work relief was so controversial in the 1930s that President Roosevelt proposed it in a separate bill that never passed. A second reason is that there are some natural opponents to job creation for the purpose of enforcing work among AFDC recipients. These include workers and employers who are threatened by the potential competition from AFDC mothers if they become workers. The Supported Work Demonstration might have run into more political opposition if it had tried to create enough jobs to serve an appreciable portion of the AFDC caseload. A third reason is that even good investments that increase government expenditures in the short run are going to have difficult political sledding in the environment of huge federal deficits.

Counterarguments have been offered. Simply because something has not been done to date does not mean that it cannot be done in the future. Every proposed change in public policy has natural opponents. Finally, even if the deficit proves to be a short-run roadblock, it will not be a permanent fixture of the political landscape. We believe that, in view of the emerging consensus that poor single mothers should be expected to work, the extent to which creating jobs for single mothers has major social benefits is likely to be the principal determinant of its political feasibility in the long run.

The Effects of Enforcing Work Requirements

We examine the effects of enforcing work requirements on the well-being, welfare dependency, and prevalence of mother-only families in the following paragraphs.

Economic Well-Being. According to economic theory, enforcing work requirements will reduce the economic well-being of all AFDC mothers who would not have chosen to work in the absence of the work requirement. Even if their incomes increased, their total economic well-being would be lower, by definition, because their behavior indicates that they would have preferred the combination of lower income and more time for rearing children, other work in the home, or leisure.

But perhaps this definition of well-being is overly restrictive. One of the most striking findings in the evaluations of workfare programs in several states is the very positive comments on the program given by the participating mothers.[30] They liked what they were doing and believed the work requirement was fair. Thus it is possible that, rather than the work requirements being coercive, the jobs created to enforce the work requirements are providing an opportunity to mothers who already want to work. It is also possible that, although the work requirements are coercive, they change the mother's evaluation of the desirability of working and, therefore, change her work-leisure choice in the longer run. That these effects cannot be quantified does not make them any less important.

The effects of enforcing work requirements on the incomes of single mothers, however, can be quantified. These effects depend on the magnitude of the increased earnings of the participants, the nature of the work programs created to enforce the work requirement, and the rules of the AFDC program. We begin with increased earnings.

Estimates of the average gain in earnings for single mothers in work and training programs range from about $600 to $1,200 per year. Some analysts have dismissed such gains on the grounds that they fill only a small portion of the poverty gap—the difference between the actual incomes of poor families and the incomes they would need to raise themselves out of poverty.[31] These analysts have compared $600 and $1,200 to the average poverty gap for mother-only families—$4,000—and noted that these programs on average fill well under one-third of the poverty gap. But if the gains are looked at in another way, $600 to $1,200 per year is quite substantial. In the Supported Work Demonstration the average increase of $900 per year in earnings represented an increase of nearly 50 percent over the earnings of the control group. And, as we have noted, the earnings increase was large enough to generate a net social profit per program participant of $8,000. Even if we

30. Gueron, *Work Initiatives*.

31. See Henry M. Levin, "A Decade of Policy Developments in Improving Education and Training for Low Income Populations," in Robert H. Haveman, ed. *A Decade of Federal Anti-Poverty Programs* (New York: Academic Press, 1977), pp. 123-88.

estimate displacement at 75 percent, this leaves us with a net social gain of $2,000 per participant. How much of the net social gain accrues to participants and how much to taxpayers depends on the relative magnitudes of the effect on earnings versus the effect on benefit receipt. If the increase in earnings is substantially greater than the decrease in welfare and other benefits, the incomes of the mother-only families who are poor will substantially increase. If employment opportunities in an economy are ample and attractive, a work program that does little more than exert pressure to enter the labor market may benefit both participants and taxpayers. But if employment opportunities are few and unattractive, beneficiaries will work less and gain less. This depends in good part on the rate of aggregate economic activity (discussed further below).

Welfare Dependence. In general, work programs may be expected to decrease welfare dependence not only by reducing the proportion of total income derived from welfare, but also by shrinking the absolute number receiving welfare. This is true because there are always some beneficiaries who are at the margin between choosing welfare and another alternative, such as work or remarriage. Requiring work in return for benefits will be enough to push some of these beneficiaries over the margin and remove them from welfare altogether.

Reductions in welfare dependence will increase with the size of the investment in job placement, work experience, and training. Giving single mothers who head families work experience or skill training costs more money initially, but in the long run, the investment pays off in higher earnings. Other things being equal, the higher the earnings of these women, the less dependent on welfare they will be.

Some research suggests that if the labor market is strong, a modest proportion of AFDC mothers need little more than good professional help in locating jobs. Preliminary evidence from San Diego, which has unemployment rates well below average, indicates that job-search assistance has been a profitable service in such a labor market.[32]

Prevalence. The effects of enforcing work requirements on the prevalence of mother-only families are ambiguous, depending on the extent to which enforcement improves the incomes of single mothers and alters the relative earnings opportunities of men and women.

If enforcement of work requirements does not increase the incomes of single mothers, welfare becomes less attractive and marriage more attractive than is now the case. If, conversely, enforcing work requirements increases

---

32. See Gueron, *Work Initiatives*.

the incomes of single mothers, they will become less dependent on welfare and less dependent on men. Recall that in chapter 3 we found that changes in the relative employment opportunities of men and women were more important than changes in welfare in accounting for the growth of mother-only families during the 1960s and 1970s. If the work opportunities of poor men as well as poor women are improved simultaneously, however, the attractiveness of marriage to both parties could increase.

At this point there is no scientific basis for estimating the magnitude of these effects, but common sense and empirical evidence both suggest that the effect on blacks is likely to be greater than the effect on whites because the economic status of blacks is so much more precarious and therefore more affected by welfare policy. The employment prospects of young, unskilled, black men are now so bleak that cash welfare must be an attractive alternative to marriage for young, unskilled, black women. Increasing the skills of young black women without doing the same for young black men could easily exacerbate an already bad situation.

The Effects of the 1984 Child Support Enforcement Amendments

Measuring the effects of the 1984 child support legislation on female-headed families is more difficult than measuring the effects of the benefit cuts. First, states are just beginning to implement the legislation, so any effects have not yet materialized. Second, there is only a small amount of research that relates child support to the outcomes of interest here. Thus we must rely on theoretical expectations and relatively crude empirical estimates.

Incomes

The income of a mother-only family can increase as a consequence of wage withholding in response to delinquency of the supporting parent, state guidelines for determining the level of child support obligations, incentives for states to increase collections for children not on AFDC, incentives for increasing interstate collections, and the particular method chosen to share the gains of increased child support collections from noncustodial fathers with the custodial mothers and their children. Thus the size of the increases will depend on how the 1984 child support legislation is implemented on both the federal and state levels. There will be few positive effects if the states enact weak standards and neither the number nor the amount of child support awards increases much; if the states fail to effectively enforce the new withholding of wages law; and if federal, state, and local resources to enforce child support are cut. On the other hand, there is a great potential for increase in the incomes of female-headed families from further strengthening public enforcement of private payments.

To estimate the potential of child support enforcement we explored what would happen if all children potentially eligible for support obtained a child support award based on some agreed-upon standard, and what the outcome would be if all such children received the full amount due them. According to the simple percentage-of-income standard used in Wisconsin, an adequate child support obligation is equal to 17 percent of the gross income of the noncustodial parent for one child, 25 percent for two, 29 percent for three, 31 percent for four, and 34 percent for five or more children. (In our calculations we tax only the first $50,000 of income for child support purposes.) Using this standard, we estimate that the incomes of families headed by women would increase by more than $10 billion if all children received the full amount due them.[33] The poverty gap would be reduced by nearly $2 billion. The estimates are not extremely sensitive to the standard chosen. The most commonly used standards lead to much the same results. But the estimates assume child support awards and perfect payment in every case. Thus a sizable portion of these gains will only be realized if the 1984 child support reforms are both effectively implemented and strengthened.

Congress has approved two alternative methods of sharing some of the increased collections of child support with low-income families on AFDC. One is now required of all states; the other is permitted in only one. The first approach is to ignore some of the child support payment in calculating AFDC grants. Congress has required all states to ignore the first $50 per month. That requirement would, if child support were more effectively enforced, increase the incomes of all people on AFDC by 16 percent. It would also increase the number of mother-only families who will continue to receive AFDC.

---

33. These estimates were derived from a microsimulation using the 1979 *Current Population Survey*, Child Support Supplement. To derive the estimates of potential child support collections, we first had to estimate the income of absent fathers. The critical assumption in the methodology is that the relation between wives' characteristics and husbands' earnings in the U.S. population is the same as the relation between the custodial mothers' characteristics to the noncustodial fathers' income. The predictions derived from this assumption were then adjusted for marital status by marital status coefficients derived from a regression on male earnings. Tests for selection bias revealed none. This work represents an extension of work by Oellerich and Garfinkel. For a more detailed description of the methodology, see Donald Oellerich and Irwin Garfinkel, "Distributional Impact of Alternative Child Support Systems," *Policy Studies Journal*, vol. 12, no. 1 (September 1983), pp. 119-29. For even more detail, see Donald I. Oellerich, *The Effects of Potential Child Support Transfers on Wisconsin AFDC Costs, Caseloads and Recipient Well-Being*, Institute for Research on Poverty special report 35 (Madison, Wisconsin: Institute for Research on Poverty, 1984), p. 140.

The alternative approach is to use increased child support collections to help fund a nonwelfare benefit that encourages work. This approach is being pursued on a demonstration basis in the state of Wisconsin under the auspices of the 1984 Child Support Act. Under the Wisconsin child support assurance system, support obligations are determined by a simple legislated formula. The obligation is withheld from wages and other sources of income in all cases, just as income and payroll taxes are. The child is entitled to receive the money paid by the noncustodial parent or an assured child-support benefit, whichever is larger.[34] Thus the savings in AFDC that results from increased child support collections is funneled back into the system to increase the economic well-being of poor families with children eligible for child support. Because the assured child support benefit will be reduced by no more than 17 cents for each dollar earned, compared to a reduction of 70 cents or more in AFDC benefits, it will improve incentives to work.

Garfinkel and Oellerich have estimated that a child support assurance program, if adopted nationally, could reduce the poverty gap of families with children potentially eligible for child support by nearly 40 percent and AFDC caseloads by nearly 50 percent. The estimated savings to the government range from slightly over $2 billion to a net cost of nearly 4 billion, depending on how much improvement there is in child support collections from noncustodial parents. If child support were ordered and paid in 100 percent of the cases, according to the Wisconsin percentage-of-income standard, the government would save $2.3 billion. Currently only a little more than 40 percent of that standard is paid. If child support collections do not improve at all, the cost of a child support assurance program will be close to $4 billion. If 70 percent of the Wisconsin standard is paid, the government will approximately break even.[35]

Prevalence

Enhanced enforcement of child support is, on balance, likely to reduce the prevalence of female-headed families.[36] We are not able to estimate the

---

34. The child's parent may also be entitled to receive an employment-expense subsidy of $1.50 an hour.

35. These estimates are reported in Irwin Garfinkel, "The Role of Child Support Insurance in Antipoverty Policy," vol. 479, *ANNALS*, American Academy of Political and Social Science (May 1985), pp. 119-31. The estimate of the effects of no improvement was not included in this article, but was developed for this book as an extension of the previous work. For a more detailed description of the methodology, see the work cited note 33.

36. For a more detailed analysis, see Murray MacDonald, "Behavioral Responses to Better Child Support: A Family Impact Analysis," in Irwin Garfinkel and Margo Melli, eds., *Child Support: Weaknesses of the Old and Features of a Proposed New System*, Special Report 32-C, vol. 3 (Madison, Wisconsin: University of Wisconsin, Institute for Research on Poverty, February 1982), pp. 117-41.

size of this effect, but in the long run it could be large—coming from effects both on out-of-wedlock births and on divorce and custody.

Stronger child support enforcement for cases involving out-of-wedlock births is likely to eventually result, in our view, in a decrease in such births by the following reasoning. Increasing the probability that men will have to contribute to the support of children they father out of wedlock will increase their incentives to father fewer children. Of course, young women's incentive to have fewer children will be reduced. However, in view of the fact that unmarried mothers are already eligible for welfare, stronger child support enforcement is unlikely to reduce the incentive for young women to have fewer children any further than welfare already reduces it. The increased incentive for men to father fewer children should thus predominate. For stricter child support enforcement to have an appreciable effect on out-of-wedlock birthrates, however, the country will have to drastically increase the proportion of cases in which paternity is established. The 1984 child support legislation does little to achieve that, but the record of other countries such as Sweden, which establishes paternity in more than 90 percent of out-of-wedlock births, suggests that improvement is possible.[37]

With respect to divorce and custody, the argument is as follows. In about 90 percent of divorces, mothers obtain custody, and fathers are usually obligated to pay child support. If child support is more strictly enforced, the prospective custodial parent contemplating a divorce will be more able to manage financially. The prospective noncustodial parent, however, will feel less able to manage the divorce. Whether this situation will lead to more or fewer divorces for middle- and upper-income families is impossible to say a priori. But for lower-income families, on balance, it should decrease divorce. Welfare already provides more security to the prospective custodial parent than enhanced child support enforcement will provide, so the prospective custodial parent's incentives will be unchanged. The effective financial obligations of the prospective noncustodial parents will be increased, reducing the incentive to divorce. Enhanced child support enforcement also should accelerate, at least somewhat, the trends toward greater assumption of custody on the part of fathers because they will be less likely to evade the financial responsibility of giving up custody.

Welfare Dependence

Increases in child support enforcement will raise the income of some poor mothers enough to enable them to get off welfare. Estimating how much,

---

37. See Irwin Garfinkel and Annette Sorenson, "Sweden's Child Support System: Lessons for the United States," *Social Work*, vol. 27 (1982), pp. 509-15.

however, is difficult. First, we would have to know how much child support collections will increase as a result of wage withholding and the new state standards. As already noted, there is no way of predicting the latter. Second, we would have to know what effects the increased collections have on AFDC caseloads.

As before, we can develop somewhat crude estimates of the potential decrease in AFDC caseloads from enhanced child support enforcement. Using existing award levels as a standard, we estimate that caseloads would be decreased by less than 5 percent.[38] Using the Wisconsin standard described earlier, we estimate that caseloads would decrease by 25 percent assuming a 100 percent collection rate. As before, the latter estimate should be viewed as an upper bound because award levels and collection effectiveness are likely to be lower than the levels projected in our estimates.[39]

As described in the previous section, the alternative methods of sharing the increased child support collections from noncustodial fathers of children on AFDC with the mothers and children on AFDC makes a profound difference in welfare caseloads. A federally assured benefit within a universal child support assurance program could reduce welfare caseloads by nearly half.

The Effects of Macroeconomic Policy on Mother-Only Families

Changes in public income transfer policy and private child support were not the only changes under the Reagan administration that affected mothers heading families. In this section we discuss macroeconomic policies, which could also have large effects.

In the two years before President Reagan took office the consumer price index rose by 24 percent. By 1981, unemployment had increased to more than 7 percent.[40] During President Reagan's first term, the United States suffered the deepest and longest recession since the Great Depression in the 1930s. Unemployment amounted to 7.5 percent in 1981, 9.6 percent in 1982,

---

38. See note 33 in this chapter for a description of the data and methods used.

39. Currently 80 percent of families on AFDC receive no child support. U.S. Department of Health and Human Services, Office of Child Support Enforcement, *Child Support Enforcement Ninth Annual Report to Congress for the Period Ending September 30, 1984* (Washington, D.C.: DHHS, December 1984), p. 90. The average number of AFDC cases for which a collection was made was almost 650,000. The AFDC caseload is over 3 million. Thus only about one in five AFDC cases receives anything.

40. See *Economic Report of the President, January 1985*.

9.6 percent in 1983, and 7.5 percent in 1984.[41] The back of the severest inflation since 1946-47 was broken at the same time. Inflation rates were 9.4 percent in 1981, 6.0 percent in 1982, 3.8 percent in 1983, and 4.4 percent in 1984.

The important question here is, what were the effects of the recession on families headed by women? We answer this by estimating what the effects would have been if alternative policies had been pursued. In developing our estimates of the effects of the recession on mother-only families, we compare the actual Reagan administration policies (Sawhill and Stone call them "cold turkey") to a set of policies ("gradualism") that would have led to a milder recession and more inflation than was experienced under President Reagan.[42]

The Effects of Unemployment and Inflation on Income

We consider first the effects of higher unemployment and then the effects of lower inflation. At least some of the effects of unemployment (and inflation) are temporary; now that the recession is over, these effects on income should end. Still, the consequences of unemployment are worth analyzing because even temporary declines in income cause suffering. Moreover, some effects may be long lasting. Wage rates depend on work experience; unemployment results in a permanent loss of experience and of concomitant wage gains. Furthermore, single women with children who become unemployed may become discouraged and stay out of the labor force for extended periods of time.

In our estimate of the effects of the recession on the incomes of mother-only families, we consider only the short-run effects. Using the estimates developed by Gramlich and Laren of the effects of previous recessions on the incomes of various groups, we estimate that if the country had experienced a milder recession, the incomes of families headed by single women would have been $3.1 billion higher during the four-year period, an average of about $0.8 billion per year.[43]

41. Isabel V. Sawhill and Charles F. Stone, "The Economy: The Key to Success," in Palmer and Sawhill, eds., *The Reagan Record*, p. 70.

42. Ibid., table VIII-1. Under gradualism the unemployment rates would have been 7.2 percent in 1981, 7.8 percent in 1982, 7.5 percent in 1983, and 6.8 percent in 1984; the corresponding inflation rates were, respectively, 9.4 percent, 7.0 percent, 5.6 percent, and 5.8 percent.

43. Edward M. Gramlich and Deborah S. Laren, "How Widespread Are Income Losses in a Recession?" in Bawden, *The Social Contract Revisited*, pp. 157-80. They estimate that for each percentage-point increase in the aggregate unemployment rate, the incomes of female heads of families decline by 0.7 percent. In 1980, mean family income for female-headed families with children under age eighteen equaled $12,743 in 1983 dollars. In 1981 and 1982, there were

This estimate suggests that the effect of the recession on the incomes of mother-only families was less than one-fifth as large as the effect of the budget cuts in welfare programs. Conversely, the losses to mother-only families from unemployment are much larger than their gains from reduced inflation. As noted in chapter 4, inflation from 1975 to 1980 eroded the real value of AFDC benefits because states failed to increase benefits to keep pace with inflation. If inflation had been higher in the 1981-84 period, states might have increased benefits by no more than they actually did. In the long run it is hard to imagine that legislators make decisions on nominal rather than real values, but in the short run this is possible. We developed a crude upper-bound estimate by assuming that legislated increases in AFDC benefits are completely insensitive to the rate of inflation. Using this assumption, even after four years real AFDC benefits were only $400 million higher than they otherwise would have been—in comparison with the income loss of about $800 million per year suffered by mother-only families because of higher unemployment.[44] If our crude estimate of the net effects of increased unemployment and reduced inflation of the 1981-83 recession on the incomes of mother-only families was the only research on the topic, we might be more hesitant to conclude that increased unemployment hurt such families much more than reduced inflation helped them. But an abundant literature provides estimates that support our conclusion.[45]

The Effects of Increased Unemployment on Prevalence

Unemployment of men, as we discussed in chapter 2, is expected on theoretical grounds to break up marriages and reduce remarriages. On balance, the empirical evidence discussed in chapter 2 provides support for the theoretically predicted effect. But estimates of the magnitude of the relation between unemployment rates and prevalence of mother-only families span a

---

5.6 million and 5.9 million female-headed families with children under age eighteen. We assumed the number of families in 1983 and 1984 was the same as 1982. To find the income base without recession, we multiplied the 1980 mean family income times the number of families in each year.

44. If the less drastic recession policy had been pursued, according to a conventional macro model, inflation would have been the same in 1981, 1.0 percent higher in 1982, 1.3 percent higher in 1983, and 1.4 percent higher in 1984 (see Sawhill and Stone, "The Economy: The Key to Success"). Assuming that state legislators would have reacted no differently with higher inflation, the real value of AFDC benefits would have been 3.7 percent higher in 1984 or less than $400 million in the year with the largest effect, compared with an average twice that (nearly $800 million) for each year for the effect of unemployment.

45. For a review of this literature, see Rebecca M. Blank and Alan S. Blinder, "Macroeconomics, Income Distribution, and Poverty," in Danziger and Weinberg, eds., *Fighting Poverty*, pp. 180-208.

wide range. Depending on the particular study chosen, the effect on prevalence produced by the cold turkey rather than the gradualist approach ranges from zero to a 3.3 percent increase per year.[46]

The Effects of Increased Unemployment on Welfare Dependence

A few studies have estimated the effects of unemployment on AFDC caseloads, and the estimates vary widely. At the low end, a study by the General Accounting Office suggests that if unemployment in 1982 had been only 7.5 percent rather than 9.6 percent, AFDC caseloads would have been increased by 0.2 percent. Another government study suggests that caseloads would have increased by 4 percent.[47] At the high end, two studies suggest that the AFDC rolls would have increased 17 to 18 percent.[48] In choosing

---

46. We limit our consideration to studies based on aggregate cross-sectional data, which, as described in chapter 2, are least subject to bias. For the lower-bound estimate, Honig, "The Impact of Welfare Payments," and also Ross and Sawhill, *Time of Transition*, found an insignificant effect for blacks in 1970. Minarik and Goldfarb also found an insignificant effect for a combined sample of blacks and whites in 1970. For the upper-bound estimate, we began with Caldwell's estimate that a 2 percentage-point rise in the unemployment rate increased the marital disruption rate by 10 percentage points. We then adjusted the estimate by the excess unemployment resulting from the cold turkey rather than the gradualism approach, that is, by the ratios of 0.3, 1.8, 2.1, and 0.7 (for 1981, 1982, 1983, and 1984) to 2.0 (for 1980, the base year). Doing this yielded estimates of a 0.15, 0.9, 1.05, and 0.35 percentage-point increase in divorce rates per year for the four years. In 1980 there were 24,634,000 families with children. Multiplying the percentage increase in divorce rates for each year times this number yielded estimates of 36,951; 221,706; 258,657; and 172,438 additional female-headed families in each of the four years, for a total of 689,752 or an average of 172,438 per year. Thus the average annual increase in female-headed families was about 3.3 percent.

47. The first estimate is derived from U.S. General Accounting Office, "Evidence Is Insufficient," pp. 52-54. Its unemployment coefficient is 0.0538. An unemployment rate of 9.8 percent for women in July 1982 translated into 715,000 unemployed, whereas a rate of only 7.5 percent would have translated into only 546,825 unemployed women. We multiplied the difference times the coefficient and divided by 3.5 million (the 1980 caseload). The second estimate is from Kevin Hollenbeck, "An Analysis of the Impact of Unemployment and Inflation on AFDC Costs and Caseloads," report by Mathematica Policy Research prepared for U.S. Department of Health, Education, and Welfare, Social and Rehabilitation Service, Project 6965, February 13, 1976, pp. 4-6. The elasticity of caseloads with respect to the unemployment rate was 0.13 (equal to the percentage change in caseloads over the percentage change in unemployment rate). The 1980 caseload of 3.5 million was used as the benchmark figure.

48. The estimate of 17 percent is derived from Robert Moffitt, "An Economic Model of Welfare Stigma," *American Economic Review* (December 1983), pp. 1023-35. Table 3 in that article, p. 1033, shows the effects of a 2 percent fall in the unemployment rate to be a decrease in participation from 0.356 to 0.295. We simply took the difference and divided by 0.356 to estimate the effect of a 2 percent increase. See also Michael Barth et al., "The Cyclical Behavior of Income Transfer Programs: A Case Study of the Current Recession," Technical Analysis Paper 7, ISP/ASPEDHEW (Washington, D.C.: DHEW, October 1975). Hollenbeck,

our preferred estimate, we rely on two pieces of data—the observed data as reported in table 10 showing slight decreases in AFDC participation rates in 1981 and 1982, and our estimates of the effects of the budget cuts on caseloads showing reductions of 9 to 14 percent—and one assumption, that nothing other than budget cuts and unemployment affected caseloads. We conclude that the recession increased caseloads by roughly 7 to 12 percent—nearly offsetting the opposite effects of the benefit cuts.

The Potential Effects of Antiabortion Policy

Twice within the recent past, public policy concerning abortion has shifted radically. In 1973 the U.S. Supreme Court struck down state laws against abortion. (Only California, New York, and a few other states had laws in 1973 routinely permitting abortion.)[49] Shortly thereafter, Medicaid, the federal medical assistance program for the poor, began paying routinely for abortions of poor women. In 1977, Congress amended the Social Security Act to end Medicaid funding for abortions.

Radical public policy shifts twice within such a short time indicate that the issue is very divisive and that policy could easily shift again. Hence the fact that President Reagan and the Republican party favor a constitutional amendment to outlaw abortion should be taken seriously.[50] What effect would outlawing abortion have on the prevalence of female headship?

In recent years there have been about 1.5 million abortions per year in the United States.[51] About 675,000 of these prevent first births among unmarried women and, thereby, the formation of new mother-only families.[52] If legal abortions were unavailable, some of the women who would have obtained legal abortions will take other action—usually illegal abortions— to prevent births. Some will carry the babies to term and marry the father or

---

"An Analysis of the Impact of Unemployment and Inflation," calculated the elasticity of case-loads with respect to unemployment to be 0.66, which implies an 18 percent increase in caseloads in response to an increase in unemployment from 7.5 to 9.6 percent.

49. By routine, we mean without requiring a special justification such as rape, incest, or threat of life to the mother.

50. See Lester M. Salamon and Alan J. Abramson, "Governance: The Politics of Re-trenchment," in Palmer and Sawhill, *The Reagan Record*, pp. 41-42.

51. Stanley K. Henshaw et al., "Abortion Services in the United States, 1979 and 1980," *Family Planning Perspectives* vol. 4, no. 1 January-February 1982.

52. About three-fourths of abortions are obtained by unmarried women and about three-fifths of all births to unmarried women are first births. Assuming the proportion of abortions for first births of unmarried is the same yields the estimate of 650,000 in the text. See U.S. Department of Health and Human Services, "Trends and Differentials in Births to Unmarried Women: United States, 1970-76," publication 80-1914 (Washington, D.C.: DHEW, May 1980), table C, p. 8.

give the baby up for adoption. Some will avoid pregnancy through better contraceptive practices or sexual abstinence.

The little research that has been done on the effects of legalizing or outlawing abortion on birthrates suggests (1) that perhaps 12 percent of the roughly 675,000 unmarried women who now obtain legal abortions would become single heads of families and (2) that the extent to which the effect is appreciably larger or smaller than 12 percent depends critically on the availability of illegal abortions.

If only 12 percent of those who would have had abortions became single mothers heading families as a result of outlawing abortion, about 80,000 such families would be added per year. A crude estimate of the annual flow into female headship suggests that an increase of 80,000 would increase the stock or prevalence of female headship by 4.2 percent.[53] This is a modest effect— but it is almost three times the 1.6 percent decrease in the stock of such families estimated to have that resulted from the 12 percent cuts in benefits to female-headed families. And the latter is an upper-bound estimate. In other words, the decrease in the prevalence of female headship that resulted from the Reagan administration's cut in benefits is dwarfed by the potential effects of outlawing abortion.

The research basis for these conclusions is as follows: Sklar and Berkov, by comparing the actual to predicted birthrates in 1971, estimated that about 14 to 17 percent of the abortions to unmarried mothers in 1971 prevented out-of-wedlock births. The predicted rates, however, were obtained by a crude extrapolation of trends.[54] Tietze, by comparing birthrates in New York City before and after abortion was legalized, concluded that about 90 percent of

---

53. In 1981 there were 375,768 first births to unmarried women. See National Center for Health Statistics, *Vital Statistics of the United States, 1981*, vol. 1, *Natality*, publication (PHS) 85-1113 (Washington, D.C.: U.S. Government Printing Office, 1985), table 1-71, p. 1-226.

There were 1,213,000 divorces in 1981 (table 2-1, p. 2-5). Fifty-five percent of these had children present (table 2-10, p. 2-11) yielding 667,150 divorces with children present. See National Center for Health Statistics, *Vital Statistics of the United States, 1981*, vol. 3, *Marriage and Divorce*, publication (PHS) 85-1121 (Washington, D.C.: U.S. Government Printing Office, 1985).

For 1981 the ratio of separations plus divorces to the number of divorces was 2.28. (This is based on data from the 1982 National Survey of Family Growth, limited to women under age forty-five, and is probably close to the appropriate population. This estimate is based on about 200 marriage breakups a year but appears stable over at least a three-year period.) Use of this crude multiplier gives the rough figure of about 1.52 million breakups a year in which children are involved.

Adding the approximately 376,000 first births to unmarried women results in an estimate of the annual flow into female headship as of 1981 of 1.9 million.

54. June Sklar and Beth Berkov, "Abortion, Illegitimacy, and the American Birth Rate," *Science*, vol. 185 (September 1974), pp. 909-15.

legal abortions replaced illegal abortions and, as a consequence, only about 10 percent of legal abortions prevented births.[55] According to a more recent study of upstate New York by Tu and Herzfeld, the legalization of abortion interrupted and temporarily reversed an upward trend in out-of-wedlock birthrates, but by 1979 the rate was again as high as the preabortion peak.[56] Tietze has noted that birthrates declined in the Soviet Union after a 1936 liberalization of abortion and more recently in Bulgaria, Czechoslovakia, and Romania after similar liberalizations.[57] Neither Tu and Herzfeld nor Tietze tried to quantify the effects.

It should be noted here that the effects on birthrates of outlawing abortion may be different from the effects of legalizing abortion. Tietze, for example, noted the experiences of two nations in which access to abortion was severely restricted following a period during which abortion was very accessible.[58] In the first, Romania, the fertility rate increased from 62 per 1,000 before restriction of access to abortion in 1966 to 140 per 1,000 in the next twelve months, and then dropped back but only to 90 per 1,000 by the mid-1970s. In the second, Hungary, the fertility rate increased from 68 per 1,000 in 1973 to 86 per 1,000 in the year following restriction of access, and then dropped back below the previous rate (to 64 per 1,000) by 1981. What these two experiences suggest is that the effects of outlawing abortion can be quite volatile and, at least in some social environments, long lasting.

In summary, these studies suggest that most, though not all, women currently obtaining abortions would find alternatives if legal abortions were outlawed. The principal alternative would be illegal abortions. Based on the estimates of Sklar and Tietze and the experiences of Romania and Hungary, a reasonable estimate of the proportion that would form mother-only families is about 12 percent.

The Reagan administration's policy on abortion is part of a broader attempt to return to more traditional values with regard to sex, marriage, and family.[59] If abortion is outlawed as part of a successful attempt to return to

---

55. Christopher Tietze, "Two Years' Experience with a Liberal Abortion Law: Its Impact on Fertility Trends in New York City," *Family Planning Perspectives*, vol. 5, no. 1 (Winter 1973) pp. 36-41.

56. Edward Jow-Ching Tu and Peter M. Herzfeld, "The Impact of Legal Abortion on Marital and Nonmarital Fertility in Upstate New York," *Family Planning Perspectives*, vol. 14, no. 1 (January-February 1982), pp. 37-46.

57. Christopher Tietze, *Induced Abortion: A World Review, 1982* (New York: Population Council, 1982).

58. Ibid.

59. For example, the administration issued a regulation soon after taking office that required federally funded family-planning clinics to inform parents of minors who receive prescription

more traditional values, the number of mother-only families resulting from out-of-wedlock births might decline in the long run despite the absence of legal abortion.[60] In the meantime, making abortion illegal could easily add 80,000 new families headed by single women to our society each year. Only widespread availability of illegal abortions will prevent the number of new female-headed families from being much higher.

A Scorecard of Achievements of the Reagan Administration

When the effects of policy during the Reagan administration on the economic well-being, welfare dependence, and prevalence of female-headed families are considered together, an interesting and ironic pattern emerges. Despite the priority the Reagan administration has given to reducing the prevalence and dependence of families headed by single women—as opposed to reducing their economic insecurity—the policies that have emerged during the Reagan administration may ultimately increase economic well-being and increase prevalence.

In the short run, the decreases in public benefits and the recession clearly reduced the economic well-being of mother-only families, but in the long run the positive effects of increased enforcement of child support may outweigh these negative effects. Although the potential increases in economic well-being of the latter are great, the extent to which the 1984 child support legislation actually improves the economic well-being of families headed by women will depend on how effectively the laws are implemented, the degree to which they are strengthened in the future, and the extent to which the increased collections are shared with the poor custodial families.

The Reagan administration's short-run policies have had little effect on welfare dependence. The effects of the benefit cuts have been nearly offset by the effects of the recession and continuing high unemployment. Increased

---

contraceptives. The administration argued that the parents of the minor had a right to know what kind of contraceptive advice their child was getting from a quasipublic agency. After provoking a storm of controversy and legal challenges, this regulation was ultimately withdrawn. Moreover, the Reagan administration cut federal funds to provide contraceptive services to lower-income women by 14 percent. Barry Nestor, "Public Funding of Contraceptive Services, 1980-82," *Family Planning Perspectives*, vol. 14, no. 4 (July-August 1982), pp. 198-203.

60. Although a return to more traditional values is possible, we should note that it is at least equally plausible that the attempt to return to more traditional values will fail and that restricting access to contraception as well as abortion will increase the number of female-headed families.

child support enforcement, however, should lead to a long-run decrease in welfare dependence as it leads to increased economic well-being.

The Reagan record with respect to reducing the prevalence of female-headed families has both pluses and minuses. On the plus side are the public benefit cuts and the improved enforcement of private child support obligations; on the minus side, recession, continuing high unemployment, and the new abortion policy. Despite all the attention that Charles Murray and a few others have focused on the relation between welfare benefits and the prevalence of female headship, it turns out that relative to either unemployment or abortion policy, cuts in public benefits are a weak reed. To date the macroeconomic policies of the Reagan administration have probably increased single female headship more than the cuts in benefits have reduced it. Should the Reagan administration succeed in outlawing abortion, the resulting increase in mother-only families can be expected to dwarf the decrease that has resulted from benefit cuts.

CHAPTER 6

SUMMARY AND
RECOMMENDATIONS

At every point in the nation's history, the United States has confronted a dilemma over whether to give greater priority to reducing the economic insecurity and poverty of mother-only families or to reducing the number of such families and the degree of their dependence on government. Such families have always been disproportionately represented among the poor, and many children who grow up in these families are clearly disadvantaged. As adults they have lower socioeconomic status; they are more likely to become single parents themselves, either through out-of-wedlock births or divorce; and they are more likely to be dependent on government. Many of these problems are traceable to the economic insecurity and poverty of the families in which they grew up. Government can reduce these economic problems by supplementing the incomes of these families. But doing so may increase their dependence on government and increase their prevalence.

The dilemma is intensified because it involves a conflict of values. Compassion, self-interest, and self-reliance—three core American values—conflict with one another on this issue. To give more is compassionate, but giving more may go against our self-interest and may undermine the self-reliance of recipients. The dilemma is further complicated by our lack of knowledge. If improving the economic well-being of mother-only families serves to multiply their number, will that action have been compassionate? And if the children of such families become burdens and threats to our children because we have not improved their economic well-being, will our lack of action have been in our self-interest? The conflict exists not just among different groups of people who support different values but within each of us.

Policymaking would be much easier if improving the lot of these mothers had absolutely no effect on their number and so improved the fate of their children that it was clearly in the nation's interest to provide them with substantially greater aid. Policymaking would be much simpler if we knew that improving the lot of single women so multiplied their numbers and worsened the fate of their children that it was clearly in the nation's interest to reduce or eliminate aid. It is unfortunate that reality conforms to neither extreme.

The confluence of two trends in the last quarter-century has pushed the dilemma to the forefront of national attention. Large increases in government benefits, particularly in the decade following President Johnson's War on Poverty, have led to substantial increases in the economic well-being of mother-only families. At the same time, there have been large increases in the number of such families and in the proportion of them on welfare. Did the increases in benefits cause the increases in numbers and dependence? If so, how large are the effects, and what are the trade-offs between income security and dependence? Are there alternatives to welfare that can increase the economic well-being of these families without having welfare's adverse effects?

A Review of the Evidence: The Growth of Mother-Only Families and the Role of Public Benefits

About one of every six white children and slightly more than one of every two black children now live in mother-only families. In the past twenty-five years the proportion of children living in such families has more than doubled, and demographers project that about one of every two children born in the late 1970s will live in such a family before reaching adulthood.

From a demographic perspective, the most important factor underlying the growth of mother-only families has been the change in marriage behavior. Among whites, most of the recent growth is due to increased disruption of marriages, whereas among blacks, the growth is due primarily to a decline in marriage. A decline in marriage increases the pool of women who may have out-of-wedlock births and thereby increases the proportion of unwed mothers. A decline in marriage also reduces the likelihood that such women will ever marry.

How much of the increase in mother-only families is due to increases in government benefits? The studies reviewed in this book indicate that the effect of increased benefits has been relatively small compared with the effect of other factors. Comparisons among states indicate that the principal effect of welfare is on the living arrangements of such families. In other words, single women with children in states with high welfare benefits are more likely to establish independent households and become household heads than to live with their parents. Setting aside the effect of welfare on living arrangements, the most reliable studies suggest that increases in benefits account for about 9 to 14 percent of the increased prevalence of families headed by women.

To say that the increase in government benefits is not the principal culprit in the growth of families headed by women, however, is not equivalent to saying that the benefit increases played no role at all. If, for example, increased benefits accounted for 30 percent of the increase in such families among the poor, most analysts would agree that this is a significant effect. Fairly good evidence indicates that girls who grow up in families headed by single women are more likely to become single parents themselves. Thus even a relatively small effect can mushroom over time. For these reasons, the effect of transfer benefits on prevalence should not be ignored. Moreover, the effects on living arrangements are a cause for concern because there is some evidence that children of single-mother families with other adults are better off than children in families in which the mother is the only adult.

If welfare is not the major cause, what is responsible for recent increases in the proportion of mother-only families? The evidence suggests that the major factor underlying this growth is the shift in the relative earnings opportunities of men and women. The roots of the shift differ by race. For whites, the shift is traceable primarily to the dramatic increase in labor force participation of women, which accelerated after World War II and has continued ever since. By working and earning more, women have achieved greater economic independence, which has reduced the costs of being single and increased the likelihood of experiencing marital disruption. For blacks, the decline in male employment opportunities—which also accelerated in the 1950s with the drop in agricultural jobs in the South—appears to be the critical factor. Male unemployment not only reduces the economic gains from marriage; it also undermines the role of the husband as breadwinner. Hence it increases marital disruption and reduces the likelihood that formerly married mothers (or unwed pregnant teenagers) will marry.

The Economic Insecurity of Mother-Only Families and the Effect of Public Programs

According to official government data, about half of all the children and mothers in families headed by women suffer from the most extreme form of economic insecurity—poverty. No other major demographic group is so poor, and none stays poor longer. The average length of time in poverty for children in such poor families is seven years: more than a third of their childhood. A large minority of black children are born into poverty and never escape.

Even mother-only families who are not poor are subject to economic insecurity and other forms of instability. Marital disruption is generally accompanied by large drops in income, averaging about 30 percent of predivorce income. During or soon after a divorce, mothers and children often change residences, which usually means a change in neighborhood and school as well. In addition, divorced mothers are likely to increase the number of hours they work outside the home, and this change may affect their children. In view of the instabilities confronting such families, it is not surprising that family members suffer disproportionately from mental health problems and use a disproportionate share of community mental health services.

Increases in government benefits quite clearly reduce the level of poverty and economic insecurity that mother-only families face. In turn, reductions in poverty and insecurity are likely to improve the mental health of mothers and children and improve the socioeconomic achievement of the children.

The official government data on poverty understate the extent to which the increases in government benefits for mother-only families have reduced their economic insecurity. The two biggest sources of benefit increases in the 1965-80 period—food stamps and Medicaid—are ignored in the official figures. According to the official data, the poverty rate for single mothers who head families remained about the same between 1967 and 1983 (around 50 percent) although it dropped during the Great Society years. If the cash value of food stamps and the cash insurance value of Medicaid benefits are added to cash income, the poverty rate for single women who head families declined from 50 percent in 1967 to between 29 and 41 percent in 1983, depending on how one estimates the values of in-kind benefits.

The extent to which government benefits reduce poverty and insecurity depends, of course, on the kind of benefit provided. In this regard, the contrast between the Survivors' Insurance program and the Aid to Families with Dependent Children (AFDC) program is quite striking.

Because AFDC and the accompanying food stamp and Medicaid programs provide benefits only to people with very low incomes, these programs do nothing to reduce the economic insecurity of divorced families who may experience income drops but do not have to go on welfare. Furthermore, although the AFDC benefit package has reduced the economic insecurity of poor single mothers, most of the benefits provided are below poverty level.

Survivors' Insurance does a much better job than AFDC of reducing economic insecurity in general and poverty in particular. Unlike welfare, Survivors' Insurance frequently provides above-poverty-level benefits. Furthermore, benefits for the children are not reduced if the mother works or remarries. As a consequence, a much smaller proportion of widows than other single women who head families are poor. Finally, unlike welfare, Survivors' Insurance does a great deal to reduce the economic insecurity of middle-income families who would otherwise experience a major income loss. The children of widows do as well as children from two-parent families on many dimensions of attainment and do better than children of divorced, separated, and unwed mothers. In view of other evidence of the importance of income on children's future well-being, it is reasonable to conclude that at least some of the higher attainment among the children of widows is due to their more fortunate economic circumstances.

The Dependence of Mother-Only Families and the Effects of Public Programs

If there were no government benefits for mother-only families, the problem of public welfare dependence, by definition, would not exist. Yet aside from Charles Murray and one or two other extremists, hardly anyone would argue that we should do away with all welfare programs.[1] From the first colonial days through the Reagan administration, it has always been a public responsibility to aid the poor. The extent to which the dependence of poor single mothers is viewed as a problem depends on the answers to the following questions. Is dependence on AFDC pervasive and does it last a time? Is it harmful? Should poor single women with children be expected to work? Would work enable these women to achieve an acceptable standard of living without government assistance? The next four subsections summarize our findings pertaining to these questions.

Is Welfare Dependence Pervasive and Long-Lasting? During the course of recent years about half of the single mothers who head families receive AFDC benefits. When AFDC mothers are receiving benefits, the overwhelming majority of them (85 percent) do not work. Most of them have no other sources of income. They are nearly totally dependent on the combination of AFDC, food stamps, Medicaid, and sometimes public housing benefits.

About 30 percent of the single mothers who ever receive benefits spend no more than two years on welfare. But another 40 percent receive benefits for three to seven years, and another 30 percent receive benefits for eight or more years. Because long-term recipients are more likely to be receiving benefits at any particular time, at each point in time they represent a large

---

1. Charles Murray, *Losing Ground: American Social Policy, 1950-1980* (New York: Basic Books, 1984).

share of the caseload. Thus, those who will receive benefits for eight or more years constitute about 65 percent of the total AFDC caseload in any given month.

Whether two years constitute a long or a short duration on welfare depends on one's perspective. If single mothers who head families are expected to work, for example, two years may seem a long time. But in terms of the possible ill effects of long-term dependence, two years may seem a short time. No matter what the concern, however, most people will agree that eight or more years is a long time to be dependent on welfare.

Thus, by any reasonable definition, nearly two-thirds of the mother-only families on welfare today, and about one-third of the current number of all mother-only families, will receive welfare benefits for a long period of time. Is such long-run dependence harmful to single mothers and their children?

Is Dependence Harmful? Many people believe that welfare harms beneficiaries by stigmatizing them and by undermining their motivation to escape poverty and make a better life for themselves. Some even argue that it creates a "culture" of poverty and dependence that is passed on from one generation to the next. There is good evidence that recipients have lower self-esteem and feel less able to control their lives than nonrecipients, but it is not clear whether welfare is a cause or consequence of such attitudes. There also is some evidence of intergenerational dependence, but again the interpretation of its cause is ambiguous. No one doubts that poverty breeds poverty, and some intergenerational welfare dependence is a natural consequence of this process. The question is, does the provision of welfare increase or reduce the extent to which subsequent generations will be poor and dependent? The answer is, we do not know.

At this point social science knowledge about the harmful effects of welfare dependence on mothers and children is too weak to warrant either the judgments that welfare does more harm than good or that society does not need to be concerned about the possible ill effects of welfare. Nonetheless, in view of the ambiguity of the evidence and the high value that society places on independence, prudence directs the nation to seek alternative methods of aiding single women with children that will stigmatize them less and will reinforce their independence more.

Furthermore, the substantial probability of long-term dependence directs the nation to seek methods of helping the poorest of all these women—unwed teenage mothers—so that they have a chance to achieve more than a life on welfare. At present, these mothers are disproportionately black, but the number of whites in this category is growing rapidly. AFDC does little to help them escape poverty, and many will spend most of their young adult lives on welfare. Perhaps the AFDC program should not be expected to provide help for recipients to escape dependence; but some program should be directed at helping these welfare recipients achieve a better life than welfare.

Should Poor Mothers Who Head Families Be Expected To Work? As we discussed in chapter 4, federal, state, and local governments have almost always been reluctant to provide cash relief to people who are expected to work. Work relief—or no relief—has been more common. Until the twentieth century, poor single mothers were generally expected to work, but cash relief was more common for widows than for able-bodied men. And it appears that until the twentieth century many of the single mothers who headed families took in piecework to do work at home or boarders and thereby earned income and took care of their children simultaneously.

From 1900 until 1960, public policy worked toward the goal of providing all single mothers—the divorced, separated, and never-married, as well as the widowed—with sufficient cash and in-kind aid to enable them to refrain from earning income entirely and to stay home and rear their children—that is, to imitate the child-care practices of middle- and upper-income married mothers. Then, nearly sixty years after professional social welfare leaders had first proclaimed this as a goal for public assistance, President Johnson's War on Poverty finally provided the necessary resources to make the goal a reality.

By the time the goal had been reached, however, ideals and practices had undergone a dramatic revolution. By the early 1970s nearly half of all middle- and upper-income mothers, even those with young children, were working outside the home at least part time. Moreover, the proportion of married mothers who earned wages has continued to grow since then. It is not surprising, therefore, that government policy toward single women with children progressed in what appears to have been an inconsistent fashion. Even as the federal government provided billions of dollars and induced states to provide billions more to finance a decent minimum standard of living for these families, it also enacted legislation first to induce and then increasingly to require single mothers to work.

Is society right in expecting these mothers to work? To answer this question, we must first know the consequences of mothers' employment outside the home for children and for single mothers. As indicated in chapter 2, the answer is not clear. There is very little research evidence to indicate that poor children of employed mothers are less well off than poor children whose mothers stay at home. And there is some evidence that the effects of employment—particularly the benefits of added income—are positive for children as well as mothers. But even the best studies are plagued with the problem that mothers who are employed may be different in unmeasured ways (such as their child-rearing abilities and coping skills generally) from those who are not employed. As a consequence, it is possible that the children of poor single women who are not in the labor force might be even worse off if their mothers were employed. The best studies have controlled for many differences among mothers, however, suggesting that the evidence so far accumulated is worth careful consideration.

In any case, in view of the great value that Americans place on self-reliance and on the high, and still rising, labor force participation of married mothers, it seems likely that the nation will increasingly come to expect poor single mothers to work outside the home, at least part time and especially once their children are in school.

Is Work Enough To Raise These Families Out of Poverty? As documented in chapter 2, most poor single mothers cannot be expected to work their way out of poverty. A small minority cannot work at all. About three-quarters of all welfare recipients cannot command high enough wages to lift their families out of poverty even if they work full time year-round. Enforcing private child-support payments will do part, but not all, of the job. Most fathers of AFDC children earn little and therefore have little to share with their children. To substantially reduce poverty among mother-only families, therefore, it will be necessary to supplement the earnings of single mothers who head families and private child-support payments by some form of government transfer. Thus if such families are to escape poverty, some government help is necessary.

Recent Policy Developments

As described in chapters 4 and 5, the three most important recent policy developments in aiding mother-only families are the large reduction in the real value of public benefits, the increasingly strong legislation either to induce or to require work by single women who head families with no preschool-age children, and the strengthening of public enforcement of private child support obligations. Each of these is summarized in turn.

Reductions in Public Benefits. In 1981 the Reagan administration proposed substantial cuts in public benefits to mother-only families. In that year Congress agreed to modest cuts in benefits to single mothers who were both working and receiving welfare. Subsequently Congress cut benefits once again by a small amount. All told, the benefit cuts amounted to about 12 percent of total federal benefits to mother-only families.

The budget cuts came on the heels of an even larger reduction in the real value of benefits—about 13 percent—that occurred between 1975 and 1980 as a result of the failure of benefits to keep pace with inflation. Taken together, the reduction in benefits to mother-only families between 1975 and

1985 was substantial—approximately one-quarter of the total real benefits available to those families in 1975.

In retrospect, the reductions in the value of real benefits during the 1975-85 period may not be surprising. We found in chapter 4 that average income is the principal long-run determinant of the level of benefits to the poor and to female-headed families. Real wages in the United States were falling during most of the 1970s and the early 1980s. The decline in the real value of public benefits reflected the decline in general living standards. More recently, incomes have begun to grow again—albeit quite slowly.

By the end of the Reagan administration's first term, Congress was no longer enacting legislation that even modestly reduced benefits and, indeed, some of the earlier cuts were restored. Moreover, early in Reagan's second term, further cuts in the major programs that aided mother-only families were specifically excluded from the stringent (Gramm-Rudman-Hollings) budget-cutting measures designed to reduce the large federal deficit. In view of both the recent growth in incomes and the recent resistance of Congress to initiate further budget cuts, it is doubtful that families headed by single women will be subjected to additional budget cuts in the near future.

Just as the large increase in government benefits during the 1955-75 period led to an improvement in the economic security of mother-only families, the decrease in benefits between 1975 and 1985 led to a reversal of some of these gains.

The decrease in the economic well-being of these families during the 1975-85 period was accompanied by a decrease—more than one-sixth—in the extent to which they were dependent on welfare. This decline reversed the increase in welfare dependence that had accompanied the expansion of government benefits during the previous two decades.

Benefit changes did not have much effect on the prevalence of mother-only families, however. The large benefit increases between 1955 and 1975 caused, at most, a modest increase in the proportion of mother-only families during that period. The smaller reductions in benefits in the 1975-85 period had little if any effect on the prevalence of mother-only families. Further cuts in benefits, even if extreme, are likely to have no more than a modest effect on the proportion of such families.

In short, we find that during the past thirty years the increases and decreases in government benefits greatly affected both the economic well-being and the dependence of poor mother-only families, but had modest effects, at most, on their prevalence.

Work Requirements. By the 1960s, as we have noted, the prevailing belief of the twentieth century—that a cash welfare program should enable poor single mothers to stay home to rear their children—had begun to erode.

At first the federal government tried to induce AFDC mothers to work by creating positive work incentives (the carrot) within AFDC. When this failed to have much impact on either work or caseloads, Congress began legislating requirements for mothers with no preschool-age children to register for work (the beginning of the stick). The Carter administration proposed a combination of the two—the expansion of work incentives within AFDC as well as a job creation and job guarantee program for AFDC mothers with no preschool-age children. The latter, in effect, also would have required work for this group of women, providing that suitable child care could be found for children below age fourteen. The Carter proposal was not enacted. The Reagan administration rejected the approach of creating work incentives within the AFDC program in favor of the pure work requirement approach—the stick alone.

To enforce work requirements, we argued in chapter 5, the government must create or locate jobs. On the basis of our review, we concluded that there is no convincing evidence that creating or finding jobs is not feasible, either politically or economically. Studies of work and training programs for women who head families generally report sufficiently large gains in earnings to make the programs profitable within three to four years, although they do cost more initially in comparison with continuing to pay only cash benefits through AFDC. Both research on program evaluation and the sociological and economic literature suggest that the postprogram earnings of poor single mothers increase greatly in percentage terms as a result of work and training programs.

The extrapolation of this evidence to what could be expected under regular national programs is complicated for two reasons. First, whereas participation has been voluntary in most of the work and training programs that have been evaluated, much of the current public discussion concerns enforced work requirements. Programs that involve significant elements of compulsion may be less profitable both to the beneficiaries and to society as a whole because unwilling workers are less productive than willing ones. Early experience with workfare, however, suggests that to date, at least, enforcing work seems to have been greated favorably by program participants.

Second, and even more important, few of the single mothers in the work and training evaluations have had preschool-age children. The child care costs for such children could be so high as to offset the earnings gains of the program. It is possible that long-run gains in earnings will more than make up for the short-term extra child care costs; but the opposite is also possible. More experimentation and study of this issue are warranted.

Enforcing work requirements in the AFDC program is certain to lead to reductions in dependence on government. Some AFDC mothers will gain enough additional income to work their way off the AFDC rolls. Others will be discouraged from applying by the hassles that accompany fulfilling the work requirement. The size of the reductions will depend on the success of the work and training programs at increasing the earnings ability of the mothers, the state of the economy, and the degree to which the programs discourage poor single women with children from applying for aid.

The effects on prevalence of enforcing work requirements in the AFDC program for single mothers will depend on the extent to which the work and training programs that implement the work requirement improve the relative position of poor women versus poor men in the labor market. If the programs lead to a large improvement for women but not for men, it is quite possible that the proportion of mother-only families will increase.

Strengthening Public Enforcement of Private Child Support Obligations. Congressional interest in enforcing child support grew as the proportion of AFDC children with noncustodial parents grew. In chapter 4 we discussed how the biggest burst of federal child support legislation followed hard on the heels of the 1965-75 growth in welfare rolls. The milestone 1976 act created federal and state offices of child-support enforcement; in other words, it created the public bureaucratic machinery to enforce the private obligation to support one's children. During the seven years that followed, several new acts strengthened the bureaucratic machinery.

Then, in 1984, Congress unanimously enacted by far the strongest federal child support enforcement legislation ever, requiring all states to enact laws that withhold from wages all future child support payments once the noncustodial parent is delinquent in payments for one month and to appoint blue-ribbon commissions to design statewide guidelines for establishing child support obligations.

The 1984 legislation requires the child support offices in each state to provide assistance to nonwelfare as well as welfare cases. Although states may charge for these services and thereby target subsidies on the poor, the service itself is provided universally to rich and poor custodial parents. The policy contrast is conspicious between the restriction of eligibility for cash welfare and the universalization of eligibility for child support enforcement services.

In chapter 5 we found that the effects of the 1984 child support legislation will depend on how well it is implemented at both state and federal levels. There will be few positive effects (1) if the states enact weak standards and neither the number nor the amount of child support awards increases much; (2) if states fail to effectively enforce the new withholding of wages in response to delinquency law; and (3) if federal, state, and local resources to enforce support are cut. But the maximum potential effects of further strengthening of child support enforcement are impressive. For example, if Wisconsin's child support standard—17 percent of the noncustodial parent's gross income for one child; 25 percent, 29 percent, 31 percent, and 34 percent respectively for two, three, four, and five or more children—were adopted nationally and perfectly enforced, the poverty gap could be reduced by 24 percent and AFDC caseloads by 25 percent.

Still, even 100 percent collection of child support obligations derived from any reasonable standard would leave the overwhelming majority of the AFDC recipients no better off than they were in the absence of the program. This is because most noncustodial parents of AFDC children do not earn enough to pay as much child support as their children are already receiving in AFDC benefits. Programs to increase the employment and earnings of poor noncustodial fathers would help. But even the best imaginable program would still leave a large proportion of the AFDC caseload poor and dependent on government.

At this time there are two alternative methods of sharing some of the increased collections of child support with low-income families on AFDC. One approach is to ignore some of the child support payment in calculating AFDC grants. Congress has required all states to ignore the first $50 per month. That requirement increases the incomes of people on AFDC. It also increases the number of families who will continue to receive AFDC.

An alternative approach is to use the increased child support collections to help fund a nonwelfare benefit that encourages work. This approach is being pursued on a demonstration basis in the state of Wisconsin. Under the Wisconsin child support assurance system, support obligations are determined by a simple legislated formula. The obligation is withheld from wages and other sources of income in all cases, just as income and payroll taxes are. The child is entitled to receive the money paid by the noncustodial parent or an assured child support benefit, whichever is larger. Thus the savings in AFDC that result from increased child support collections is funneled back into the system to increase the economic well-being of families with children eligible for child support.

We estimate that such a program could reduce the poverty gap among American families potentially eligible for child support by nearly 40 percent and would reduce AFDC caseloads by nearly 50 percent, at little extra cost and perhaps even with some small savings. As before, the estimates assume that 100 percent of the child support obligation resulting from the Wisconsin standard would be collected. How close the actual results come to these estimates will be known when the demonstration is completed.

One criticism of the child support assurance program is that for AFDC beneficiaries who live in states that pay higher AFDC benefits than the assured benefits, the latter will benefit only those mothers who work. These mothers constitute about half the national caseload. For those in high-benefit states who are unable to work or cannot find jobs or who simply prefer to stay at home with their children, the program provides nothing. Thus the success of the child support assurance approach will hinge on the extent to which both poor custodial mothers as well as poor noncustodial fathers work. The $50 per month set-aside that Congress enacted in 1984 is in sharp contrast. It provides more for custodial parents on AFDC who do not work than does the child support assurance program.

Where Do We Go From Here?

As our book has shown, the dilemmas inherent in designing a government policy to help families headed by single mothers are difficult. Different observers will resolve them differently, depending both on their reading of the evidence and on their value judgments. This section indicates how we come out.

Work and Welfare Do Not Go Together

Throughout most of U.S. history, welfare was provided only to those who either could not work or were not expected to work. During the 1960s, however, AFDC was reformed in order to provide incentives for mothers to work their way off the rolls. For a small minority of welfare recipients, AFDC became a supplement to earnings. Enthusiasts for this policy argued that work and welfare go together.[2] But do they, or should they, go together?

Assume for the moment that AFDC will be used to assure a minimum standard of living for single women with children who are temporarily or permanently unable to work either because of disability or because of the lack of a job. Then the question of whether work and welfare go together becomes, should AFDC also be used to supplement the earnings of people who do work?

If promoting work among poor single women with children is a primary objective, the answer is clear. Extending welfare to supplement the earnings of people who can work will do more to discourage work than supplementing the earnings of these poor single mothers through a separate program. This is so for two reasons.

---

2. Sar Levitan, Martin Rein, and David Marwick, *Work and Welfare Go Together* (Baltimore, Maryland: Johns Hopkins University Press, 1972).

First, trying to use the same program to aid both the people expected to work and those not expected to work is problematic because the benefit structure most suited for each group differs so dramatically. The benefits required to supplement the earnings of the poor single mothers who work are much smaller than those required to assure a decent minimum to the poor single mothers who cannot work. In a single program, the only way to reduce the benefits for those with no earnings to the level required for supplementation is to reduce benefits rapidly as earnings increase (that is, impose a high tax rate on earnings). But doing this reduces the incentive to work.

The second reason for separating programs that supplement earnings from those that substitute for earnings is that the resulting demarcation between total dependence and partial dependence promotes work. Persons aided by the welfare program are clearly dependent; persons aided by a separate program designed to supplement earnings are only partially dependent by virtue of the fact that they are employed. For a society that values work, a clear distinction reinforces the values of work and independence. If there is only one program, reinforcing work and independence is difficult because the question becomes, how much work is enough? There is no clear answer. With two separate programs, the answer is obvious. Those poor single mothers who are physically and mentally capable of work should work enough to be independent of the welfare program. By creating two separate programs, the social message to those who temporarily cannot find work and therefore must have recourse to welfare is clear: society expects their dependence on welfare to be short term.

In short, by supplementing incomes through programs apart from welfare, work will be encouraged both through better economic incentives and through strong, clear social messages.

The U.S. Education and Social Security Tradition: Heavier Reliance on Universal Programs

To promote self-reliance and to reduce the economic insecurity of poor families headed by single mothers, the nation should rely more heavily on universal programs that provide benefits to these families, whatever their incomes, and should place less emphasis on welfare programs that provide benefits only to the poor. Free public education, Social Security, Medicare, and the newly emerging child support collection system are universal programs. AFDC, food stamps, and Medicaid are welfare programs.

The first argument for universal programs is that they integrate beneficiaries into the social mainstream; welfare programs segregate them. Free public education has been one of the principal social institutions in America.

It is difficult to imagine that the United States would have had as much social mobility if the public had paid for only the eduction of poor children. Welfare and other income-tested programs place beneficiaries in separate programs. They create special bureaucracies to deal with the poor alone. In universal programs one bureaucracy deals with rich and poor alike.

The second argument for heavier reliance on programs that benefit citizens of all income levels rather than just the poor is that doing so will promote work among single mothers who are poor. In the previous section we concluded that the earnings of families headed by women should be supplemented by separate, nonwelfare programs. The programs for supplementing earnings should provide lower benefits than AFDC and should not be reduced so drastically as under AFDC when earnings increase. A benefit provided to all—that is, a universal benefit—is not reduced at all as earnings increase. Thus universal benefits give the greatest incentive for the poor to work.

Put another way, programs that aid only those with low incomes must reduce benefits as the income of beneficiaries increases. In so doing, these welfare programs impose tax (benefit reduction) rates that are higher than the tax rates required to finance the programs. This is equivalent to imposing regressive tax rates in our overall tax-transfer system. Whereas the rich lose part of what they earn through taxes, the poor lose an even bigger part of what they earn through benefit reductions. We fail to recognize this regressivity because it is imposed not by institutions that tax all of us, but by special institutions that are designed to, and do indeed, provide help to the poor.

Precisely because welfare programs lead to this regressivity, they are not a desirable means of supplementing the incomes of the poor who are expected to work. The poor can earn less in the market than the nonpoor. Regressive tax rates exacerbate this inequality; they stack the deck against the poor who try to achieve through hard work—the way Americans are supposed to achieve. Hence these rates reduce rather than enhance equality of opportunity. Furthermore, owing to their higher tax rates, welfare programs create greater incentives for the poor to work more at intermittent, informal, and even illegal jobs where the earnings need not be reported.

But the greater is the number of people who receive benefits, the more costly the program will be to nonbeneficiaries. Programs that provide benefits to everyone, such as public education, will be more costly to upper-middle-income and upper-income people than programs that provide similar benefits only to the poorest. Thus, because universal programs cost them more than welfare programs, the narrow self-interest of citizens with above-average incomes will lead them to favor welfare programs. Only if a universal program offers substantial advantages to people with above-average incomes will the extra costs be worth it to these people.

The more pervasive a problem is, the greater is the case for resolving it with a universal program. When the problem affects the middle- and upper-middle-income groups, they may have more to gain from a universal than a welfare program. Poverty is the most extreme manifestation of economic insecurity. But economic insecurity is not confined to the poor. Unemployment, for example, is most severe for the poorest, but it is often severe even for middle-income and upper-middle-income Americans. The fact that unemployment insurance provides benefits to all Americans rather than to only the poorest reflects the pervasiveness of the problem of unemployment and society's commitment to reduce the economic insecurity of the unemployed population regardless of their poverty status. That is why the United States and every other Western industrialized nation has an unemployment insurance program. Similar arguments exist for Old Age Insurance and Survivors' Insurance.

Are the economic insecurity and poverty of mother-only families pervasive social problems or are they confined to a small segment of our poorest citizens? The evidence clearly indicates that they are pervasive. Nearly half of such families are poor. Most of the others have suffered large drops in income but do not qualify for welfare benefits. We think it is hard to avoid the conclusion that welfare is no substitute for a program that would provide support for all single mothers.

Despite the fact that women obviously have a disproportionate interest in how such families are treated, this is not just a woman's issue. Nearly one of every two fathers who has a daughter today can expect her to head her own family. Similarly, one of two fathers can expect his child to live in a mother-only family before growing up and leaving home. And nearly one of every two men in the next generation will grow up in such a family. Because any of us could be affected, it may be in the best interest of people of all incomes to provide some benefits and services to all mother-only families rather than to only the poorest. If a man's daughter, for instance, runs the risk of divorce but not of poverty, it may be cheaper for him to pay more taxes for an efficient, universal, child support collection system than to pay less taxes for a system that serves the poor alone. For in the latter case, he may be forced to provide the only support his daughter and her children will receive (with those children's father getting off scott-free). And, finally, surely it is in the long-term self-interest of Americans, whatever their income, race, or ethnic group, to increase the economic security and self-reliance of the family form in which one-half of the next generation can be expected to spend part of its childhood, especially if it can be done without encouraging—and indeed perhaps even discouraging—the prevalence of this family form.

Basic Recommendations

In this section we present three approaches to reforming the nation's system of providing economic security for mother-only families. The first two involve the adoption of two new universal programs: a child support assurance program and a child-and-adult allowance program. In both cases, the universal programs grow out of existing policy directions. Each would increase the economic well-being of such families while reducing their prevalence and welfare dependence. The third involves the conversion of AFDC from a cash relief to principally a work-relief or guaranteed-jobs program. This reform would reduce dependence but, by itself, might also reduce the economic well-being of families headed by single women with children. In combination with child-and-adult allowances and child support assurance, however, work relief would greatly enhance the incomes of such families.

These three approaches to reform are certainly not the only ones that would increase economic security and promote work and self-reliance. We focus on them because we have studied them sufficiently to be confident that they will simultaneously achieve these goals, reduce the prevalence of mother-only families, and reduce their dependence on government at little or no additional cost.

This section includes programs that both achieve desired social objectives and require little or no increases in taxes. In any fiscal environment such programs make sense to most people and will command public support. In the current fiscal environment, where deficit reduction is a high priority, such programs are even more attractive.

Our concluding section then recommends two proposals that would increase program costs. We do this because, in our judgment, even in times when fiscal constraint is essential, it may be judicious to raise taxes somewhat to achieve desirable social objectives.

A New Child Support Assurance System

The 1984 federal child support legislation, enacted unanimously by Congress, moves the country in the direction of a child support assurance system. This is especially true of the two provisions that require all states to (1) initiate a process to withhold child support from the wages of noncustodial parents who are delinquent in their child support payments for one month, and (2) appoint blue-ribbon commissions to devise statewide advisory guidelines for child support. Although advisory guidelines and withholding in response to delinquency are unlikely to be as effective as legislated standards and universal withholding, respectively, they are big steps in the right direction. The 1984 legislation contained another provision that moved even closer to a child support assurance system; it gave the state of Wisconsin the authority to modify AFDC rules and regulations in order to conduct a demonstration of a child support assurance program. More important, federal funds that would have been spent on AFDC in the absence of the child support assurance program may be spent by the state of Wisconsin to help defray the costs of the assured benefit.

By adding a socially assured benefit to the withholding and standard features of a child support assurance system, we would have a universal benefit that would reduce economic insecurity and poverty, promote work and self-reliance, and reduce the prevalence of female-headed families. A legislated standard of support and universal withholding of child support obligations would reduce the economic insecurity, poverty, and welfare dependence of a large number of mother-only families. They would also reduce prevalence somewhat. The assured benefit would further reduce poverty and the extent of dependence on government by providing a universal benefit, which when combined with earnings, would lift many such families out of poverty and remove them from welfare. Custodial parents accepting employment would not face a dollar-for-dollar reduction in their child support payments, as they do under AFDC. Any reduction in their payments would be small and would occur only if the absent parent was paying less than the assured benefit. Thus custodial parents would have the usual incentive for acquiring jobs—the knowledge that by so doing they would be enhancing the well-being of their families. Moreover, benefits would no longer be seen as charity but as contributions to which all children eligible for child support were entitled. In short, child support assurance has all the features of the kind of program that should be used to supplement the earnings of single mothers.

How much would a new child support assurance program cost? As described in chapter 5, if the federal government collected 70 percent of the money due according to the Wisconsin child support standard from all non-custodial parents (17 percent of gross income for one child, and so on), the federal government could afford an assured benefit that would reduce AFDC caseloads by one-half and poverty among children potentially eligible for support by 40 percent—at no extra cost. How much more or less such a benefit would cost the government will depend on how much child support enforcement improves. Given the Wisconsin standard, currently only 44 percent of the money is collected. Will collection be closer to 50 percent, 60 percent, 70 percent, or 80 percent of the Wisconsin standard ten years from now? If enforcement does not improve at all, the extra costs could be as high as $4 billion. If child support collections improve to 70 percent of the Wisconsin standard, the cost would be zero. We think 70 percent is a reasonable goal. It is halfway between the current dismal situation and perfection. If it were achieved, a cost-neutral child support assurance program would reduce AFDC caseloads by 50 percent and poverty among families eligible for child support by 40 percent. It is worth careful consideration.

Child-and-Adult Allowances

A child allowance is a monthly government payment to all children under age eighteen, common in all industrialized countries except the United States. The United States has a close relative of a child allowance in the personal exemption for children in the federal income tax, which is subtracted from income in calculating tax liability. President Reagan has proposed that personal exemptions be nearly doubled: from $1,080 to $2,000. Converting a $2,000 child exemption in the income tax to a $300 to $400 child allowance would create another universal benefit at little or no extra cost.

The major argument advanced in favor of raising the personal exemption is that doing so would lighten the tax burden of the poor. A child allowance of equal cost would help the poor more. Most important, it will actually give them more income. More than 90 percent of the poor already pay no federal income taxes; increasing income tax exemptions will be of no help whatsoever to those poor. Even for the minority of the poor who do pay taxes, a child allowance will increase their incomes by a greater amount than an exemption increase of equal cost. More generally, such an allowance is likely to be of greater benefit than a personal exemption for the bottom half of the income distribution.[3]

A small allowance for children has all the attributes of the kind of benefit that is desirable for supplementing the earnings of female heads of families expected to work. It is small; it is not reduced as earnings increase; and it goes to everyone, rich and poor alike, so there is no stigma attached to receiving it.

Because child allowances would go to two-parent as well as to mother-only families, they would diminish the current discrimination in favor of the latter and perhaps reduce their prevalence. Presidents Kennedy, Nixon, and Carter all recognized the desirability of providing aid to two- as well as one-parent families. As a consequence, they proposed extending AFDC, a cash

---

3. Public finance economists are agreed that an equally costly refundable tax credit, compared to a personal exemption, will be of greater assistance to the poor. For a discussion of the relation between the negative income tax and demonstration grants such as child-and-adult allowances, see Jonathan Kesselman and Irwin Garfinkel, ''Professor Friedman Meet Lady Rhys Williams, NIT vs. CIT,'' vol. 10, *The Journal of Public Economics* (1978), pp. 179-216.

welfare program, to two-parent families. As we explained in chapters 2 and 4, however, providing cash welfare to two-parent families may increase rather than decrease marital breakups. Food stamps may have the same effect. Prudence suggests therefore that two-parent families should be aided primarily through nonwelfare programs, such as child allowances.

A somewhat smaller assured benefit in the child support assurance program combined with a small allowance for children is better from the point of view of prevalence than only an assured child support benefit that is as high as the sum of the somewhat smaller assured benefit and the child allowance. This is so because the higher the assured benefit is, the greater is the number of people who would profit financially from a marital breakup. It is also better from the point of view of equity and poverty reduction. There are, after all, many children in poor and near-poor two-parent families. A higher assured child support benefit is of no help to them. Indeed, it could hurt them if it toppled a wobbly marriage through offering bigger financial incentives to separate. A child allowance would help children in low-income two-parent families both directly by increasing their family's income and indirectly by decreasing incentives for family breakup.

Liberals in the United States have been the traditional advocates of child allowances. Former Senator Paul Douglas and Senator Daniel Patrick Moynihan have been two of the most notable liberal advocates. Recently some influential conservative thinkers, including David Stockman and George Gilder, have also proposed child allowances.

Rather than doubling the personal adult exemption, we also would advocate converting it into a $300 to $400 *adult* allowance. The arguments are the same as for the child allowance. It would create another small universal benefit of the ideal type for supplementing earnings; it would not be reduced as earnings increased; and the loss to upper- and upper-middle-income families would be slight while the gain to poor and near-poor families would be great. An adult allowance of $300 per person a year would be no more costly than a $2,000 personal exemption but would further reduce poverty and welfare dependence. A small adult allowance is superior to increasing the assured child support benefit because it creates no incentive or reward for being a single parent. In that sense it is identical to a child allowance. One additional advantage of an adult allowance is that, relative to a child allowance alone, it would reduce the relative advantage to becoming a parent. In each case, two small benefits are superior to one benefit twice as large.

Although converting the personal adult exemption in the federal income tax to an equally costly adult allowance is a sensible policy that, by definition, would require no additional taxes, we recognize that it would require political boldness. No other country in the world has one. Unlike children's allowances, which have influential advocates in both the Democratic and Republican parties, adult allowances as a substitute for adult exemptions in the federal income tax have never been advocated by any politically influential figure.

Work Relief and Guaranteed Jobs

No matter how successful the universal programs are in drawing poor women with children into the labor market and off welfare, there will always be a need for a program to provide cash assistance. Some of these women will be unemployed for a time; others will be incapable of working. Those with disabilities should be identified and medically certified. The current method of aiding this group—cash relief in a combination of benefits including disability assistance and AFDC—appears to us to be quite sensible. Because the nation achieved a consensus that poor mothers with no preschool-age children should work, however, the federal government may choose to provide more work relief and less cash relief to those who are unemployed.

Work relief programs are now advocated primarily by conservatives and are opposed primarily by liberals. During the 1930s, however, exactly the opposite was true. Liberals now favor guaranteed-job programs, which conservatives vehemently oppose. In view of the fact that work relief and guaranteed jobs are at least first cousins, this is a perplexing state of affairs. To understand the relation between work relief and guaranteed jobs for custodial parents, consider how AFDC would be changed if it were to become principally a work-relief rather than a cash-relief program.

The first step would be to limit the amount of time that the heads of AFDC families could receive cash benefits without either working or progressing satisfactorily in an education or training program. Exactly how many days or months this time limit should be would depend on the answers to several questions. For example, how long will it take welfare departments to efficiently place beneficiaries? What are the relative costs of providing jobs versus providing cash benefits to beneficiaries who are expected to receive benefits for only two or three months? We have not systematically explored the answers to these or related questions, but we suspect that two or three months would be a reasonable time limit.

The second step would be to provide the jobs to make work relief a reality. If there are no jobs for welfare beneficiaries, then work relief becomes at best an empty slogan. At worst, it becomes a nuisance to beneficiaries. In other words, if work relief is to be effective, there must be a guarantee that there are enough jobs for all beneficiaries capable of working. All that is left between work relief and guaranteed jobs is haggling over the terms of employment.

If the wage rates in these guaranteed work-relief jobs were equal to the federal legal minimum wage of $3.35 per hour, we believe that after an initial period when costs would increase, assuring full-time work to all people now eligible for AFDC would cost about the same or only a little more than the amount the nation is now spending on AFDC. By assuring the availability of minimum wage jobs, the government can make the minimum wage truly effective. At the same time, paying only the minimum wage will minimize the number of workers who will leave private employment for a work-relief job, create a slight incentive and a clear social message that private employment or civil service public employment is preferable to work relief employment, and thus help to make the cost of the program politically acceptable.

The third step would be to provide services to facilitate independence. Evidence abounds that these services are sound investments for single mothers heading families. The most important would be education and training. For many very young single women with children, completing high school or obtaining some vocational degree may be a better investment from their own as well as society's point of view than working at a work-relief job. Similarly, despite the popular view to the contrary, evidence shows for many single women of all ages who have children, short training programs are likely to be a better investment than work relief. Making satisfactory progress in an education or training program, therefore, should be considered as equivalent to work in a sensible work-relief program.

As we stressed earlier in this book, because of the extra public day care that will be required, it may be less profitable to invest in work and training for women on welfare who have preschool-age children than to invest in women without such children. There are almost certainly important distinctions within this group: between, for example, the overall social desirability of requiring work in the marketplace or job training of poor mothers who have children under one year of age vis à vis requiring work of those with children aged three to five. Individual states and the nation will have more than enough challenge for the next few years to provide sufficient jobs at the minimum wage for AFDC custodial parents with no preschool-age children. At the same time, since the issue is so important, the federal government should support some state and local experiments with work relief for poor mothers with preschool-age children of various ages. To the extent that these efforts prove to be beneficial for various subgroups, the states or the federal government can extend the programs accordingly.

Converting AFDC from a cash welfare program to primarily a work-relief or a guaranteed jobs program would reduce welfare dependence. If such a program were enacted without the other two programs we have endorsed, however, it could reduce the average economic well-being of mother-only families. The benefits provided by a child support assurance program and child-and-adult allowances, however, would more than outweigh any losses incurred from converting AFDC from a cash-relief to a work-relief program. In combination, the three programs would substantially reduce the poverty, welfare dependence, and prevalence of mother-only families.

Extensions of Basic Recommendations

The reforms singled out for discussion in the previous section would, as noted, cost little and might even save a small amount of public funds within four to five years. The two reforms suggested in this section are extensions of the same basic principles that would increase government costs—at least over a four-to-five year period and probably longer than that. They are (1) to make child-and-adult allowances sufficiently high to completely substitute for the food stamp program and (2) to extend eligibility for the AFDC work-relief jobs to all parents of poor children—both custodial and noncustodial parents and stepparents as well.

Increasing the Child-and-Adult Allowances to the Food Stamp Benefit Level

We have argued for the adoption of child-and-adult allowances or re-fundable tax credits equal to at least $300 to $400 per person. They would cost little or no more than the $2,000 personal exemption proposed by the president as part of his 1985 tax revision proposal. In our judgment, the nation should aim for sufficiently large child-and-adult allowances to eliminate the food stamp program. In 1985 dollars, that would mean a credit of about $800 per person per year. A credit of this size would increase the costs to upper-middle and upper-income taxpayers by a significant amount over the proposed exemption. Exactly how large the net average cost would be for the families in the top third of the income distribution is not yet known, but we would be surprised if the figure exceeded $1,000 per year per family. At the same time, a credit of this size would make a sizable additional dent in both poverty and welfare dependence.

Historically, enacting the food stamp program was a big step forward because it effectively provides a nationwide negative income tax paid in food coupons to all needy individuals and families. But the program separates beneficiaries from the rest of society both because it is means-tested and because it pays benefits in a special, very visible and debased currency. In addition, every research study indicates that the additional amount of food bought by beneficiaries as a result of providing the aid in food stamps rather than cash is minuscule because most beneficiaries already spend more on food than the food stamps they receive. Finally, the rest of society pays more to administer this program than is necessary because the special currency—food stamps—has to be distributed, collected, and monitored by the government.

Extending Eligibility for Work-Relief Jobs to All Parents

Converting AFDC from a cash-relief to a work-relief program will require the initial cost increases, as we have seen, but the evidence suggests that this investment will pay for itself in the short run. The initial costs required to extend eligibility to all parents is much greater. Also, there is little reliable evidence that the investment would ever pay off, although we believe that it would. In chapter 3 we reviewed the evidence in support of the claim that rising unemployment among the black population is the principal culprit in the deterioration of the black family and perhaps poor white families also. Although hardly conclusive, the evidence is strong enough to warrant suggesting that if the nation seeks to reduce the prevalence of mother-only families, it should assure a job to all fathers as well as mothers who want to work.

A guaranteed-job or work-relief program also could have a substantial effect on child support. Noncustodial fathers cannot pay child support if they cannot find a job. Part of the cost of work relief for a noncustodial father would be immediately recouped because it would be deducted in child support. Moreover, if a minimum-wage job were guaranteed, noncustodial parents would have no excuse for being unable to pay a fair share of the earnings of a minimum-wage worker in child support. In this case, social opportunity and social control go hand in hand. A guaranteed job would provide a route out of poverty for people inclined to take advantage of the opportunity; at the same time, it would enable a noncustodial father to fulfill his obligation to help support his child and provide a test of the noncustodial father's willingness to fulfill that obligation.

Postscript

The reforms we have suggested here are almost certainly only a subset of those that will ultimately prove to be workable. We chose the first three reforms because we knew enough about them to feel confident that they could accomplish a lot at little or no extra cost to the government. The last two reforms were chosen because, though we were less certain about the benefits and costs, we still knew enough to feel confident they are at least good bets and worth experimenting with in some states. We hope that our confidence in them, and our review of the evidence that we do have, will lead to careful consideration of their merits by others.

INDEX

191